HEN

Mistress of Mayhem

Praise for Darren Coffield

'Darren Coffield, another of those magicians who (probably without knowing) knows how to imbue pieces of printed matter with light.' – David Sylvester, author of *The Brutality of Fact: Interviews with Francis Bacon*

'Coffield's book ... lobs a multicoloured grenade into the frigidity of the present moment.' – Andrew O Hagan, *London Review of Books*

'It is brilliant! I couldn't put it down once I started it.' – James Birch, curator and author of *Francis Bacon in Moscow*

'Every boringly serious art historian, good or bad should read it ...' – Norman Rosenthal, art historian and curator

'Entertaining, shocking, uproarious, hilarious ...' – *Sunday Times*

'An elegy to a vanished world.' – *Daily Mail*

'The escapist read I needed.' – *Guardian*

'Wonderfully evocative.' – *Times Literary Supplement*

HEN

Mistress of Mayhem

A Portrait of Henrietta Moraes

Darren Coffield

foreword by Sarah Lucas

The History Press

Also by Darren Coffield

Factual Nonsense: The Art and Death of Joshua Compston
Tales from The Colony Room: Soho's Lost Bohemia
Photographers of the Colony Room Club
Queens of Bohemia and Other Miss-Fits

First published 2026

The History Press
97 St George's Place, Cheltenham,
Gloucestershire, GL50 3QB
www.thehistorypress.co.uk

British Library Cataloguing in Publication Data.
A catalogue record for this book is available from the British Library.

ISBN 978 1 83705 109 0

Typesetting and origination by The History Press
Printed and bound in Great Britain by TJ Books, Padstow, Cornwall.

MIX
Paper | Supporting responsible forestry
FSC® C013056

The History Press proudly supports
Trees for Life
www.treesforlife.org.uk

EU Authorised Representative: Easy Access System Europe
Mustamäe tee 50, 10621 Tallinn, Estonia
gpst.request@easproject.com

For
Marianne Faithfull
1946–2025

Contents

Foreword by Sarah Lucas

My first encounter with Henrietta Moraes was Maggi Hambling's fabulous sculpture, *Henrietta Eating a Meringue*. I saw it at Maggi's studio. The studio was quite cluttered at the time, and although it wasn't prominently displayed, it managed to attract me like a magnet in all its abstract, fluffy, messy white voluptuousness. I asked what it was and Maggi said, 'It's Henrietta *Moraes* Eating a *Meringue*, of course'. Once seen never forgotten.

Later I encouraged Maggi to make a larger version of this sculpture for an exhibition I was putting together called *BIG WOMEN*. Approaching this larger version had a mesmeric effect – like being drawn towards a muscular cloud that's ready to swallow you up, should you be brave or foolish enough to dive into it.

Although I never met Henrietta in person, I did frequent many of the same Soho establishments. Maggi and I met for the first time at an old haunt of Henrietta's, the Colony Room Club. It was on our birthday. We were introduced by a mutual friend, Sebastian Horsley, who, knowing us both, announced to us that we shared one.

Sometime later I moved to Suffolk and crossed paths with Maggi more often … she published a book called *The Works* focusing on her portraits of people and animals that have been important to her. Reading this compelling, short, autobiography led to my second encounter with Henrietta … she and Maggi had fallen in love, and love, naturally, is very inspiring. Maggi's book includes many drawings and paintings of her muse.

As often happens when reading a very good book, I was left wanting more. I'd become curious about Henrietta. I looked next to her memoir, *Henrietta*, which charts her wayward progress through life; despite all its travails, mishaps and (often) lack of funds, she paints a vivid and romantic picture.

It's a charming book: traversing the countryside in bow-top wagons with horses and dogs, camping in the fields of hospitable farmers and rock stars, and barging around on canals. A life spent chasing a dream. It became a favourite book of mine, for a while. I was delighted by this unconventional life of freedom and, again, I found myself wanting more.

Maggi says that Henrietta intended to write a second volume of her autobiography. In the first she had been very nice about everyone and everything. In the second she planned to write the nasty version (goody!) but, unfortunately, she died before that happened.

Her compact first volume, so far as I know, was, until now, the only glimpse we had into the life of the legend. A full biography has been eagerly awaited, certainly by me and, I imagine, by many of you.

Here it is.

Time to dive in.

Introduction

The working title for this biography was *Studies for a Portrait of Henrietta Moraes after Francis Bacon*. Using the word 'Studies' in the same manner as the artist Francis Bacon, who called his paintings *Three Studies for a Portrait of Henrietta Moraes*. You may be wondering why *Studies for a Portrait*? Well, a portrait is an artistic representation of a person. It can be created in any media, from traditional oil painting to photography, sculpture and even mixed media. Furthermore, the notion of a series of 'studies' is that they are open-ended and never quite finished … as we know, some of the best portraits have an eerie, abstract quality, where eye sockets become gaping voids and open mouths echo emotional chasms.

The portrait is also a literary genre and can act as a parallel to the pictorial portrait. A written portrait gives deep insight and often oscillates between reality and fiction. When making a portrait the artist aims to capture some elements of their subject's character, but the artist can also convey messages of their own.

Over the years I have obtained glimpses, flashes and insights into Henrietta Moraes' life from the interviews I've conducted whilst researching my previous books, *Tales from the Colony Room* and *Queens of Bohemia*. From these literary fragments and my own experiences, I formed a thumbnail sketch of Henrietta and began to flesh out a portrait of a truly remarkable and unique woman. But the enigma central to the story remained: who *was* Henrietta Moraes?

Henrietta was a half-Indian beauty, muse and model. She was one of the stars of bohemian London who drank in Soho and became part of a hedonistic set that bedded one another and included artists such as Lucian Freud and Francis Bacon who partied with hard-living aristocrats, East End villains and, of course, the irrepressible Henrietta, whom they both painted.

Born Audrey Wendy Abbott in India in 1931, Henrietta's father had served in the Indian Air Force, but when he found out that his wife was pregnant with Henrietta he tried to strangle her before deserting the family home in the foothills of the Himalayas. Henrietta was then brought to England by her mother and sent to boarding school aged just three – where she was so afraid, she was sick all over her bed. Terrified at the sight of what she'd done, she ate it all back up, every little bit, and held it down. Then, as if in some twisted fairy tale by the Brothers Grimm, her mother abandoned Hen to her wicked grandmother, who finding her too wilful a child, badly mistreated her.

It was whilst attending convent school that Henrietta developed a crush on a girl called Valerie who slept with T.S. Eliot's poems under her pillow and, in an amazing twist of fate, went on to marry the poet himself. Henrietta also gravitated towards artistic circles and fell into the non-conformist bohemian lifestyle of the period. She went to the 100 Club on Oxford Street, became a jazz groupie and (being an eager teenager) lost her virginity to a young trumpet player with very smelly feet before sleeping with most of his friends. Like many young women of that era, she attended secretarial college as a type of finishing school – before stripping off to become an art school model. During the 1950s she became the prototype rock 'n' roll wild child a decade before the term was invented and, in the process, broke all the social taboos designed to hold women back in a society controlled almost exclusively by men.

Henrietta possessed a fearless naivety and an uncanny antenna for adventure as she drank and caroused in the Colony Room, the Gargoyle and the French – all of the legendary names and exotic watering holes where she became a regular face. In 1951, she met (and eventually married) the filmmaker Michael Law; a ubiquitous figure in Soho's clubland who introduced her to the artist Francis Bacon. Being gay, Francis was one of the few male admirers who did not want to sleep with her. Instead, he painted her more than twenty-three times over the next two decades and drank with her every night in Soho. Yet even though he owed much of his inspiration to her, Francis never gave her any of the pictures he painted – despite promising he would. In later life, when she was living in a cramped room on skid row and Francis' portraits of her began to fetch millions at auction, Henrietta realised the profit being made off her back and continued to complain about it until the end of her days.

Prologue

Today will be her last day.

It is 6 January 1999, and, as a new millennium dawns, the doom-mongers are predicting that a 'millennium bug' will cause computers to crash, planes to fall from the sky and that the end of the world is nigh. Whether it is the best of times or the worst of times, it certainly seems to be the only time they have left *together*. Henrietta's latest lover, the artist Maggi Hambling, telephones her but on getting no answer she worriedly drives towards the World's End, Chelsea. Upon arrival, Maggi finds Henrietta's door jammed and Hen hollering down from her bathroom window, complaining how ludicrous it is that she can't get out.

With her steely blue eyes, Maggi sizes up the situation on the street below as the clock remorselessly ticks down. In desperation, Hen rapidly lowers her beloved dachshund, Max, from the window in a travel bag attached to a length of electrical cable. Once safely down, Henrietta challenges Maggi to climb through the same very small window which, with extraordinary effort, she does.

Clambering into Henrietta's tiny bedsit, Maggi discovers our heroine lying flat out on her bed beside a large pile of unpaid bills. She asks Maggi how long it was before he died that Oscar Wilde had said those 'funny things' – referring to Wilde's famous wallpaper quote, when he had quipped on his deathbed, 'This is a duel to the death. One of us must go, and I fear it must be me' – and with her smouldering eyes staring up intently from her bed, Henrietta recites it perfectly.

Realising time is of the essence, Maggi protests that Hen needs medical help, but Henrietta just tells her to calm down … to give her a hug and another cigarette. Not easily deterred, Maggi insists Hen must try and speak to her doctor and miraculously manages to get straight through to him. Then, as Maggi is fiddling with some flowers by the sink and Hen is being hilarious, joking with her doctor on the phone, her voice suddenly changes – as if hitting a punchline – and she dies in an instant, dropping the receiver.

But to understand what gave rise to the killing joke, we need to go back to the beginning …

Chapter 1

Law of the Jungle

When Henrietta first arrived in 1950s bohemia, Soho was still a village in the West End of London. Its hub was the French pub, formerly known as the York Minster, now officially named The French House, but forever known as 'the French' to the locals. Of all the surviving pubs, the French is still the truest to the spirit of Soho: no fruit machine, no jukebox to drown the conversation and *definitely* no television.

For someone who led such an unconventional lifestyle, Henrietta's days fell into a set pattern. They would usually begin late morning when she'd leave the attic of the Queen Anne house at the top of Dean Street (where she lived) and amble south down the road with her boyfriend, Michael Law, until they reached the Café Torino on the corner of Old Compton Street. The place reeked of old rubber and disinfectant as a long sticky strip of paper swayed from a central light fitting, brown with glue and black-dotted with dead flies. Here they sat at one of the marble-topped tables listening to Spanish anarchists and Republicans discussing how to overthrow Spain's fascist dictator Franco. It was nicknamed 'The Madrid' and became a favourite haunt of Hen's because the café sat betwixt the Colony and the Gargoyle clubs, from which vantage point she could observe the familiar faces of her quarry going by. It also commanded a clear view of the French, so Hen and Michael would wait at the café to watch the pub fill up before entering the premises by the left-hand door.

A Genius of a Landlord ...

The pub itself was pretty basic, but part of its appeal with women was that they could go unchaperoned and not get hassled, which was unusual back then. Women were often segregated in the other pubs or refused admission altogether. Each day at noon, the French was where Hen would congregate with kindred spirits. It was run by Gaston Berlemont, a balding middle-aged gentleman of Gaulish heritage, who sported a dark suit and had twinkling eyes and a long twirly handlebar moustache. He was also gracious to the working girls – the local prostitutes – who regarded the French as a sanctuary. Once inside they were off-duty and would complain bitterly to Gaston if any man tried to pick them up. The pub's oak interior had a defiantly French ambiance, the walls lined with faded sepia photographs of the many famous French artistes who'd drunk on the premises between the wars. In keeping with the continental atmosphere, Gaston never served pints of beer, only half pints, and refused to serve Coca-Cola because he said he didn't like the type of person that drank it. But he did sell quarter bottles of champagne, that's how stylish the French was – as a woman you could go into a pub and order a quarter bottle of champagne for yourself or (as in Hen's case) persuade an unsuspecting admirer into buying you one.

One of the quirks of the French was that Gaston ran it more as a club than a pub. There were two ends of the bar, one end was for the 'intellectuals' – artists, poets, writers, publishers, etc. It was very cliquey. When you first entered through the left-hand door, you'd see all the regulars at the other end of the bar, drinking. After a few years drinking at the 'Shallow End' of the bar you'd become established as a regular and slowly be allowed to move down the bar in a southerly direction towards the 'Deep End'. The cash register in the middle of the bar marked the demarcation line where both ends met. Once you'd got there, you'd made it to the 'Deep End' or V.I.P. (Very Inebriated Person) area.

To reach it was considered an honour, despite it being where the grim reaper was regularly harvesting his crop, and Gaston expected those who'd graduated to undergo an initiation ceremony. He would bring out a bottle of 1912 pre-Prohibition French absinthe, and with all the ceremony of a high mass he would also set out paraphernalia; the bottle, the glass, the perforated spoon upon which he would place a sugar lump that helped shoot the alcohol into your system. However, some said his rare bottle of absinthe tasted suspiciously like the house Pernod …

Gaston had his favourites, and Henrietta was certainly one of them. He remembered her as 'smashing, voluptuous', and confessed, 'It was as much as any red-blooded man could do to keep his hands off her'. For Henrietta, Gaston was a genius of a landlord, welcoming her with a cheerfulness that lit up her day. Once she became so bored listening to a man complain about his life that she threw her glass of champagne in his face. The pub fell silent, and everybody expected Gaston to bar her. But instead, he twirled his handlebar moustache and smiled, 'Madame, I see that your glass is empty. Please allow me to refill it for you'. He was very diplomatic with drunks too: 'One of the two of us will have to go, and I'm afraid it's not going to be me!' And he would throw people out with such courtesy that they wanted to thank him.

For those bohemians perpetually short of cash, such as Henrietta, Gaston proved a very generous landlord too. The first words she'd utter upon entering were, 'Good Morning Gaston, could I have a glass of Pernod please and could you possibly lend me a fiver?' Whereupon he'd proffer a rolled banknote, handing it over to her discreetly with a nod and a wink and the reassurance that he was willing to wait for repayment. By the till he kept a list of people and their debts written in tiny handwriting in black ink. He said he loaned people money because: '9 out of 10 people pay it back, 1 in 10 don't but the amount of money they spend coming in here explaining why they weren't paying me back far exceeds the debt.' So, cultivating customers like Henrietta was a shrewd business move. But Gaston was less generous in other respects. If someone had the cheek to ask for an extra cube of ice to go with their drink there would be outrage, and if a man wanted to have a crap they had to go through the indignity of asking for the key to the gents washroom, whereupon all the customers' heads would swivel in unison as Gaston bellowed across the bar: '*Who* wants the key?'

In this environment stood Henrietta and her lover Michael Law, he a hopeful but impoverished film director and she an Amazonian beauty in a dark dress and cream-coloured coat. With her mop of black hair, aquiline nose and dark, smouldering eyes she pitched her voice so everyone else at the bar could overhear. 'Aren't I right, Michael?' she demanded of him at the end of every sentence. '*Of course* you are,' he'd concur, as they hung out waiting to see what might happen. Maybe a rich friend would buy them lunch? It was Michael Law who taught Hen the 'Law of the Jungle' – survival of the fittest – eat or be eaten. Upon spotting his prey, Michael would let out the hunting cry, 'Henrietta, look!' Henrietta would clap her hands delightedly, jumping up and down like an excited little girl, as their meal ticket walked in. It was usually one of those bored aristocratic rich kids who took them everywhere to keep himself entertained – but never bought or gave them what they actually needed, as Henrietta loudly complained:

> Really it is *too* bad. Tony Hubbard took us to the Caprice last night which was marvellous but he *refused* to give us the money for a taxi home so we had to walk *all* the way. I ask you. Could you believe that anyone so rich could be so *mean*!

Tony Hubbard loved to toy with them, such was the sadistic sense of humour that permeated Soho. One day, in the French, he said he was going upstairs to eat when he asked: 'Would you like to join me?' Then, halfway up the stairs, he turned round and enquired if they had any money. Of course they hadn't, so he told them: 'If you like, you can come up and watch me eat.'

Neo-Romantic ...

Another of Hen's wealthy benefactors was the artist Johnny Minton, heir to the Minton ceramics empire. Everyone said Johnny looked 'like an El Greco painting'. Rather posh, buck-toothed and wiry, with the physique of a matchstick and a long, drawn face topped off with a mop of dark hair, Minton was a 'neo-romantic' painter who liked to splash the cash and have a good time. Hordes of people benefited from his largesse whilst he dissipated himself to the hilt. His loyal band of followers was known as 'Minton's Circus', and Henrietta was more than happy to provide the entertainment. As an art tutor, Minton would regularly gather up his students and take them to Soho, where they might catch a glimpse of Dylan Thomas sitting slumped on the benches that used to run under the windows of the French or that Queen of Bohemia, the artist Nina Hamnett, outside the door to the ladies loo lying in a pool of her own piss.

Henrietta was a natural fit in the French. Like Soho itself, the pub attracted a lot of people who were orphans or, as in Hen and Francis Bacon's case, had been written off by their families. Like many orphans, Hen had an extraordinarily vivid fantasy about one day meeting her father and lied by telling everyone she had once done so in the Hyde Park Hotel. A lot of teenage runaways from all parts of Britain congregated in Soho's social and sexual melting pot where (if they were lucky) they formed new friendships and became part of a wider, bohemian family. Henrietta had grown up not knowing her parents and her hedonistic mother eventually ran away to South Africa to start a new life without her. As Henrietta told *Queen* magazine:

> All my life I have been on the wrong side of the fence. It started off by my having no father and living with a very belligerent grandmother. My mother was known to me, until I was about seven, as Mummy Judy, and appeared once a year dressed in startling and very beautiful black clothes. I was sent to … an enormously expensive and snobbish secretarial college for young ladies. Deep down inside me I had never made this grade. I got into trouble three times for pawning typewriters.

So, Hen went to one of those red public telephone boxes and looked up the numbers of all the London art colleges in the phone directory. She telephoned them all and told them she was the most beautiful and talented model in London but, she lamented, without realising what low standards art schools had. As figurative painting fell out of fashion during the 1950s, many models switched from working for artists to art students. The days of the celebrity artist's model had gone – along with much of the romance of it.

On the first day, she arrived in a building teeming with art students her own age. It reminded Hen of her first day at boarding school, the memory made her feel sick, but somehow she managed to hold it down. Unlike her boarding school, the art school was well heated and the students were friendly. She felt like an interloper in the life studio where the young people were silently working from the static nudes.

Henrietta found modelling at art school awful because she kept on fainting in the middle of exams. Nobody ever talked to her, and she soon developed a pathological hatred of art students. For such a deeply undisciplined person as Henrietta it was pretty hellish. She was expected to arrive at the appointed hour, fill in her contract of employment and be paid by banker's cheque, something which would have caused the bohemian models of yesteryear to faint, as they'd never seen a bank, let alone a cheque. However, Henrietta's real problem with modelling in the hallowed silence of a life studio was her gregarious nature, she just couldn't keep her trap shut, a trait which had caused her a great deal of trouble as a child.

Her mother had abandoned her with her grandmother who had once lived a colonial life with a fleet of servants in India. Now back in Britain and having to cook, clean and fend for herself (all of which according to Hen she did badly) she would take her frustration out on her granddaughter, becoming very violent towards her. She'd tie Henrietta's hands behind her back and push her into a dark room for hours on end before reappearing with a leather strap and viciously whipping her. A terrified little Hen resolved that she would not give her sadistic granny the pleasure of seeing her cry or beg for mercy. So, she took it all, without a murmur.

Terrorised and Enchanted ...

As an adult, Henrietta met a lot of kindred spirits in Soho who'd also had difficult childhoods. They knew that life wasn't going to give them anything so they'd have to grab what they could with both hands. Perhaps it was this approach to life that made the French so loved by artists, writers, actors and musicians. When Hen first met Francis Bacon they seemed to have an immediate rapport. She was overwhelmed by his disarming charm and cherubic features, his shiny rouged cheeks and pouting lips. His bleached blonde hair and lithe figure belied his age and, like many, she found Francis' feminine features at odds with the violence inherent in his paintings.

Along with the baby-faced Francis, other regulars included John Deakin, the rubber-faced fashion photographer for *Vogue*, whose scruffy, hungover appearance seemed incompatible with his glamorous subject matter, and Britain's first celebrity television interviewer, Daniel Farson, a sadomasochist with a penchant for wearing ladies' lingerie. It was Daniel Farson who told me that Picasso and Francis Bacon stood apart from all the other painters in the twentieth century because they never let fashion encroach on their art and both were exceptional in their selfish single-mindedness. As for Henrietta, Daniel thought she was the most beautiful woman he had ever seen: 'wildly attractive, fussing over her cigarette, with an arrogant upturned nose.' He said she could stop people dead in their tracks and make them turn around, others were shocked by her unique mixture of caustic wit and beauty. As her friend, the pop star Marianne Faithfull, put it:

> Henrietta was one of the great beauties of the 1950s – the epitome of that bohemian life that's now gone. Her reckless intensity of spirit magnetically attracted people to her. Hen had friends from the gutter to the aristocracy whom she both terrorised and enchanted.

But we must remember that at this point in the early 1950s Henrietta and Francis Bacon were almost completely unknown. According to another friend and former model, Diana Melly:

> Back then, Henrietta wasn't really known for anything apart from being outspoken and part of the bohemian scene … what was it about Henrietta that attracted so many artists to paint her? Well, she had incredibly striking features – almost too striking to be beautiful. There was nothing soft about her features at all. They were incredibly strong like her personality. People did talk about her in Soho as a beauty, formidably attractive and witty – she was very much part of the bohemian gang.

Henrietta became part of a new generation that fundamentally altered the character of bohemia into something brasher, drunker and more *risqué*, as the easy, convivial amiability of old bohemia gave way to the professional jealousy and infighting of the 1950s. At its core was a group of individuals who met at noon each day at the 'Deep End' of the French, and collectively formed the Monster Club. In Soho, one didn't call someone a Monster just because they were annoying. Monsters don't just behave badly; in fact their success is mostly due to their enormous charm. Along with Francis Bacon, John Deakin and Daniel Farson, Henrietta graduated to the exclusive Monster Club too. The label 'Monster' was an accolade and you had to fulfil some basic requirements before you could qualify. You didn't call someone a Monster at random. A Monster was pretty special; they had to appear to be totally selfish and egocentric, only interested in their own importance and often plotting for their own gain. Monsters were completely unscrupulous, lacking in any modesty or restraint. They were often noisy, shouting down people cleverer than themselves. Eating and drinking with abandon, Monsters ignored the rules of good behaviour but were often refreshingly funny and made surprisingly good company. According to Marianne:

> Hen inhabited a sort of enchanted space where the oddest, most unlikely things happened. She was the perfect muse for Francis Bacon … she travelled on her own loopy groove, avoiding the straight world entirely.

The Golden Age ...

Henrietta was an eighteen-year-old called Audrey Wendy Abbott when she began hanging out at the 100 club on Oxford Street. It had become a hip jazz venue where Diana Melly's future husband, George Melly, often sang with his jazz band. There Hen met her first boyfriend, a jazz trumpeter, and lost her virginity to him before sleeping with all his friends (by her own admission, it never occurred to her to say no). A year later, aged nineteen, she met the thirty-five-year-old filmmaker Michael Law at the 100 Club whom she described as a 'white-faced, pale-eyed medievalist with hammer toes'. He was almost twice her age and became the kind of father figure she'd never had. It was Michael Law who renamed Audrey Wendy Abbott, Henrietta, after his first girlfriend, Henrietta Swan. He then took her across Oxford Street from the 100 Club to Soho, a bohemian world she knew nothing about. Problem was, Michael was already married to the dancer Maria Ralph, with whom he lived beneath a Soho brothel. So, the starstruck lovers needed somewhere else to shack up. They'd heard on the grapevine that a well-known literary figure was away and his house left unoccupied. However, he was a powerful figure in British culture who knew everyone worth knowing. Not the sort of man you'd want to annoy. So, without a second thought, they decided to break in ...

After a long weekend away, Cyril Connolly arrived back home to discover that his wife, Barbara Skelton's, earrings had gone missing and the money left out for the housekeeper had disappeared. Someone had fleeced them, and after going through the expense of having all the locks changed the mystery deepened when they found a pile of human excrement by the back door. Only then did Cyril Connolly discover Michael and Henrietta, holed up in his former lodger's quarters. Barbara Skelton resented the intrusion bitterly and was forever banging on their door complaining about the noise, so the lovers moved on to the attic of a Queen Anne house at 86 Dean Street, Soho – a former brothel – where Zoe Hicks (daughter of Britain's most famous living painter Augustus John) resided with her husband the composer Alwyn Williams, whom Hen had previously danced with at the 100 Club.

It was more by accident than design that Hen landed in the beating heart of bohemian Soho and wound up living on the same street as the unholy trinity of Soho drinking dens: the French, the Colony and the Gargoyle. For Henrietta, Soho was like a village, peopled by all these wonderful characters whom her boyfriend knew, such as Fred the Wings and No Knickers Joyce:

> Sid the Swimmer delivered our logs. We knew every shopkeeper, every pub and club – Italian, French, Spanish, Polish, Swiss and African. The new Hi-Ho down the alleyway was full of deviant whores and their protectors. Big Jean and Stout Sally fought with dustbin lids on Friday evenings. And the Lagos Lagoon opposite our drawing-room windows was packed with gambling-crazy Africans.

For Hen, Soho was one big pantomime but as the local 'People's Poet', Paul Potts, put it: 'She was a pantomime and the whole of the year was Christmas'. Hen admitted they found her very easy to put up with, 'particularly Francis. I never talked about painting, he loved that'. Francis Bacon did not tolerate bores. Despite being stereotyped in various art history books as a wild reckless drunk, Henrietta was a fiercely intelligent and entertaining woman whose boyfriend was well connected too. Born in 1917, the son of a clergyman, Michael Law's parents divorced whilst he was young and his mother moved to Chelsea, where her friends included the artist Augustus John and the author Naomi Mitchison.

Michael had been educated at the posh Westminster School and won an art scholarship to Chelsea Polytechnic, where he was taught by Henry Moore, but soon abandoned his studies to become a runner for Strand Films and fell headlong into bohemia. Despite being much in demand as a director and winning the Grand Prix d'Or at Cannes, he is now remembered mostly for his love life. This perplexed Paul Potts who considered Michael the only real friend he ever had whom he did not and never could understand: 'His chief occupation in life was women. As a sideline he was in films.' But it was Michael himself who best summed up the situation:

> In those days everybody was thinking what was in it for them – a time not so much of greed as naked pleasure-seeking. There were a lot of loose cannons finding their way. There's never been such a collection of people together in one place … doing what they wanted to do.

And what Hen and Michael really wanted to do at 3 p.m. every afternoon was to carry on drinking. But the licensing laws were different back then. All the pubs closed in the afternoon and you could not consume alcohol in a public bar between 3 p.m. and 6 p.m. So, unless you were a member of a private club, there was nowhere to drink. The attraction of the Colony Room was that when the pubs were forced to shut in the afternoon, the Colony Room opened. As Gaston called last orders, Francis Bacon could be heard complaining:

> These ghastly English laws, you can't have a drink, can't do anything. Do you think they'll ever change them …? I can take you up that awful Colony Room if you like.

So, off to the Colony they went.

Chapter 2

The Colony

To reach the Colony Room Club, Hen and her entourage would turn right as they left the French and head north, picking up a few stragglers as they passed Café Torino on the way. The Colony was located at 41a Dean Street; its dingy passageway was dirty and dustbin-lined, with empty wine boxes from the Italian restaurant which occupied the ground floor of the building. The waft of garlic and the waiters screaming at each other in a foreign tongue gave you the feeling of being abroad. As Henrietta walked off the pavement, into the dark anonymous passageway, passers-by would glance at her as if she were a call girl.

The club itself was a not-very-comfortable small front room on the first floor of a tiny Georgian house; however, the fascination was with the assortment of people who went there. Before she became a regular, Henrietta hadn't realised what alcohol could do to a face and had never seen such well-trodden ones. The bar was mahogany with gold-painted bamboo striated all along the front. The glass and mirrored shelves behind the bar sat holding bottles of spirits and various shaped drinking glasses. In the middle of the shelving was an old metal till and in front of the bar sat several bar-stools, on one of which, next to the door, sat the proprietor Muriel Belcher. The club's cream-coloured walls contrasted with the lush greenery of the large tropical plants which dominated the place. The bar-stools and banquettes were all upholstered in leopard skin, which made the place look like a sophisticated jungle.

A Kind of Salon …

The club was dominated, indeed created, by two personalities – that of its owner and founder Muriel Belcher, who opened the Colony in 1948, and the artist Francis Bacon, who was one of Muriel's first customers. For Henrietta's homosexual friends, Francis Bacon and John Minton, the club provided a support network in a hostile world. It was a bolt-hole at a time when 'queers' needed somewhere to hide and was filled with luminaries who didn't dare appear in the gay pub (The Golden Lion) down the road. Muriel loved them being around because they were funnier, brighter and spent more. She had realised the power of the pink pound long before anyone had coined the term, but you certainly didn't have to be homosexual to be a member.

In a regimented and sexually repressed post-war London, the Colony attracted professional drinkers to a man, woman or something in-between, since sexual non-conformity always played its part in the mix. The club itself was asexual. Your sexuality was your own concern, but occasionally the subject of learned debate. 'I think you should wear heels, dear, and a nice frock,' Muriel might say to some upright city gent in a pinstripe suit, 'and you'll feel happier in yourself.'

The Colony was the closest thing to a Paris café London could offer since the great days of the Café Royal. On any given afternoon at the bar, you would find the jazz singer George Melly in a loud suit; the bookish-looking author Colin Wilson in a beige duffle coat locked in conversation with Daniel Farson; the penniless poets George Barker, Paul Potts and Dylan Thomas; the artists John Minton and Lucian Freud; and, finally, Francis Bacon who was always centre stage. Muriel knew there was something extraordinary about Francis, long before he became famous. As Henrietta recalled: 'He exuded this incredible energy. If there is a force field around people, his was ten times as strong.' Francis briefly worked as a 'hostess' for Muriel bringing interesting people into her orbit, such as Henrietta, to whom Muriel became a combination of mentor, critic and guru. She was a life-enhancer, an inspiration by example. It seemed to Hen that Muriel had all the essential qualities one needed in life: a formidable capacity for alcohol, an admirable vocabulary of expletives, extreme generosity, shrewd judgement of character, a fervent champion of the underdog, purveyor of scurrilous gossip and, above all, a knack for extracting and happily betraying everyone else's innermost secrets.

At the time there were dozens of different afternoon drinking clubs in Soho: crooks' clubs, police clubs, jazz clubs, even taxi drivers' clubs – but Muriel's was to do with fun. She ruled over a kind of salon – a gathering of people with an inspiring hostess, held to amuse, refine the taste and increase the knowledge of the participants through conversation, by deciding the subjects of their meetings whilst mediating and directing the discussion. She encouraged socialising between different social ranks, races, sexes and sexualities; breaking down the social barriers and taboos that other establishments operated under. But Muriel's was not a salon of civility, polite conversation and reasoned debate. According to George Melly it was a salon of absolute freedom of expression, to the point of nihilism:

> I think the problem looking back is we embellish things with hindsight. If you'd gone up to Muriel Belcher and asked her if she'd started a club to help make the world a freer, more liberal place, she'd have said 'fuck off'.

To which Muriel's friend and former barman, David Marrion, concurred:

> Muriel was the attraction. She was a good conversationalist and read the papers back to front every day before she started work. She was slightly built and about 5 feet 4 inches tall. It was her face and hands you noticed most. She had a very unusual face, very sharp features, her long boney nose arched and protruding over her shallow cheeks, proudly revealing her Jewish ancestry … Her face defied anyone to challenge her authority or her request, 'Which one of you lot are going to buy me a drink?'

The Fascination of Forbidden Fruit ...

In Muriel, Henrietta found a witty, foul-mouthed mother figure and a generous hostess to boot. As Hen's friend, Sandy Fawkes, said: 'It was drinks all round and that included poverty-stricken poet Paul Potts and every down-on-his-luck actor, writer or painter present who could not dream of returning the compliment.' However, if you didn't walk into the club with confidence, Muriel would verbally slaughter you: 'Shut that door! The wind is blowing right up *my cunt.*' Famous for her wit and infamous for her devastating put-downs, Muriel's humour was infectious – the delivery, the body language, the coarse juxtapositions and the sense of shared absurdity. Henrietta said that from the moment they first met they hit it off:

> Her greeting was 'Hello Cunty!', which could be quite frightening if you were feeling frail. But her club was definitely her home, where she reigned and her word was law.

Muriel's, as the club was affectionately known, worked so well because the members were friends of Muriel, attending her slightly mad party. Upon entering the premises, the club's pianist, Mike McKenzie, would break off his current tune to play each new arrival in with a theme song he'd chosen for them – either flattering, like '*You Go To My Head*', or in Hen's case, one loaded with innuendo – as she once again came nose to nose with Muriel, 'Hello Henrietta, how are you love?' Then looking at whoever or whatever was in tow, 'Is this cunt with you? Sign them in then ... *Hello cunty*, what's your name?' Henrietta would have forewarned her companions whilst ascending the stairs that if Muriel called you a cunt twice in quick succession it meant she liked you.

Those who frequented the Colony could clearly remember the first time they went there. Like the recipient of a major shock, or stumbling upon a murder scene, Muriel left her mark on anyone who entered. Everyone who walked in through that door had to be examined: 'Who are you? *Members only!*' she'd shriek. But she liked the purses and the handbags being opened: 'How's your handbag today, dear? *Get that handbag out, girl!*' The only unforgiveable sin in the club was to be boring. Muriel was keen on the money, but if you were too boring that was it:

> 'Members only', dearie, and get a facelift on the way! I can't stand respectability just for the sake of respectability. Nor people who bore the shit out of me … unless I feel in the mood for a bit of camping.

Hen's best friend during this period was a beguiling blonde called Caryl Chance, together they formed something of a double act. Like the characters in the eponymous Hollywood movie *Thelma and Louise*, they were always breaking the rules and behaving so recklessly they might career over the edge at any moment. They had taken to preying on expensive restaurants – Caryl always found someone to offload the bill on and Hen provided the chutzpah, the sheer devilry that gained them the initial entry. Hen loved Caryl because, like Muriel, she never bored her.

For Hen and Caryl, the Colony held the fascination of forbidden fruit, a tiny one-room world, where they could be found at 4 p.m. on a sunny afternoon, gossiping their lives away. The club became an impromptu performance space where Muriel was the ringmaster and their feverish conversation made the very room where they drank into a theatre. Some would recite poetry, others might burst into song, but Hen told extremely funny stories, like the time she was at the opening party of Francis Bacon's exhibition at the Hanover Gallery, Mayfair. The paintings were still wet and when Henrietta became pressed against one in the crush, she walked away with a Screaming Pope on her back … and she continued to make everyone laugh that afternoon when she relayed a recent anecdote about her and Caryl dining in the deep gloom of a posh restaurant. Hen had pulled out at random from her handbag one of the Havana cigars she was partial to smoking. No sooner had she done so, then as if by magic a waiter popped up and lit it for her. He should have then disappeared but instead began giggling as he struck match after match trying to light it. Wondering why her Havana was the object of such hilarity, Hen stared at her cigar and realised she was puffing on a Super Tampax.

Muriel's Kingdom ...

Very little is known about Henrietta's mother figure, Muriel Belcher. Born in Birmingham in 1908, she came from a strict Jewish family who were always running away from creditors. When her father died she moved to London and became part of Soho's clubland. Muriel had a black girlfriend, Carmel Stuart, from the Colonies – Jamaica – after whom she named her club the 'Colony Room'. Unlike the rest of British society, there was never any racial, religious or sexual division in the club. It was never an issue. With most private clubs you join a clique or crowd and must behave accordingly. However, George Melly told me that at the Colony there was no clique, no way to dress or act and no required station in life in order to become a member:

> Muriel was a kind of magician, a witch, not necessarily a very kindly one. She could turn on people, she was rather mercenary, she weighed up whether someone was valuable ... she could tell if someone had potential immediately and she would cultivate them. In retrospect, it was extraordinary to think it was there. She kept this cauldron on the boil and would occasionally throw in another ingredient that took her fancy.

But it was Francis Bacon who best summed up its unique appeal:

> It's different to anywhere else. Here we laugh more, we enjoy ourselves more. It's because of Muriel. Her tremendous ability to create an atmosphere of ease. After all, that's what we all want, isn't it? A place to go to where one feels free.

In the Colony, Henrietta met some very strong female figures such as the Canadian poet Elizabeth Smart and the artist Elinor

Bellingham-Smith, who was currently riding high after a successful exhibition on Cork Street. But there was one woman (other than Muriel) whom Francis seemed particularly close to: the artist, spy and pornographer Isabel Rawsthorne. She was a former lover of the sculptor Giacometti, who compared her to a wild cat: 'a man-eater.' Isabel's ear-splitting shrieks of laughter cut through the club's dense foliage like the cry of a wild beast in the jungle. Another notable regular was the Queen of Bohemia, Nina Hamnett, who would exchange anecdotes of her glory years for drinks. She was one of the truly great characters of her age, but one whose artistic talents were ultimately washed away by booze. By the time Henrietta had met her in the Colony, Nina was living in penury. The once great beauty's face creased almost beyond recognition. All her front teeth had recently been extracted and to make matters worse she'd become incontinent and frequently wet herself on Muriel's bar-stools. Nina stood as a monument to pre-war bohemia and a stark scarecrow-like warning to Henrietta of what she might become if she didn't change her ways.

Her Slightly Mad Party ...

For those operating at the fringes of polite society, such as Henrietta and Nina, Muriel's was not just a bar, it was also a psychiatrist's couch, unemployment bureau and marriage guidance centre too. Many relished listening to Muriel's malicious gossip concerning mutual friends – until they departed and her knife inevitably became firmly planted in their backs too. Henrietta's friend, the ex-jailbird and bestselling author Frank Norman, was a tough nut but even he had to concede:

> I have yet to meet someone who is a match for Muriel when it comes to a verbal punch-up. I have seen her render even the toughest of her members helpless under a barrage of abuse, the intensity of which leaves them inarticulate chattering imbeciles.

The weird thing was that even amidst all the verbal punch-ups Henrietta and the other members would observe one another indirectly in the pieces of mirror dotted around the Colony's walls. The long shards acted like one of Francis Bacon's paintings, pulling Henrietta to bits and putting her back together in unlikely ways – evoking the dislocation of things. And with the skilful use of these mirrors, Muriel could carry on a conversation with a volley of asides to the people stood behind her: 'Can you keep a secret, Henrietta?' she'd ask Hen who'd laugh, 'Of course not, Muriel.' Then, to someone who'd just entered, 'Hello, darling, where's your beautiful wife?', before continuing the conversation conspiratorially, 'Well, Henrietta I'll tell you anyway …'

As Muriel's tongue wagged, her dog 'Nosher' (slang for someone who performs cunnilingus) sat on her lap, ears pricked up, eavesdropping in. Henrietta said Nosher was the best-informed dog in London and should have had his own gossip column. Whilst gossiping away and not holding a glass, Muriel would clasp her long bony hands, twisted by Paget's disease, in her lap – raising them in mock horror, relief or joy of good news or a joke, or sometimes coming down on some unsuspecting member who'd not bought her a drink like a clap of thunder.

Alcoholics can never remember people's names so Muriel gave her members ones that would stick in her memory. Many members were known only by their nicknames. The monikers made sense once you got to know them … Henrietta was 'Hen', John Minton was 'Minty', the poet Stephen Spender was 'Brenda' and another was known simply as 'Miss Hitler'. Muriel and Francis Bacon's relationship was so close he would call her 'Mother' and she in return called him 'Daughter'. Besides, none of them took themselves too seriously – how could they with Muriel's razor-sharp ability to prick pomposity? 'Look, she's got a new frock!' Muriel would cry at a city banker who arrived in a new Savile Row suit, and then turning to Henrietta, 'Look! She's wearing trousers today!' Muriel loved to swap the genders round. Her club was gender-fluid decades before the term was coined, as Francis Bacon fumed:

> That's happening all over now – it's called unisex, and she's been doing it for years. Her language has become very exaggerated and she turns on 'he and she', like 'Hot and Cold', until she doesn't know who 'he and she' are any more and that vaporises the atmosphere for a start. She creates this state where people feel free to talk about themselves and their desires. I love her looks. I think she's extraordinary looking. She has a very grand air about her. There's something there that has come from an ancient world – perhaps the Babylonian world.

When it came to Francis, I think Henrietta and Muriel were rather flattered to have become the subject of so many of his artworks, which in a strange way demonstrated their profound lack of physical vanity. To be immortalised by Francis demanded a certain detachment: 'Muriel is Francis's friend? If that's how Francis paints his friends, I'd hate to see how he treats his enemies!' quipped Muriel's mate, David Marrion.

Don't You Have Any Nice Cottages to Go to?

The club was particularly busy between 3 p.m. and 5.30 p.m. The afternoon hours were always best to meet the most eccentric and exotic members, people who didn't actually have to *work* for a living. It was a happy hunting-ground for Hen who was only too happy to help relieve the young aristocrats of the burden of their inherited wealth and it became a rite of passage for many upper-class youths to spend a year or two slumming it around Soho.

Henrietta and Caryl's benefactor at the time was Tony Hubbard, heir to the Woolworths retail empire, who had a lavish house on Regent's Park Terrace where he kept his artworks by Francis Bacon. Hubbard had recently cut a swimmer's foot off with the propeller of his motorboat on the French Riviera and had, by so doing, earned himself a place in *The Guinness Book of Records* for shelling out £50,000 in damages (a considerable sum of money in those days). Hubbard was rich, spoilt and loved extravagant gestures.

John Deakin nicknamed him 'Poor Little Rich Boy' and, according to Daniel Farson, Hubbard was devoted to Deakin, one of the few people who dared tease him. Although Hubbard's temper and generosity often see-sawed dramatically, he entertained Hen and Caryl to endless lunches and visits to Muriel's where buying a round of drinks could prove ruinous. Her alcohol was said to be the most expensive in London. 'They can't be so clever if they pay my prices,' laughed Muriel. She allowed her members to run up bills and pay them off in instalments. 'Muriel Belcher. Muriel Belcher!' cried one member's angry bank manager, threatening to return his cheques, 'Who is this woman you're keeping?'

The Colony operated under a traditional afternoon drinking club licence of 3 p.m. to 11 p.m. As far as Muriel was concerned, she'd rinsed their handbags clean of cash and had got the best out of them by 11 p.m., by which time she would call last orders at the bar with the refrain: 'Don't you have any nice cottages to go to?' This was the signal for everyone to down their drinks and head across the road to the Gargoyle, the entrance to which was situated on Meard Street (pronounced *merde* – French slang for shit). Once through the door you took a rickety caged lift to the top floor, and walked down a flight of stairs into a ballroom made up of hundreds of small pieces of hand-cut shimmering mirrors. The concept for the décor had come from the French painter Henri Matisse, whose paintings and prints had originally hung in the club. But by now the Gargoyle had been open for a quarter of a century and was beginning to look rather jaded. When it had originally opened in 1925 it was the favourite hunting-ground for exotic femmes fatales such as Tallulah Bankhead. Openly bisexual, Tallulah smoked, drank and swore in ways which outraged polite society and, in her own small way, Henrietta was unwittingly keeping the tradition alive.

Into the Swing of Things ...

Despite its glory days being far behind it, the Gargoyle was still the place to be and the same bohemian crowd attended night after night: Cyril Connolly, Barbara Skelton, Elizabeth Smart, Isabel Rawsthorne, John Deakin, Francis Bacon, John Minton with an entourage of twenty sailors and the ubiquitous young artist Lucian Freud. When she first began going there, Henrietta felt terribly shy and intimidated to be in the company of a bunch of intellectuals who revelled in being rude to one another. But she soon got into the swing of things – drunkenly tugging on the odd beard, and hurling the club's gilded chairs across the dance floor to the tune of Alexander's Ragtime Band playing the *Charleston*. Hen was the youngest person there and inevitably became mesmerised by Lucian Freud's hypnotic stare. Despite standing at only five foot six, Freud was an imposing figure, with a fierce gaze likened to that of a hawk. As they hit the dance floor Hen said, 'I want you' and the next morning they consummated their relationship on the edge of a very cold and cumbersome china sink, whereupon she fell in love (or was it lust?) with Lucian.

Anyway, that night at the Gargoyle, Henrietta was with her sidekick Caryl Chance, who could be heard yelling out of the ladies' loo: 'Jesus Christ! I married one millionaire by the time I was nineteen. I'm certainly going to marry another before I'm twenty-two.' Caryl had set her sights on milking their friendly cash cow Tony Hubbard, who ticked all the boxes: rich, spoilt and a helluva lot of fun. At the Gargoyle, Hubbard had once got hold of Henrietta by the legs and spun her across the dance floor until she went into the band's bass drum – headfirst – right between the kilts of those otherwise inseparable Scottish artists, The Two Roberts.

That night, as Hen and Caryl hit the dance floor two men appeared at the top of the stairs in raincoats and broad-brimmed hats hollering: 'This is a raid.' They rapidly held up the bar on the top floor and robbed the takings before walking slowly down the steps onto the dance floor, holding something resembling a pistol in their pockets whilst repeatedly yelling: 'This is a raid!' Hen was pretty drunk by this time and a half-cut Caryl just spun round and dismissed them with her loud nasal drawl: 'Oh, don't be so silly, darlings, you look absolutely lovely and I'm going to dance with one of you,' and threw her arms around the nearest crook, which acutely embarrassed him, causing his face to turn bright crimson.

Of course, you can only hold up a place if people believe that you really are a dangerous gangster, but nobody in the Gargoyle (apart from Caryl) took any notice of them at all. By this time, the barman upstairs had managed to untie himself and telephone the police who came haring up through the fire escape and nabbed the crooks … at the sight of which all the clubbers started shoving drinks up their jumpers, because it was 'after hours'. The bemused crooks were overheard complaining: 'I've never seen such disgraceful behaviour in my life!' 'Oh yes,' concurred the arresting officer, 'it's *not* the sort of place to come to.'

So, the police and the crooks left, commiserating with one another as the band struck up again and Henrietta danced with Lucian until the sweat poured down their faces.

Chapter 3

Chelsea Girls

It's difficult to imagine now, but 1950s Chelsea was still a cheap area and home to a bunch of bohemians nicknamed the 'Chelsea Set'. The district today has almost nothing in common with the Chelsea that emerged from the Second World War. It was more like a tranquil market town and artisan's quarter. The King's Road was still a quiet residential street with chemists' shops, family grocers and a few inexpensive restaurants. Adding to the bohemian atmosphere was the artist Augustus John, like a character out of the nineteenth-century novel *Trilby*. With his pointy beard, felt hat and swirling cloak, Augustus could be seen swaying down the road, as *The Naked Civil Servant*, Quentin Crisp, effeminately sashayed up in the other direction, looking every inch a dandified dame, with his candyfloss hair.

Prototype Rock 'N' Roll Wild Child

Against this backdrop Henrietta became a 'Chelsea Girl' and entered the life of the once well-known but now largely forgotten artist Elinor Bellingham-Smith, who lived in a large Georgian house on 155 Old Church Street, just a few doors down from the Chelsea Arts Club. Her studio was housed on the top floor and her living room was decorated with paintings by eminent artist friends such as William Coldstream. It was from here that Elinor ran her artists' salon crammed with *objets d'art*. For most of the

1950s, the '155 Salon', as it was affectionately known, became a lodestone for those returning from the services like the author and art critic Colin MacInnes. Over the years regulars included the artists Prunella Clough, Nancy Sharp, Elizabeth Frink, Lucian Freud, Francis Bacon, The Two Roberts, John Minton and of course Henrietta herself.

It was the art critic David Sylvester who introduced her to Elinor's 155 Salon where she perfected her prototype rock 'n' roll wild child persona. Henrietta often stayed over and Elinor's teenage son, John Moynihan, became besotted with her:

> My mother always had a flair for grouping interesting people into sets, and making sure these sets were not only fiercely loyal, but seemingly impregnable ... It was Elinor's sense of fun ... that enticed people to join ranks and enjoy a daily party.

Elinor's Salon was also conveniently placed just a few doors down from the Queens Elm pub, which had become the favourite meeting place for local artists. Low key in a rather dreary brown mahogany, the colour of the place came from its customers. It was also convenient. The Chelsea Arts Club resided in the same road (as did Elinor's Salon) and the Chelsea School of Art was nearby. After the pub everyone would walk down to 155 where Elinor produced piles of sausages and mashed potato to sober them up. Ever since she'd suffered a miscarriage during a German bombing raid in the war, Elinor had wanted a daughter. She took Henrietta under her wing, and everyone became bewitched by Hen's beauty as she threw herself around Elinor's front room to the strains of the *Washboard Rag*.

By her own admission Henrietta had grown up with no role models, but throughout this period she was enjoyed and indulged by her two adopted mother figures: Muriel Belcher and Elinor Bellingham-Smith, who'd originally trained as a dancer until a back injury put paid to her career. So, she went to the Slade School of Art and became an artist. Although Elinor was now grey-haired and middle-aged, she still danced on top of tables and refused to grow old gracefully. She enjoyed bedding young men, she liked the daring of it – breaking one of the last female taboos – and, in return, Henrietta enjoyed Elinor's outrageous sexual jokes and pornographic drawings which were considered the steamiest around.

Whenever reminded of those days Henrietta would laugh: 'I wasn't very girlish, definitely a tomboy.' But Paul Potts credited Henrietta with more intelligence than the others: 'Exposure sharpens the senses. Some people called her a slut; if she was, she was a slut of heaven.' However, her boyfriend Michael Law got so exasperated by Henrietta's lust for Lucian that he went off to work in Rome and told her that if she ever wanted to get married she should write to him, but Henrietta was besotted with Lucian. She visited his studio every day for a year because she found him 'infinitely mysterious and frightfully good-looking'. She loved the romance of it all until she found another woman's menstrual stains on the bed sheets. So, she left Lucian to marry Michael Law, but with Michael in Rome (and having nowhere to stay) she took up residence at Elinor's once more. As her son, John, said: 'Even Henrietta had her let-downs.' As Elinor recorded when Hen turned up after another row with Michael Law:

> Henrietta is staying here. She's going to the country tomorrow. But she got herself into such a state of nerves that she had to go to bed with calming pills (sedatives). With a bit of sensible quietness, I hope, she will recover. She's a bit of a problem, but she seems to have nowhere to go.

Another row involving Hen and Michael ended in a bust-up, which reached the press with the front-page headline: 'Queen's Painter Arrested!' Elinor's husband, the painter Rodrigo Moynihan, had been fined for taking part in what the newspapers described as a brawl, in which a police officer's helmet had been knocked off. But according to Elinor, the police were beating up Michael Law in the street and when Rodrigo asked them to stop, they gave him a good hiding too.

At Apollo Place ...

Henrietta went on to marry Michael Law in a civil ceremony in Rome, where large swathes of the American film industry had relocated to escape Senator McCarthy's witch hunt, which was then purging Hollywood. They shared an apartment with former Gargoyle habitué the screenwriter Ivan Moffat, with whom Michael was busily working on the film *Attila the Hun*. But Hen became lonely and depressed ... she cut her wrists and, after a year away, they returned to London.

The Chelsea Set was incestuous, everyone slept with one another sooner or later. Once back in the fray, Henrietta became besotted with John Minton's latest crush, Norman Bowler. A bodybuilder and amateur wrestler of Adonis-like proportions, even the most 'straight' artists marvelled at Norman's physique. Minton lived just down the road from Elinor at the end of Cheyne Walk, where he had a small house in a cul-de-sac called Apollo Place in an area ominously known as the World's End.

The World's End and its boundaries are never very clear. It forms the lower reach of the riverside at Chelsea, the furthest point from the King's Road from Sloane Square and incorporates the streets and houses for 300 metres in either direction of the World's End pub. If the Sloane Square end of the King's Road was the poshest and most respectable, then the World's End was the opposite. In the 1950s it was where the most extreme forms of anti establishment counter-culture began to cluster. From artists, writers and poets to underground record shops and boutiques.

John Minton's home, at 9 Apollo Place was always full of rough trade (saucy sailors he'd picked up for sex) and became the site of numerous wild parties. In Minton's case, the road was aptly named after the Greek god of music and the arts. Apollo symbolises eternal youth and Minton marvelled at the male physique in the same homoerotic way as the ancient Greeks did. The World's End was a kind of playground for rich kids slumming it and a form of purgatory for the poor living in its slum dwellings. Needless to say, John Minton and Francis Bacon loved it there – partying away on 'Queer Street' – and Apollo Place soon developed a reputation with the local police.

The constant partying also led to casualties. One of Minton's sailors became so neurotic, he told Henrietta he was sick and tired of 'Minton's Circus' and was going to end it all. He careered into the kitchen and stuck his head in the oven. Several minutes later there came a blood-curdling scream as the sailor shot back out of the kitchen with his head sizzling; it was an electric oven. He ran outside to the Embankment and vaulted over the wall, straight into the River Thames. But it was low tide, so the sailor became stuck in the sludgy mud with his smouldering good looks and charred head leaving a vapour trail. However, according to Hen (and despite his promiscuity), Minton was always on the lookout for love. He was as romantic as his paintings and craved affection. So, to replace the half-singed sailor he installed the object of his desire, Norman Bowler, at Apollo Place.

Of an evening the members of the Chelsea Set would congregate at the Queens Elm, which slowly filled with the most unlikely people. The road to Soho was then taken either by taxi or the number 19 bus. Upon arrival, everyone regrouped at the Colony Room to consume Muriel's gossip and numerous alcoholic refreshments, before hitting the Gargoyle where they wedged themselves in. The dance floor would be dominated by 'Minton's Circus' with the artist himself at the centre dancing away, whilst the muscle-bound Norman Bowler charmed the pants off everyone by the bar.

Over breakfast Elinor liked to give a post-mortem of the previous night. John Minton and his new crush, Norman Bowler, featured in much of the gossip: 'Johnny's boys come and go fast ... he picks them up in pubs, you know. Nice boys but very naïve.' Norman had joined 'Johnny's Circus' just as his father was preparing him to take over his watchmaking business, which was not an exciting prospect for young Norman. Trying to think of ways to make money, he'd heard that the Royal College of Art was looking for models – a move which changed the course of his life and introduced him to the bohemian world of Soho. He was then asked to sit for a tutor at the Royal College of Art, John Minton. On the way to his first sitting, Norman's motorbike had broken down and he was late. Rushing in, he apologised for looking a bit of a mess. But Minton went weak-kneed at the sight of the butch biker who'd bowled in like Marlon Brando in *The Wild One*. They hit it off immediately. Norman liked his sense of humour and Minton marvelled at Norman's physique. He'd finally found the ideal man he'd been looking for: young, attractive and original, with a sense of humour that was infectious.

Manic Bingeing and Promiscuity ...

Norman was soon feeling very happy to be in the company of an affluent artist who drove around in a Rolls Royce and painted pictures of him barefoot in crotch-tight trousers. Whilst he sat for Minton at Apollo Place, another young man turned up called Jeffrey Bernard, who also modelled for Minton and was looking to borrow some money. Jeff knew of a party in Soho that night, so they all ended up there. It was the start of a long friendship. Jeff was the same age as Norman. Minton paid Jeff a weekly allowance to accompany him on his jaunts around bohemia as queer 'eye candy'. The former art student Jo Reed Turner told me Jeff was a close friend of Henrietta's too, and they often hung out together, cadging drinks from whomever they could:

> Henrietta represented fun. Always laughing, always up to no good ... I walked in to the French early one day and saw Jeffrey and Henrietta killing themselves, laughing in the corner. When I asked, 'What are you doing?' Jeffrey put on his 'little voice' and said, 'Henrietta's starting at that end of the bar and I am starting at the other end and we are going to meet in the middle and see who's got the most fivers. The loser buys lunch'. It was a little game they played, cadging money as they worked their way around the bar. I was mesmerised, watching Henrietta ensnare a city gent ... she got him in her sights then locked on and did the 'business' on him – she'd perfected it down to a fine art. After which he bought her drink after drink after drink ... and there was always one going around the corner for Jeffrey. She was really good at it.

Jeff had been at prep school with the Woolworths heir Tony Hubbard. He was well educated with a posh voice, but once he'd left school Jeff just did odd jobs and drifted. He was a toyboy long before the term was invented and became very good at bumming off rich homosexuals like John Minton. In many ways Minton personified the post-war art set often remembered more for their louche lives – manic bingeing and promiscuity – than their art. Henrietta had developed a crush on Minton, who in turn was in love with Norman Bowler, whom Henrietta then proceeded to seduce. Confused? Well perhaps the situation is best summed up by Norman himself:

> Soho in the fifties became a myth. Those few who are still alive get wheeled out by interested and ignorant journalists and their foggy minds forget what is true and what is not. Stories are often taken out of the mouths of others and put in their own. Forgotten are the suicides, the attempted suicides, the spitefulness, the bitterness and the loneliness. But it produced a talented period in England like no other ... I had seen Henrietta Law around the Soho Clubs and pubs, sometimes with her husband Michael ... I heard that the marriage was one of convenience, both having open liaisons elsewhere. You could always be sure that Henrietta would turn up at a good party. Outspoken, intelligent, she would not suffer fools gladly – and at your peril did you make her an enemy.

Forever trying to turn his life into one long party, in 1955 Johnny Minton threw one in his home for fellow artist Denis Wirth-Miller. From the outside 9 Apollo Place looked like an Arabic little house with a small door and bare walls but inside it opened out into long passages and high ceilings with a kitchen and bathroom. Beyond this was a flight of red-carpeted stairs which led up to Minton's huge studio with exposed beams and rafters; here sat a rather large table serving as a bar, manned by one of Minton's matelots and a dance area blasting out loud gramophone music.

The place was heaving and amongst the throng of frenetic dancers was Henrietta and Minton's crush, Norman Bowler. By the bar area stood Jeffrey Bernard telling tall tales of the punishment beatings he'd experienced at school, whilst Francis Bacon reminisced about the illegal gambling parties he'd held in Minton's studio. Then, an excited Henrietta and Norman whirled past, making their way downstairs together, pausing only at the bottom to turn and look back up. As Norman later admitted: 'It was pretty obvious that we were getting on more than just "well".' Not moving from his flat for two days, they then fled to a caravan in the country to escape the Soho rumour mill. They decided to elope and live together, but not having any income (having just felled their magic money tree, Johnny Minton) Norman worked and they borrowed where they could. Meanwhile, back in bohemia, John Moynihan witnessed a bereft Minton thrashing about in an emotional chasm:

> It caused quite an uproar in Soho and Chelsea at the time and the effect on the lover scorned was acute. Elinor offered Johnny her Arpeges-scented shoulder to weep on, which he constantly did at Muriel's. Minton's drinking escalated alarmingly, after Norman's marriage to Henrietta at Hampstead registry office. His health began to show signs of deterioration.

Elinor's daughter-in-law, Clare Moynihan, told me that Minton was drawn to Elinor because she knew all about sadness. Elinor adored Minton: 'I'm the only woman to have ever slept with Johnny Minton,' she'd say, followed by a big laugh. But from here on in, it was a downward spiral for Minton. He'd helped so many people, including Francis Bacon, but their friendship had steadily deteriorated into jealousy. At the Colony, Minton insulted Francis' paintings and in retribution Francis poured a bottle of champagne over Minton's head and massaged it into his scalp whilst repeating his mantra: 'Champagne for my real friends, real pain for my sham friends.' Deeply wounded, Minton found the public humiliation too much to bear. The news that Henrietta had fallen pregnant by Norman didn't improve matters either, but being magnanimous in his grief, Minton gave Hen and Norman £1,000 to set up a family home together, and in 1955 they moved into 357 Liverpool Road, Islington, which Johnny Minton would occasionally visit. He loved Hen's little boy, Joshua. He used to make him giggle.

But money still constantly slipped through Hen's fingers like water. Tony Hubbard took pity on her when she complained she didn't have a good overcoat: 'Go down to Harrods and buy yourself one and put it on my account.' So off she went, but that coat wasn't the only thing she bought and she quickly burnt a hole in Hubbard's wallet. But the debt was soon repaid when, at the Gargoyle, a man walked in whom Hubbard hated: 'Oh God, I'd give a hundred pounds to see that bastard on his back,' he cried. 'Would you *really* darling?' said Hen as she calmly strolled over to the unsuspecting man and asked him to dance. Unable to believe his luck, he jumped up as she casually bent down and grabbed him by his ankles then flipped him on his back. Hen said it was the easiest £100 she'd ever earned.

Meanwhile, her ex-lover, Lucian Freud, had been featuring regularly in all the gossip columns. Despite being married to Kitty (the daughter of Britain's most famous sculptor, Jacob Epstein), Lucian was publicly wooing the Guinness heiress, Caroline Blackwood. Lucian then forced Kitty into a humiliating public divorce and married Caroline to much fanfare. After their honeymoon in Paris, the married couple moved back to London where Caroline paid £1,000 for a flat at 86 Dean Street, the same seventeenth-century Queen Anne-panelled house once occupied by Henrietta and Michael Law. Just like Hen before her, living in the epicentre of bohemian Soho, Caroline had dinner with Francis Bacon nearly every night of her marriage to Lucian. She also dropped into the Colony daily, to meet Henrietta with whom she had attended Queen's Secretarial College some years earlier. Caroline had obtained a position at *Picture Post* magazine, but as alcoholism began to bite, she soon gave up her journalistic career and (like Hen) grew closer to Francis Bacon. Hen and Caroline became bosom buddies, but I wonder if Caroline ever knew that during all those months Lucian was mooning around town like a lovesick puppy – loudly proclaiming his love for the Guinness heiress – he'd been sleeping with Hen and her best friend Caryl.

The Siren's Call ...

Amidst all of this, John Minton seriously went off the rails. His next crush after Norman Bowler was a James Dean lookalike whom his best friend, Elinor Bellingham-Smith, seduced and stole from him. An apoplectic Minton began to go around to Elinor's son's home to scream at him what a *slutty bitch* his mother was. Then, a few weeks later (and after a dismal Christmas to boot) Minton took his own life on 20 January 1957. The star that had shone so brightly and lit the way for so many other artists was snuffed out. The unfinished painting on his easel, *The Death of James Dean*, seemed poignantly symbolic considering the loss of his James Dean-like lover.

The funeral haunted Minton's friends who'd all but deserted him during his downward spiral. The service was theatrically staged with a circus of Minton mourners. He'd died at the youthful age of 39, but, to many, he was already a burnt-out case often to be found drunk, and unconscious, under a table at the Gargoyle. Whenever someone commits suicide those left behind often feel guilty about not having done enough to stop it and Henrietta was no exception. Her initial reaction was anger when Norman informed her that Minton had killed himself. She loved him very much and thought, as people often do, that if she'd been around he might not have done it – but on reflection she conceded he would have – and so that, I thought, was that, until Diana Melly gave me an interesting coda:

> When Minton committed suicide, he left Henrietta Apollo Place because he thought if Henrietta had a home of her own, she'd leave Norman and go and live there which is what eventually happened. If you were a woman living the life of a bohemian, as Henrietta did then, you were bound to meet unconventional men. You really weren't going to end up with a stockbroker and live an ordinary 9 to 5 existence. I made a commercial for Henrietta's first husband, Michael Law – he seemed rather nice. Then there was Norman Bowler: he didn't treat her badly and she had two children with him.

According to Norman their marriage ended after three years because he'd decided to use his love of the theatre to become an actor – or, as Henrietta put it, he'd been sleeping with their lodger Caryl Chance. Furious at the deception, Hen moved out of their Islington home and journeyed to the World's End. Caryl begged to go with her but Hen was having none of it. Amidst the suicides, attempted suicides and spitefulness, Norman knew that he had to leave bohemia behind to survive and sold their family home to Hen's ex-lover, Lucian Freud, before moving on. But the siren's call proved too strong for Henrietta, who was heading for the rocks.

Chapter 4

Dom

As you may have realised by now, dear reader, nothing is ever clear-cut or straightforward when it comes to Henrietta. During the last year she lived with her second husband, Norman Bowler, she'd hired a nanny with whom she left her son, Joshua, and took a job working in a bookshop café where she became besotted with a shy eighteen-year-old Indian boy called Dom Moraes.

Dom's father, Frank, was a former Oxford man and the best-known journalist in India as editor-in-chief of the *Indian Express*. By the age of sixteen, Dom had travelled to half a dozen countries with his father and met the poet Stephen Spender (then a well-known British literary figure) who'd visited India in 1954. Spender was so impressed by Dom's poetry he offered to publish some in *Encounter* magazine and helped Dom get a place at Jesus College Oxford. The following year Dom travelled through Europe before going to Oxford to read English aged eighteen. In 1957, when he was nineteen, he'd already hooked up with Henrietta and published his first book of poems, *A Beginning*, which Dom dedicated to her and caused considerable waves in literary London. But to fully understand what's going on let's go back to when Dom first arrived in Britain.

A Village Inside a City ...

Most Sundays Dom lunched at the Spenders' house with Stephen Spender's wife, the pianist Natasha Litvin, a tall, beautiful woman whose brisk manner concealed her sweet nature. One of the other guests was Spender's best friend, Cyril Connolly, that literary lion in whose house Henrietta had once literally squatted and defecated by the back door. Connolly, who could be intimidating, interrogated the terrified Dom, 'Where did you buy that suit? It does not fit you!' Then, to clear the air, Stephen Spender produced some of Dom's poems, and showed them to Connolly who read them furiously, before declaring they were exquisite and proceeded to shower Dom with some of the best criticism he'd ever had in his entire life. Connolly's wife, the literary femme fatale Barbara Skelton, then read the poems and purred, 'They're very sexy, aren't they?', which surprised Dom as he'd never thought of them that way.

Some weeks later Stephen Spender invited Dom to lunch in town with two other poets. After the meal, one of them said to Dom: 'Care for a drink?' This young man was called Oliver Bernard, elder brother of Hen's friend Jeffrey. Oliver wrote verse but had not yet had much published. Then he said, 'Shall we go on to a club?' So they walked down Dean Street and entered a basement, a long room with a bar in the middle, and tables and chairs hugging the wall. It was half-lit, which Dom thought was fortunate because it contained some of the worst paintings he had ever seen. A small, well-worn woman called Jenny served them. 'This is Jenny's place,' said Oliver as the bar started to fill with scruffy drunks. Dom was terrified when a tall, skinny Scotsman, with a face wrecked by whisky, made a pass at him. Oliver explained, 'That's Robert Colquhoun, he's a famous painter.' As the air filled with drunken laughter and manic music, Colquhoun kept stumbling back over and making lewd passes at a somewhat delicate Dom, who, unused to drinking burpy British beer, started to feel bilious and took a taxi home.

The next day, as Dom nursed the mother of all hangovers, he received a note from Oliver, apologising for the previous day and inviting him to pop by his small flat. Oliver's girlfriend had just left him and the place was in chaos. Dom said that they ate baked beans on toast and exchanged poems like salutes. Afterwards, they went back to Soho for a drink and the bohemian lifestyle began to bite. It fascinated Dom: the chaos of Oliver's flat, the baked bean cuisine and the Soho bars were exactly what he had dreamed literary life to be like. Before long he was hooked and found himself going to Soho *every* night:

> The pungent smell of exotic food and people in the street, the pretty, waif-like girls in the pubs, the sense of inhabiting a village inside a city intoxicated me.

He even became friendly with the drunk painter Robert Colquhoun and his boyfriend (and fellow painter) Robert MacBryde. Once they discovered Dom was not homosexual, they did not make any more passes. The pair were nicknamed 'The Two Roberts' and had a reputation as the *enfants terribles* of the art world. Dom said that when sober they were marvellous to be with. Colquhoun was very gentle and intelligent and MacBryde was malicious and very funny. He was the domesticated housewife of the pair, forever fretting and fussing over Colquhoun. But when drunk they became intolerable, often physically attacking each other and sometimes arriving covered in bandages and plaster casts.

Eccentrically Orientated ...

In Soho, rumours of a house party often spread from bar to bar like wildfire. Whenever this occurred, everyone downed their drinks and went. No matter whose party it was, Dom always found them depressingly the same: lots of scruffy poets and painters drinking rough red wine and then the playing of a gramophone record that triggered off the pairing up of couples indulging in the preliminaries to copulation. Dom was too shy and inhibited to approach a girl, though the girls at these parties were very approachable. He would just stand there and watch enviously as the couples paired off, that is until fate intervened, and he was pulled into Henrietta's orbit via David Archer's bookshop.

One afternoon, after drinking with Oliver Bernard in Jenny's club, Oliver suggested they call on David Archer. Dom didn't know who Archer was. 'He's just started a new bookshop,' Oliver said as they walked round the corner into Greek Street and entered a beautiful new shop opposite the Palace Theatre. Its only occupant was a tall middle-aged man who held himself rigid in a regimental way. This was David Archer. He began by asking Dom if he'd met any poets. 'You ought to meet some, really,' he said. 'Fun for you, *what?*' For some reason Archer always talked like a P.G. Wodehouse character and there was something distinctly Jeeves and Woosterish about him: 'What, *what?*' For Dom, Archer was a godsend. In his fifties, bald and bespectacled with kind, blue eyes. Archer walked with a Prussian stiffness and a bundle of newspapers always clamped under his left arm to help disguise his withered hand. Henrietta, who loved Archer deeply, variously described him as gently born, eccentric, altruistic, kind and perceptive.

Archer had come to Soho via a circuitous route. He had moved his original Parton Street bookshop from Bloomsbury in London via Manchester to wartime Glasgow, by which time it had evolved into some kind of arts centre where he met The Two Roberts, Colquhoun and MacBryde. In 1956 he opened his last bookshop, back in London. The sign read 'David Archer Bookseller Parton Press' and it resided at 34 Greek Street, Soho. The Italian designer Germano Facetti designed the bookshop at a cost of £3,000, a huge sum in those days. Dom said it was a beautiful establishment spread over two floors. Beside the bookshop section was a large library, a coffee shop and an art gallery where homeless poets often slept. The poet Paul Potts said the bookshop was always on the edge of bankruptcy, due to Archer's habit of never accepting any money from his customers. Perversely, he often gave them whatever he had in the till, saying they looked like they needed a good meal:

> The actual physical way in which he gave money, was the most beautiful thing about him. It was as if he was conferring the order of merit on you ... He really believed his function in life was to look after people who couldn't look after themselves, provided they had some talent.

It didn't take long for Henrietta to latch on to Archer, who attracted a large circle of bohemians and was respected because he helped people. The very first exhibition at his bookshop's gallery was for his boyfriend, John Deakin, who exhibited his photographs of Paris. The catalogue was written by another important mother figure in Hen's life, the poet Elizabeth Smart – but more of her later. Oliver and Jeff's younger brother, Bruce Bernard, helped hang the show and, as Henrietta recalled, it was Deakin's first ever exhibition:

> David Archer and his friend John Deakin were old friends of mine. I spent my early youth drinking in the same places as they did, and this bond, once forged, is impossible to overlook. Archer was a man the like of whom will not be seen again … a left-wing Fascist and patron saint of the 40s and 50s poets – he had first published Dylan Thomas, George Barker, David Gascoyne, Sidney Graham … his publishing house was called the Parton Press and it was entirely financed by David. He was so generous-minded that he let his authors own their own copyright … of course he never managed to recoup any money. As soon as his authors became successful, which they invariably did, they would transfer to a bigger house with greater powers of distribution. Of course, what David wanted was a literary salon in the style of Madame de Staël – and he got it. Colin Wilson, Christopher Logue, Colin MacInnes, Michael Hastings and many others, came in every day, drank endless cups of coffee and talked voraciously, but never bought a book.

In the basement of the bookshop was the coffee bar run by Henrietta, who Bruce Bernard had nicknamed 'Piss Off Darling'. There was a three-metre-high photo of Henrietta at the back of the bar, which Deakin had printed. As Henrietta explained in the BBC documentary on David Archer, *A Gentleman in Soho*:

> He was an entrepreneur … he didn't want a bookshop at all – he wanted a Salon – that's why he wanted a coffee bar in it … David talked more about the coffee bar than the books when he was setting up the business … he talked about how people would sit

> around and have wonderful conversations. What he never talked about was how it would pay for itself. The point of the bookshop was that it was to be an arts centre for Archer, it was his life.

Henrietta explained that David Archer wasn't motivated by money, nor did he have any concept of making any. Archer lived through other people, he couldn't bear to be alone and would soon go on to publish the first collection of poems by Henrietta's future husband:

> One afternoon David and I were drinking in the Colony Room. 'Hello, cunty' Muriel ... greeted me as usual. We sat down on a banquette and David pulled some crumpled sheets of typescript from his pocket. 'I wish you'd read these poems,' he said, 'they're by a young Indian boy called Dom Moraes. I might want to publish them. What do you think?' I said I liked them and he seemed relieved and stuffed them back in his pocket.

Whilst Hen ran the café, Dom became Archer's shop assistant along with Robert Colquhoun and Ralph Abercrombie (son of the poet Lascelles Abercrombie) who took over as manager. A dryly witty man, one day Ralph was drinking with Dom across the road in the Coach & Horses pub when a destitute old man, with a slightly mad look in his eyes, shuffled in. He half stumbled up to Dom and Ralph and produced a battered copy of the Bible before demanding, 'Half a crown please Ralph'. Ralph gave him the money and as the man handed over the Bible and hobbled off, a mystified Dom enquired who he was. 'That,' said Ralph ruefully, 'was the manager of David's last bookshop.'

A Man of Importance ...

News of Archer's largesse had spread like wildfire on the Soho grapevine and the Parton Press bookshop was now rammed full of people, none of whom were paying customers. Every young writer around used it as a club, borrowed books and drank free coffee. For weeks nobody was able to enter the lavatory because the poverty-stricken playwright Bernard Kops had locked himself in it to write *The Hamlet of Stepney Green*. The play became a considerable success and Kops confessed he owed it all to Dom:

> Dom, gentle and quiet, and not yet out of boyhood, had a different aura, with his white suit and touch of eastern promise. He had a little money and was extremely generous … We all fell in love with Dom immediately. 'You've written a play, I hear. But is it a masterpiece?' were his first words to me. 'I do hope it's a masterpiece.' Me, in my green arrogant years replied, 'Yes. It probably is a masterpiece.' – 'Actually, I am a poet,' he said, earnestly. Surely, he could not be as awful as that. All poets were shits; the higher the art the greater the shit. But in a world where everyone was self-absorbed, Dom actually listened. That morning … Dom introduced me to David [Archer] and sang my genius, although he had not read a word of mine. I was not embarrassed, and did not contradict him … David pointed me in the right direction. There and then, he commanded me to ring an American producer, and my writing life and career was born.

Another literary talent who joined the scene was Christopher Logue who'd arrived from Paris with his hat, cloak and stick, looking like a character from Weimar Germany, and was surprised to find Archer's bookshop:

> open, fresh, friendly, with people standing about, talking, trying to catch the eye of the black haired, sumptuous beauty, whose name I soon learnt was Henrietta … working the coffee machine that stood at one end of the shop's counter, assessing new customers in loud, always on the verge of laughter voice: 'What's your name? Have you come to buy a book? Or borrow some money? That's David over there. The only gentleman you're likely to meet in this part of London' … David, now quite forgotten, was a man of importance where poetry was concerned. Nervous with a mild stutter, never still, always anxious to help others, courtly in his ways, David, the homosexual son of a Wiltshire landowner who hated him, gave together with the fortune he inherited, to poets and to their work

> … [whilst] Henrietta came and went as she pleased with this poet or that painter.

According to Henrietta, Archer had an aristocratic prejudice against taking money from customers and would recommend them to another bookshop down the road. Hence his dire financial state, as Christopher Logue concurs:

> David … preferred to give books away rather than sell them. If you asked to buy a particular volume, David would say: 'Oh, please, do you mind. I need that for the window. Try Better Books.' Then, fearing that he had offended, he would rush to the nearest off-licence and buy a bottle of wine … a customer of David's who looked like a schoolboy wearing a three-piece suit was going through the shop's magazine rack … [he was] the playwright, and future novelist, Michael Hastings. Michael's black hair bristled upwards. Now and then he ran a comb through it. His eyes darted about. A handsome lad. Henrietta came over for a closer look … But Henrietta's (to me) exciting décolletage made no impression on M. Hastings … 'Oh I've got to run.' And without more ado he hurried away out of the shop. Henrietta, neglected, sniffed, put her nose in the air and went back to her coffee machine.

Dom was having a drink, across the road in the Coach & Horses, when Archer marched in and stood looking at him twitchily for a while, then, in the slightly awkward and embarrassed way of someone requesting a personal favour, he enquired: 'Would you mind very much if I published your poems? As a book I mean … *what?*' Dom stared at him, shocked. Of course, he wouldn't mind being published by the Parton Press, with its unique record, in fact it seemed to him an honour. But then, on second thoughts, Dom protested that Archer had not read any of his poems. 'But, my dear boy,' he said, 'I only ever read detective stories. I never read any of the poets I published. But I can smell a poet, if you see what I mean … *what?*' Archer then introduced Dom to his boyfriend, John Deakin, whom Dom considered one of the world's greatest living photographers because his eye was so restless.

Deakin shot a set of promotional portraits of Dom posing against mosaics and the iron arch of a Victorian railway station before taking the train from London to Oxford and pursuing Dom back to his digs. As well as artistic portraits, Deakin also loved pointing his camera at flea markets, forgotten alleyways and graffiti-covered walls. Dom chose one such photograph for the cover of his soon-to-be-published book of poetry, which he dedicated to his new secret crush, Henrietta.

Piss Off, Darling. Can't You See I'm Busy?

Dom had first seen Henrietta perched on a stool at the Colony surrounded by men, whose idle chit-chat she ruthlessly punctuated with her noisy, emphatic laughter. She was twenty-five and Dom was struck by her pale skin, long dark hair and the radiant intensity of her eyes. Dom noticed her escort was a tall, handsome young man with a kindly face who stood a little back from Hen's entourage, nursing a beer. When he asked her if she'd like another drink, Hen turned and declared with a dramatic flutter of the eyelashes: 'Piss off, darling. Can't you see I'm busy?' Her high-pitched voice emphasising certain syllables like a well-rehearsed actress. For Dom, the words conjured up the atmosphere of the 1920s and reminded him of one of those Bright Young People from Evelyn Waugh's *Vile Bodies*. She was everything Dom imagined a literary muse to be, but being far too shy to make the first move he was introduced to her by Archer. 'She's a one, really,' he beamed.

Together, Henrietta, Dom and Deakin formed a tragicomic trio that drank together and became party to horrendous accidents, rather like The Three Stooges. On one occasion Deakin burst into the pub and demanded a glass of white wine, which the barman mistakenly poured from a glass bottle containing bleach. Deakin downed it in one, fell to the floor unconscious and had to be carried off to hospital to have his stomach pumped. Shortly after, at the opening of a Francis Bacon exhibition, a brass bolt from an overhead window came loose and plummeted down, striking

Ralph on the head and knocking him out. It was through these incidents that Dom slowly became aware of the ominous nature of David Archer's bookshop and noticed that everyone connected with it seemed to become increasingly accident-prone as the omens of doom abounded.

As things began falling apart, Archer himself became more and more nervous. He began to disappear from the bookshop for long periods and employed a young painter who had just been discharged from a psychiatric hospital, as a shop assistant. On his first day, the painter dusted the books with a long feather duster. Unnervingly, he did this studiously to the exclusion of everyone and everything else that went on round him in the busy shop. On the second day, having run out of books to dust, he began to dust David Archer, who freaked out and fled. The painter then dusted the manager, Ralph, before moving on to Henrietta, and finally Dom. In quick succession, one by one, they followed Archer to the pub across the road. From the window of the Coach & Horses, Hen and Dom peered apprehensively at the shop, observing the casual entry of customers and their eager exit, pursued by the demonic painter wielding his duster. They didn't know what to do, so they telephoned the psychiatric hospital from which the painter had been discharged and a van called round to cart him away.

In this doomed atmosphere, Henrietta and Dom's relationship blossomed. After a date at the cinema, the shy teenager found the inner courage to invite her to lunch, which soon became a daily fixture. Eventually, they started having dinner together too and passed much of the day in each other's company. For Hen, Dom was a beautiful and slender fawn-eyed boy and, for Dom, Henrietta's qualities which had once deeply disturbed him now seemed beautiful. She told him that she'd had an unhappy childhood, and he felt deeply sorry for her. When she threw bread rolls at the other diners in Wheeler's restaurant, Dom realised Hen's insecurity made it impossible for her not to be the centre of attention in any given situation. This he accepted unquestioningly, along with her being twice married with a baby boy in tow and, being six months pregnant, with another well on the way ... then it suddenly hit him:

> I realised that I was in love ... Though my behaviour must have made this fairly obvious, I took pains not to actually declare my feelings. I did not aspire to share the pedestal on which I had placed her. She began to tell me how much she would miss me when I went up to Oxford.

He knew he would miss her too and he wished he didn't have to go.

Chapter 5

University Challenge

Dom found he had a few spare evenings left before the start of term at Oxford that October. So he took Henrietta out to dinner at Wheeler's. Many people in Soho consider the French to be the most important building in the entire city. But others of us would happily swap an afternoon in the French for the wonder of Wheeler's fish restaurant on Old Compton Street. The great granddaddy of seafood restaurants, Wheeler's was once to Soho what the Eiffel Tower is to Paris. Inside its hallowed walls could be savoured the fruits of the sea, mountains of sole mornay, strata upon strata of shellfish, bottomless lakes of parsley sauce and a seemingly unending supply of wine.

After dinner, as they walked down Old Compton Street towards the Colony Room, Henrietta turned to him with a glint in her eye and said, 'I've got the keys to someone's flat. They're away. We could go there if you like.' Dom appeared perplexed at the proposition, so she elaborated further, 'You could make love to me.' Dom was shocked. He hadn't felt any sexual desire for Henrietta, who, after all, was many months pregnant with her second child. The poet in him had set her high on a pedestal, far from the bed. 'I couldn't possibly,' deflected Dom. Artfully amused, Henrietta simply shrugged her shoulders and suggested they go for a drink instead.

The day before Dom was due to leave for Oxford, Henrietta became very ill. Some very elegant rose-shaped marks had appeared on her swollen stomach. But Hen being Hen, she couldn't just contract any *ordinary* illness and had the dubious honour of being one of the few people in the British Isles to be diagnosed with typhoid. She'd contracted it whilst dining at Wheeler's with Dom; according to Hen it was the result of twelve oysters and a *sole Véronique*.

David Archer was also very worried, not so much about Hen, but that the health inspector had called about the typhoid and told him that his bookshop might have to be quarantined. As he sat at his desk contemplating a pile of unpaid bills he began to despair, 'Dear, dear, dotty me. I really shan't be able to pay these ... *what?*' However, he reassured Dom that he'd paid the printers for his forthcoming book. But Dom didn't want to leave him like this, suffocating under the weight of unpaid bills which he felt were partly his fault as Archer was publishing his poetry. He also fretted over Henrietta being in hospital, which he also blamed himself for, because he'd fed her the typhoid-ridden oysters. So, under a somewhat doom-laden cloud, Dom departed for Oxford.

During his first week at Oxford, the other new male undergraduates sported their college scarves and applied themselves to pursuing all the nurses from the local hospitals. 'Lovely crumpet,' they said, talking of their triumphs as Dom rolled his eyes and daydreamed of the damsel in distress he'd left behind. He consoled himself by composing sad letters which snailed their way back along the sixty long miles to Henrietta's bedside.

Fortunately for Dom, he struck up a friendship with fellow poet Peter Levi who, among other things, was studying to be a Jesuit priest. Peter was tall and handsome with dark hair combed back from his pale face. He was as romantic and complicated as Dom, who remembered Peter as having the awkward grace of an antelope in a clerical collar, as he showed him around Oxford, whilst Hen was sent to another hospital, ranting and raving with a high fever. Some days later she came back to a kind of normality and found herself in the strangest of places – the abortion ward of a fever hospital, which she declared 'a damn sight jollier' than the polio ward.

A Student of Life ...

Dom's head wasn't in Oxford. Although Henrietta and Soho were far away, they still dominated his reality. To him, sleepy Oxford seemed *unreal*. Once back in London he called on Henrietta. She was over her typhoid but had been ordered to stay in the hospital in case of complications with her pregnancy. Petulant, frustrated and puffing fiercely on a fag in her hospital bed, he found her chastising the friends that sat around her, but to Dom she was charm personified.

After a trying first term, Dom took rooms in London for the Christmas vacation and visited Henrietta in hospital every day. Her bitterness surprised him, but he felt sad for her. He was certain that she had been wronged by life, although he couldn't quite work out how. So, he sent her a constant stream of flowers and books for which he received a stern letter about the dire state of his finances from his bank manager. However, he soon discovered that Soho was the same as ever, populated with the heavy drinkers and bohemian bullshitters who now bored him. He did not frequent it as often as before, except to visit David Archer, who sat in his shop surrounded by piles and piles of unsold books and unpaid bills. The bookshop had failed and Hen's coffee bar at the back was closed. But Archer was determined that Dom's poetry would still be published. As they lunched together, Archer spun Dom stories of how he'd met poets like Dylan Thomas and published them before anyone else. Before admitting, 'Frankly, I never read a word they wrote. But I *sensed* they were good.'

Whilst Dom was wrestling with his conscience, Hen was making the most of her time in hospital and noticed that the patients changed every three or four days. Her bed was next to a small operating theatre from where the surgeon would appear in shiny surgical white blood-spattered boots and gloves, waving to everyone. It was a rigid routine for the other patients, but, in that ward, Hen was above reproach, she was the loved one. She was in a situation that was unique to her in that space: she was pregnant and she thrived on it. Whilst most people had one bath a day, she had three. Despite being heavily pregnant, she was allowed to smoke all day long in bed and receive visitors whenever they showed up – often at antisocial hours when the pubs were shut. Every day she saw a wonderful female psychotherapist who would come into Hen's glass cage and tell her, contrary to her most sincere beliefs, that having a baby was going to be a piece of cake.

When Dom asked David Archer over lunch what he should do about the heavily pregnant Hen, he replied, glowing with embarrassment: 'Er, well ... I don't really know, you know. It's difficult to say, isn't it? She is ... er, a very lively girl, isn't she? You ought to bear that in mind.' He intimated that Henrietta had had many lovers, which depressed Dom, but he consoled himself with the thought that they'd all taken advantage of her trusting nature.

But Hen was no fool, and as a high-flying student of the University of Life she studiously observed the patients and staff at the hospital and once described a hideous scene where a staff nurse, bizarrely named 'Angre', was striding up and down the ward haranguing the patients for being no good. By now Hen had realised that there was not one patient in the hospital who wasn't as troubled mentally as they were physically:

> There was a poor Turkish lady who had no clothes and could speak no English and whose husband had deserted her. She was never allowed to leave the hospital because she had no clothes. She tried to run away each night but was always brought back by the porter on the gate.

Soho Swallowed Him

After the Christmas vacation, Dom visited Hen in hospital just before he returned to Oxford. He was her only visitor and Henrietta stared at him, her dark eyes smouldering in her pale face. Then, as he rose to leave, she asked, 'Do you love me?' Caught off guard, he shakily answered, 'Yes.' 'I love you too,' she said, and Dom drifted back to Oxford elated. Later that evening a fellow student popped around for a drink and Dom told him his predicament. 'I think you're very unwise,' the student said, 'all you can do is wait till she's left hospital.'

A few days later David Archer telephoned to say Henrietta had in fact left the hospital – having given birth to her baby daughter. So, Dom broke his promise to the College Principal and immediately left for London, without seeking permission. Then, to make matters worse, he began leaving for London twice a week, every week, to take Hen out to lunch at Wheeler's, where he noticed that she seemed more beautiful than ever, and as they held hands under the table Dom felt an extraordinary intensity of feeling radiating from her.

But, alas, this did not happen every day because even Henrietta could not always extricate herself from the demands of having a young family, despite employing a nanny to deal with her young son and newborn baby. When she couldn't extract herself, Dom continued the routine by himself, because he found it pleasurable. On days when she couldn't get away, Hen was unhappy and the next day, to his delight, she would tell Dom how unhappy:

> Everything she said I absorbed with pleasure, each remark she made a new shaft driven into her mind, opening it up to me.

We have now reached the point, dear reader, where Hen claims in her memoir to have made love to Dom in his Kensington boarding house and that they then remained lovers for the next ten years (1957–1967), but, as with so much she recalled, the dates just don't add up. It would have also been around this time that Henrietta claims to have left her second husband, Norman Bowler, over his affair with her best friend Caryl Chance, which may have just been a convenient excuse for Hen to leave the matrimonial home, as Johnny Minton had recently committed suicide and bequeathed her his house.

However, what is beyond doubt is that Dom quickly moved into Apollo Place with Henrietta and from here on led a double life between Oxford and London. He was nineteen and in his first year of university; she was twenty-five. Looking back on it, Dom said he enjoyed Soho too much: the company of other poets, the eccentric behaviour and, of course, the booze. He'd been easily assimilated into bohemia by Henrietta, but not into 'normal' English life, which was alien to him ... as the entertainer and female impersonator Michael Southgate told me:

> I met Dom Moraes in the French pub with Henrietta, they both used to be there a lot. Dom was a very sweet, charming man. He was the complete opposite to Henrietta in character. I never understood why she was considered such a beauty. She always looked so hard with her jet black hair and leathers. None of those artists models were very beautiful ... If you saw them in the street you wouldn't be struck by what a beauty she was but she was very sculptural and dramatic looking.

Dom admitted that 'Soho swallowed him.' Henrietta had frequented Soho for several years since the age of eighteen. She knew all the clubs and the restaurants and moved through them like bohemian royalty, hallo-ing her friends like an actress in the loud, deliberately affected voice which she liked to project in public. With Hen, Dom lost whole days to alcohol – albeit punctuated by some very expensive meals – and as Bernard Kops clocked it:

> Dom drifted away ... he got involved with the upper demi-monde, the hard drinkers of the French Pub, the environs of Hades – the vicious, lost, successful souls like Francis Bacon and Lucian Freud, and Henrietta, a beautiful, sexy, booming Junoesque empress.

Dom loved the atmosphere of the French at opening time, Gaston discussing the previous night's incidents, the leathery taste of the first whisky of the day, which made his mouth feel wet, witty and full of zest. He and Hen laughed and enjoyed themselves till it was time for lunch at Wheeler's, after which came the Colony, where everyone made bawdy jokes, and then to bed. As Dom's friend, the writer Ved Mehta verified:

> Henrietta was about the only person who could keep up with Dom's drinking. Dom would have a double whisky as an eye-opener at

half past ten and would be drunk by noon. When he was flush with money, he would stand drinks to practically anyone and everyone in a pub. He would throw money around the way he would drink. We accepted his drinking – and everything else about him – because he fitted our notion of the poet, right down to the toes. The fact that he was sometimes incoherent and feckless seemed to us a mark of his general gaiety and genius. He and Henrietta went through at least one bottle of whisky a day each.

The Romance of It All

Hen and Dom were drinking in the French one day when one of her previous lovers came in looking decidedly dishevelled. Having clocked him, Hen began talking rapidly in a loud voice. The young man didn't look at Dom, but Dom looked intently at him and read the unhappiness in his face. He was taken aback by the bitterness in the man's eyes as he suddenly swung round and walked over to their table. 'Oh, *piss off*, darling!' hissed Hen contemptuously. He stared at her, bewildered, before slapping her hard across the face. Then, as Dom was about to come to Hen's defence, the young man struck him too and, in doing so, cut his hand on the whisky glasses strewn across the table. When Gaston asked them to leave, Dom said to the young man, 'We'd better go somewhere and talk.' He went around the corner to the chemist's and bought a bandage for the hand of Hen's former lover. As he hypnotically wound the bandage round and round her ex-lover's hand, Dom felt he was trying to repair a wound that cut much deeper than mere glass.

As we now know (and as Henrietta's previous two husbands could testify), hanging out with Hen could be hard work. Dom had no sooner scurried back to Oxford for a tutorial when he found an urgent message waiting for him that he should immediately phone a friend in London. When he did so, a flat dispassionate voice told him that Hen had been sent to the hospital having taken an overdose of sleeping tablets and that he'd better come as soon as possible. The days that followed must have been hell for Dom as trains slowly shuttled him back and forth between the hallowed spires of Oxford and the languid skies of London.

When Hen was discharged from hospital, she came to Oxford for a few days to recuperate. Dom's rooms had previously been occupied by T.E. Lawrence (aka Lawrence of Arabia) and the romance of it all appealed to her. On one of the rooms' windowsills there was a deep hollow. Dom informed Hen that it was worn away by Lawrence's elbow as he lent on the sill morning, noon and night, staring intently at the view outside. She didn't know whether or not to believe him, although the window did look directly out over the men's public lavatory on Market Street.

Out in the lazy sunshine, Dom punted her on the river and they lunched at the best hotels. She ate strawberries and cream and quaffed champagne. Dom was keen to show her off to his friends. The hammer of her loud laughter and her boisterous beauty fascinated them. None of them had ever met anyone like her before, she seduced them all, they thought she was marvellous. Hen bathed in her reflected glory, blossoming in the adulation, as did Dom, in the slipstream of her afterglow. He was wonderfully happy and, imbued with the false feeling that all their problems had been solved, they discussed marriage.

But as you and I know, this idyllic quality applies only to the start of an affair and, as they soon discovered, nobody is perfect in reality. Hen could be very touchy and constantly looked for hidden subtexts in everything Dom said. A casual remark could draw a sudden adverse reaction from her. She needed to be reassured and often asserted angrily that what Dom *really* wanted was to get shot of her. He would then withdraw into himself, slightly paranoid, wondering if what she said was true. Her naked aggression shocked him, it made her voice ear-splittingly shrill. This behaviour brought back horrible memories of his childhood, since he forever associated such naked hostile emotions with his mother. The pairing of Hen and his mother in his mind shocked him, so much so that he withdrew even further into himself, unwittingly increasing the desperately sad violence of Hen's behaviour. 'It was my fault,' he would say, to which Hen would reply, 'No, mine, I had an unhappy childhood.' For Dom these repeated phrases after each and every violent argument tolled like funeral bells marking the long, drawn-out death knell of their relationship.

Cheerful and Cynical

Their relationship may have changed and the violence had increased, but the pattern of their London life remained the same. They went into Soho every day. Always drinking and eating in the same places. Always seeing the same people, many of whom were destitute. Their conversation became circular and entirely devoted to a discussion of whom they could borrow money from, or who could be persuaded to pay for lunch. The cheerful and cynical manner in which such remarks were made struck Dom as bohemian. He had grown up being taught that punctuality and courtesy were virtues but, in Hen's world, it was thought smart to be neither courteous nor punctual. In his domestic life, too, his habits altered. Dom always had a great feeling of ritual in his life. Each day was ordered and highly structured until he'd hooked up with Hen. But now, as alcoholism began to bite, he found he was unable to write, his days became shapeless and unplanned, leading nowhere except to the bottom of the next bottle. Worries prevented him from writing ... so he simply washed them away with whisky and, once drowned, hoped they didn't learn to swim.

By now their relationship had entered a new phase. Dom had always been something of a quiet loner, but Hen demanded constant reassurance that she was loved and craved continuous conversation and company. When Dom was in a silent mood, Hen compelled him to talk to her. Her unquenchable craving for reassurance led her to engage in more and more provocative behaviour to get some sort of reaction from Dom but had the unintentional effect of driving him to retreat further and further into himself, which made Hen worse. She may have been insecure about many things, but not about her physical attraction. When she swept into a bar, men turned and stared. In the centre of the room, Hen stood with her drink, throwing back her head and laughing noisily, surrounded by admirers. This made the usually shy and unassuming Dom rage with jealousy, but bizarrely brought him closer to her. Dom had a gentle voice and an unassertive manner. As a person, he seemed very different to the other members of the Monster Club they hung out with. He had a lemur-like quality, lithe and smooth-moving. Everyone was taken with his looks. He could be nervous and shy as well as witty and deft. He was completely different to Henrietta's first two husbands, Michael Law, a promiscuous father figure, and Norman Bowler, a no-nonsense macho man. In stark contrast, Dom was quiet and thoughtful, a shy pretty boy whom Hen loved to push around.

Amidst all this emotional turmoil, Dom's bank account rapidly dwindled. Supporting Hen's lifestyle was expensive, and then there were his Oxford bills. As he frittered away all his father's money, he rapidly slid into debt, like his friend David Archer who had let the main floor of his bookshop to an agency and retreated into the basement, the clutter of which was added to by the arrival of numerous crated copies of Dom's book of poetry, the aptly titled *A Beginning*. It was the first time Dom had seen a copy. As he turned it to and fro, the book looked handsome and he felt powerful in the knowledge that he was now a published poet. He noticed that David Archer flapped round and round the books, like a hen who'd just produced an egg, and was even more proud of them than the poet himself. Archer took an armful to distribute around the Soho pubs, which seemed the only way anyone would ever read them. As there was no distribution system in place Dom hawked them around London too, armed with a briefcase full of copies. Many bookshops refused to stock them as they said poetry didn't sell. But Dom's friend Ved Mehta remembered the poems as 'rather small-scale, fine things, almost like light pencil sketches' and, as we now know, they became a literary sensation. The critics were soon comparing Dom to Dylan Thomas.

Chapter 6

Fin de Partie

The arrival of the blind Indian writer Ved Mehta at Oxford was warmly welcomed by Dom. Ved had been educated at a school for the blind in America, and from there gone up to Harvard. Dom said Ved intensely disliked people who tried to help him. Anyone who took his arm to assist him across the street was given short shrift. His relationship with Ved was different to that of his other friends because he was also Indian, but, unlike Dom, he spoke fluent Hindi and intended to return home, to live in India. Ved was a dapper dresser with a waspish wit. He led a different life from that of any other university writer in that he had a secretary, and Ved was equally impressed by his new friend who seemed to know everybody who was anybody, not only at Oxford but also in London:

> That was partly because of his father and partly because of his own success as a poet, but mostly because he simply turned up everywhere unannounced and made a great impression.

By now, Dom had begun affecting the manner of Henrietta's mother figure, Muriel Belcher. A peculiar type of 1930s camp he'd picked up from the Colony, where everything ended in 'kins' or 'ette' and other words were prefixed by the word 'tiny'. So, for example, he'd turn to Ved and say, 'Vedkins how about a tiny drinkins? Let's go to the tiny pubkins.' Ved found the language particularly cosy and noticed that Henrietta and her circle used it as a type of private language – as if it were gang talk.

Talented Eccentrics ...

Ved and the other students felt that it was right for Henrietta and Dom to live in a carefree manner; they did the things the rest of them would have liked to but did not dare to. Hen and Dom felt like family to Ved. He found it easy to become the third member of the *ménage à trois* and admitted he adopted the role of a child when he was with the couple, but, because of his blindness, he could not lay claim to many of the things that they took for granted.

None of the university's dons or undergraduates were disapproving of Hen and Dom's relationship, possibly because it was so 'out in the open'. Even if some secretly did disapprove, that didn't stop them from having Hen and Dom round to dinner. Far from being cold-shouldered, they were seen as a couple of talented eccentrics with the glamour of a bohemian lifestyle. It's said that one of the most striking aspects of Dom's life in Oxford was that he lived openly with Henrietta who had been married twice and had two kids. Their contemporary, the poet Patrick Garland, compared Dom bringing Henrietta to Oxford to letting Cruella de Vil loose in Battersea Dogs Home:

> She cut a great swathe ... through the impressionable undergraduates of the late Fifties, a heady whiff of Bohemian Soho. She was an almost Parisian figure in those inhibited, repressed times. We were virginal – and she wasn't.

For many the 1950s were a period of sexual innocence. This was before the proliferation of the contraceptive pill and couples could not live openly together out of wedlock unhindered. According to Ved, most women arrived at Oxford as virgins and left as virgins. Many females looked down upon the women who had sexual relationships since, for many, preserving their virginity was the only way for them to complete their studies. Henrietta was older than the rest of the undergraduates. Ved said she was 'provocatively sexy' and liked to challenge men. She could also alternate between being 'boisterous, flighty, and hoity-toity'. All the students liked her, but Ved was also frightened by her. Forever making jokes or trouble, he said she seemed to find daily life without a drama boring:

> Part of what made her personality so attractive was that it was riven with contradictions. She was dazzling, destructive, and volatile …

More fun to be with than anyone else when she was in a good mood, but definitely someone you couldn't wait to get away from when in a bad one, Ved found Hen worldly with a childlike immediacy. She would brush Dom off like a fly, but whenever she wasn't in Oxford Dom was forever talking about her, the wonder of the World's End and its bohemian temple at Apollo Place. He was captivated, entranced and bewitched by her. He would go to see her and disappear for weeks at a time. Ved considered the whole situation extremely exciting, not only because Hen belonged to another world but also because she and Dom lived at the edge of it and carried on as if there were no tomorrow.

Fin de Partie

As if Henrietta's frequent transgressions weren't enough, her children were there too. Ved remembers that one of the first times he met Dom he was stuck at Oxford with Joshua, Henrietta's four-year-old son, so that she could go abroad. Dom looked after Joshua by himself for almost a week, taking him round to friends' student digs, university lectures and even the pub. Contrary to all the rules, Dom and Henrietta co-habited, at a time when an undergraduate could be sent down for having a person of the opposite sex in their room. Whenever Hen was there she'd stay too late and have to hide in the morning when the scout came over to wake Dom up or else attempt to climb over the college wall without impaling herself on the spikes. They once had to hide in two dustbins to avoid the moral tutor roaming the area. Hen said she and Dom looked like the two characters in a dustbin from Samuel Beckett's *Fin de Partie*.

To help pay the mounting bills, Henrietta got a secretarial job in London. A friend she met in the French, Geoffrey Rigby, gave her a job as his assistant at an advertising agency. She wasted no time chatting up the company accountant and managed to wangle herself an expense account, which she blew on long boozy lunches and taking taxis everywhere. However, Hen wasn't happy with her nanny despite her heroic efforts to deal with a toddler, a newborn baby and a chaotic household, as well as cooking and cleaning. Hen suspected (and clearly judging her by her own exacting standards) that her nanny was necking all her booze and getting screwed in the afternoon when she should have been walking the children. Henrietta desperately needed a domestic goddess who – after placing an ad at the local newsagent – came in the shape of a little old lady (Mary Grice) nicknamed Nana, who magically took over Hen's domestic life with the effortless ease of Mary Poppins.

As an earthy plain-speaking Irish woman, Nana freely gave her advice whether you wanted it or not, letting Hen know which of her friends she should keep clear of and of which she approved. Hen said Nana's advice was always right and soon came to regret it whenever she ignored it. Nana loved Dom, 'such a lovely boy!' He was her favourite. She always called him 'Dommie'.

A Terrible Knot of Pride ...

Hen's new role in the advertising agency meant she was now only around at weekends. So, every weekend Dom tore down to London to see her, which caused yet more trouble. Undergraduates who lived in college were supposed to sleep there, but Dom didn't. He was always whizzing off to London whenever he felt like it and was constantly in trouble for not writing his essays. Ved said he had an 'atmosphere of vagrancy' about him and emanated mystery. Anyone but Dom would have been sent down for his constant flouting of the rules, but Dom said his tutors were so fond of him they were frequently making excuses for his behaviour:

> Nobody had ever expected me to finish my three years at Oxford. I was always in trouble. When I felt like going to London, or even abroad, I always went; I brought up trainloads of drunken poets who turned the college into shambles overnight; I didn't turn up for tutorials. My college, however, had endless patience. This was especially due to my Principal. He shielded me from the wrath of the disciplinary authorities. Occasionally, in the quadrangle, he winked at me. We understood each other.

Despite this, Dom had a series of difficult interviews with his peers and, finally, the fellows of the college met to decide whether or not they should send him down. He was constantly absent and, by his own admission, his work was very poor. In an attempt to placate the Master of Jesus College, Hen and Dom threw a sherry party. She filled Dom's room with white flowers, hoping for the best, radiating beauty, and so somehow Dom clung on at Oxford, although the precarious nature of his stay was the least of his worries. For his entire life he'd taken it for granted that there'd always be money about, lots of money, to pay bills and indulge himself, but now there wasn't any. What with his and Henrietta's louche lifestyle, debts in London and overdrafts in Oxford, he had very little money to play with. In retrospect Dom realised that he was too young for Henrietta. She was accustomed to men with money to milk – cash cows – and, apart from his poems, Dom had no means of creaming it.

Conversely, Henrietta viewed Dom's inability to foot the bills for Apollo Place as proof of his lack of love. So he became quiet and evasive. Spinning stories about the imaginary stash of cash that would soon arrive to cover the bills. When the money did not materialise the public scenes Henrietta caused were worse than ever. Their life together was almost that of enemies: neither one trusting the other. Their mutual tensions, once sexually released in bed, returned at dawn. As their once happy innocence became an endless cycle of feuding, fighting and fucking, Dom felt a terrible knot of pride tied them together.

They had become the Elizabeth Taylor and Richard Burton of bohemia. A notable power couple whom everyone marvelled at and wanted to rub shoulders with. When Burton wrote of Taylor, 'Bewitched, bewitched by her cunt and her cunning', he could have been speaking on behalf of Dom. But for many of his contemporaries at Oxford, to witness the dreamy teenage poet going around with 'a woman of experience', was to perceive him as something akin to a hapless small furry creature in the grip of a hawk. She had an intense way of eyeing him, as if she wanted to eat him, and she radiated instant hostility towards any other female that came near her quarry. A fact backed up by the writer and curator Jane Rankin-Reid:

> My mother, Lee Hinde, met Henrietta when she first went to London from Sydney in the 1950s. As a 'beard' for a gay journalist friend, they saw each other quite frequently at the Colony Room and at the French and were introduced by mutual friends. My mother remembered not liking Henrietta terribly much. There may have been some rivalry between them. Henrietta was dominating and compelling, my mother was wily and flirtatious. Behind their distaste for one another lay my mother's crush on Dom Moraes. She adored him, though it is highly unlikely that my mother's affections were reciprocated. There is no mention of this vivacious Australian femme's presence in Moraes' diaries or other literary works. But to her dying day, the mere mention of Henrietta brought out a rarely seen side of my mother that was never particularly flattering.

Ved Mehta mentioned that there was an unmistakable whiff of physical violence between Henrietta and Dom, which he found quite disturbing, although he never witnessed any fights. Sometimes she was girlish and coy with Dom, at other times she treated him like an irritated mother who liked to physically punish her children, as witnessed by Patrick Garland:

> She partly doted on him, partly tormented him. She saw her role as a femme fatale ... in one way very devoted; but part of me felt that she was enjoying walking in the footsteps of Caitlin Thomas – enjoying the melodrama.

Ved thought there was something quite rancorous about Hen too. She could hit out at people and shower them with spite. She and Dom often seemed to be spatting. She indulged in histrionics and bullying, to which Dom mostly replied in monosyllables, 'Yes,' 'But,' 'No,' 'But,' 'Yes,' often with involuntary guilty little giggles in between. Ved noted that this atmosphere of violence also existed among their friends in London, where they'd meet up with the Monster Club and start drinking in the 'Deep End' of the French. Friends would drift in and join them as they washed away their hours in whisky and wine. Regulars included the poets Stevie Smith and George Barker, the novelist Colin MacInnes (who despite being militantly gay said that Henrietta was the only woman he'd like to marry), the playwright Frank Norman, the painter Francis Bacon, the journalist Francis Wyndham, the photographer John Deakin (who was always scouting around for someone to photograph and tout round the fashion magazines) and Dom's publisher, David Archer. Some of these friends, like MacInnes and Norman, were known for having a violent streak and were long-standing members of the Monster Club.

Added to this mix was the Indian artist F.N. Souza. Many members of the Monster Club, such as Frank Norman, became the subject matter for Souza's tortured paintings. Like Dom, Souza had also been championed by the poet Stephen Spender and both were seen as the artistic geniuses of Britain's former colonies … although both had, in fact, come from the Portuguese colony of Goa. Like Dom, Souza had also developed a disastrous drinking habit, which had got to the point where his hands shook so badly he couldn't hold a paintbrush, but that didn't stop him from painting Henrietta's portrait.

Swimming in the 'Deep End' of the French's shark-infested waters with Souza, Dom was completely out of his depth. He was always trying to see the best in everyone, even someone as impossible as Henrietta. He felt she had many admirable qualities and they could have probably been best friends, but the fatal mistake was to become sexually involved. They were too different to live successfully together. However, unlike Ved, Dom didn't picture himself as that hapless small furry creature for Hen to play with and devour. No, the poet in Dom heroically portrayed himself and his lover as a pair of those magnificent fighting hawks that fall, claws fastened on each other, in a long slow spin, crashing headlong towards the earth, as if in some wildlife documentary.

The Naked Lunch

The Easter vacation was soon upon them, a time of resurrection from death in the Christian calendar. In an attempt to resuscitate their dying relationship, Hen and Dom headed to Paris, spending their mornings at the Deux Magots and lunching at Lipp's, before fucking up their afternoons in the Café de Flore. On their first morning they saw two ragged young men racing towards them. Dom recognised one of them as Allen Ginsberg, an American Beat Poet whom he'd met in London a few weeks before; the other was a fellow poet, Gregory Corso, a little faun-like man with black curly hair and a triangular face. Corso not only looked like the great god Pan, from one of Nicolas Poussin's Bacchanalian paintings, but behaved like him too. Corso and Ginsberg both dressed in blue jeans and checked flannel shirts. They were extremely friendly and eager to please. Corso seemed to delight in being Ginsberg's sidekick and would pepper the conversations with phrases like 'They're as crazy as daisies, man!', to which Ginsberg would garnish, 'Yeah Baby, we're the wildflowers!'

Ginsberg and Corso lived in an attic at the top of a hotel, which they shared with the *Naked Lunch* author, William S. Burroughs. The attic contained three beds and a quantity of Beat literature which Ginsberg and Corso scattered over one of the beds and told Dom to read, while Burroughs rolled up his trousers and introduced Henrietta to the hellish tapestry of his hypodermic needle-marked legs. 'I hate women,' he told her, 'women are like birds,' and went into one of his long nasal drawls. Then, Corso produced some marijuana from under the bed and proceeded to roll everyone large spliff cigarettes. He showed Dom the correct way to 'toke' on his joint whilst Dom noticed, rather worryingly, that Hen seemed to have all too quickly got the hang of it.

When Ginsberg and Corso came to Britain some weeks later, Dom got them a poetry reading gig at the New College Poetry Society, Oxford. He and Hen had to go to London to collect them from the parental care of the patron saint of peculiar poetry, David Archer. Dom said Corso had the charm of a wicked schoolboy and sat smoking marijuana on the train up to Oxford. Fortunately, they were the carriage's only occupants. Then, to Dom's horror, the inspector arrived to check their tickets. 'Funny smell,' he remarked. 'They are American cigarettes,' explained Hen, 'these gentlemen are from America.' 'I've never tried American cigarettes,' mused the Inspector. 'Try one,' cried Corso as he waved a giant joint to and fro under the inspector's nose, happily ignoring Dom's frantic hand signals to desist. 'Thanks,' said the Inspector, unwittingly toking on his first joint, before floating away with a bemused look on his face.

Upon arrival at Oxford train station they were met by Peter Levi in his clerical collar and an eager welcoming committee of other poets including Quentin Stevens. When they finally arrived at the New College Poetry Society, that bearded Beatnik freak Allen Ginsberg poured out his poem *Howl*, all about how the best minds of his generation were being destroyed. When Ginsberg began to recite his poetry, poor Corso naturally felt left out so he leapt up onto a table and started taking his clothes off yelling, 'People who wear clothes are creeps! Flowers don't wear clothes!' Corso then read his poem in praise of the hydrogen bomb, unimaginatively titled, *Bomb*, which went down like a cup of cold sick.

Corso wasn't praising the bomb but rather the shape of it. However, that went over the heads of the left-wing audience who denounced him as a disgrace, 'An American Imperialist'. How dare he praise 'The Bomb' they fumed, and in the sanctity of the socialist poetry society, of all places! Corso's poem had metaphorically lit the blue touchpaper of protest. Someone threw their shoe at him; fortunately they missed, but that lonely soul of a shoe did not remain so for long, as it was soon joined by a flurry of others, all hurled in the same spirit as the wearers had once marched in protest on Trafalgar Square chanting: 'Ban the Bomb.' Not easily deterred, Corso continued to read his poem to an accompaniment of thuds and scrapes from high heels, sandals and the odd walking boot. After the poetry reading, the room descended into chaos as the students hopped about on their one remaining shoe, looking for its companion before trotting off and tut-tutting in their Trotskyist way, at what they'd witnessed. As they exited, Ginsberg goaded them all and denounced them as bunch of 'assholes'. Undeterred, the next day the Beat Poets went on a tour of Oxford's colleges scattering cannabis seeds like confetti wherever they went, much to Hen's amusement, and Ginsberg and Corso stayed on in Dom's digs for several days afterwards.

Some weeks later, back in London, Dom was awarded the Hawthornden Prize for *A Beginning*, the book of poetry David Archer had published. It was the first time the prize had been awarded for fourteen years. Henrietta told Ved that the Hawthornden Prize was prestigious, 'Everyone who's anyone will be there ... if you're not there, everyone will know you're a nobody,' she beamed. Dom was not only the youngest person ever to win it, but also the first non-British writer to do so. The presentation ceremony was midway through Dom's summer vacation. He and Hen lunched at the Ritz with the judges, during which Hen was all smiles. Ved said the award ceremony was chock-a-block with practically every leading poet and writer of the day, amongst whom mingled a mishmash of friends from Oxford, the French and the Colony Room.

Afterwards, the three judges sat on the platform with Mrs Pandit, the Indian High Commissioner. Lord David Cecil made a speech and after a few references to the rapturous irony of Dom's verse, the prize-winning poet popped up to the platform to collect his award. Afterwards, as they all sat drinking tea, a stranger approached Dom and congratulated him: 'Her Majesty the Queen has read your book of poems.' Apparently she had enjoyed them!

Later that evening Henrietta threw an after-party at Apollo Place and, apart from Stephen Spender, it was Monster Club Central – Frank Norman, Colin MacInnes, George Barker, etc. etc ... with John Deakin drunkenly photographing everyone as Stephen

Spender informed Dom, 'You'll be winning the Queen's Medal next.' But before long everyone was bursting for the loo because some Monster or other had passed out in the lavatory. So, they sent another one up to climb in through the toilet window and unlock the door. During the kerfuffle David Archer managed to fall off the roof and into a dustbin in the courtyard down below, where he remained resolutely stuck, like a character from *Fin de Partie*.

Everyone was in a state of euphoria and, for the first time, Dom felt he'd done something worthwhile. When the party fizzled out, Hen turned to him and said flatly, 'You don't need me anymore,' before striding off into the bathroom leaving Dom standing in an emotional chasm, amidst the detritus of what should have been his moment of triumph. After a pregnant pause, he slowly followed her into the bathroom, witnessing her there perched on the edge of the bath, chipping away at her wrists with a razor blade. She looked up, wild-eyed, and declared, 'You made me do this.' Blood covered both the bath and floor. Then, without a word, Dom leant forwards and gently took the blade away from her.

Unaccustomed Squalor

Worryingly, for the next few weeks, Hen was quieter than before. Her tranquillity was eerily disquieting and unsettled Dom. He compared it to quicksand, deadly calm on the surface but inherently untrustworthy beneath. However, Dom could never stay mad with Hen, he worshipped the shifting sand she walked on and their life remained much the same, as they slowly corroded their souls in Soho, with those witty and wicked Monsters. There was a shortage of news that month – and a lack of drama on the world stage – and so Hen began to see Dom's face writ large over all the newspapers. He even appeared on television answering questions about poetry.

In the meantime, Dom's benefactor David Archer had abandoned the bookshop and now lived in unaccustomed squalor in a box flat off the Edgware Road. Having been bled dry by almost every member of the Monster Club, his financial situation was worse than ever, and although he tried to find employment with several publishers, they were all suspicious of his eccentric literary talent and refused to employ him. Down but not out, Archer was still brimming full of ideas and unfounded optimism: 'Have you heard about my Bin Book?', 'Dustbins?' enquired a disinterested Dom. 'Loony Bins. I want them investigated and improved. I want to see the conditions are really good by the time I get there.'

Another literary outlaw who became part of Hen and Dom's social circle was Anthony Carson. Bespectacled and bow-tied, Carson belonged to a now extinct species of writer going back to eighteenth century Grub Street: steely and smart, but spendthrift. Always in constant fear of debt collectors, taxmen and landladies, he'd worked in film for a while, alongside the poet Dylan Thomas, and once dreamed up a 'This Is My Job' type documentary which featured a public toilet attendant known as Dan, The Lavatory Man. The film ends with Dan foiling a Nazi secret agent whose coded messages were disguised as graffiti on the toilet walls. Dan heroically dies for his country and the closing shot shows a monument to his courage being unveiled, a giant lavatory pan engraved with the legend: 'WE ALL HAVE TO GO SOMETIMES.'

Carson wrote some extremely funny prose and had recently enjoyed quite a success with his book, *A Rose by Any Other Name*, a phrase adopted and much used by Francis Bacon when referring to his sexuality. Carson was often in the Colony and engaged in the daily contest of insult throwing with the other Monsters. He usually came out on top, as he'd studied rudeness under a true master, that bohemian bad boy Brian Howard. Despite being big and powerful, Carson was placid by nature, until one afternoon he found himself being attacked by a furious Lucian Freud. What Carson had done to anger him Hen and Dom never knew – Carson did not know himself – but Freud was in a frenzy, kicking, scratching and attempting to bite him. Carson put up no resistance, except occasionally brushing him off with a mighty arm. It was like a big bear being buzzed by a petulant wasp and, in the end, the journalist Paul Johnson had to drag Freud off. According to Johnson, Muriel was not on her perch, otherwise the incident would never have taken place. But Carson just shrugged his shoulders. 'The fellow has a short fuse,' he said, his eyes still dancing with the light of battle. 'Some people are like that,' he laughed.

Days later, Dom wandered into Soho without Hen, to find the Colony full of the usual faces, none of them benevolent. Amongst them stood an old friend of Hen's, a deeply cynical Monster who was eyeing up a young man who'd recently arrived from the sticks. The young man wanted to be a writer but was currently swaying around the room, very drunk. 'He's got no money,' roared the Monster, 'and nowhere to sleep. Take him away, will you?' Dom helped the young man downstairs, and after sobering up in the cold air he asked Dom for a coin to phone a friend and find a bed for the night. Dom stood by the red telephone box as the young man, not getting the response he wanted, proceeded to smash all the glass panes of the phone box with the receiver before staggering out and suddenly seizing Dom's sleeve spluttering, 'What has happened? What has happened to me?' Disturbingly, in the young man's booze-blank eyes, Dom saw a dark reflection of himself.

The Requisite Air of Affluence

The start of another new term at Oxford set off a series of explosions in Hen and Dom's personal life. From London, Hen constantly phoned and wrote to him in a melodramatic manner, threatening to commit suicide. Dom couldn't understand the sudden new twist in their personal soap opera. So, a dutiful Dom made endless trips down to see her, as a result of which he skipped many tutorials and his peers at the college met once more to decide whether or not to expel him. No matter what he did to placate and reassure her, Hen's disturbed mood dominated Dom. There had always been calm passages in their stormy relationship, but now there were none. Despite being emotionally buffeted around by Hen's emotional swell, he felt he could not leave her. But Dom was deluding himself that he had any say in the matter as our hawkish Hen had no intention of lessening her grip.

Then Dom's father, Frank Moraes, turned up at Oxford and everyone succumbed to his easy charm. Frank was a man of the world, a grand figure in his own right. Dom's friends noticed that Frank, like Dom, had an aura of romance and the easy self-assurance of someone who had been everywhere and met everyone. Like Dom, Frank also had a touch of sadness about him, which caused him to drink even more than his son and yet somehow never appear inebriated.

Ved Mehta noticed that the contrast between Dom's father–son relationship and that of his own could not have been starker. Frank and Dom openly talked about each other's mistresses, like old-world aristocrats, and were beyond the normal moral code, whereas Ved would have been mortified to mention any affair of the heart to his own father. Frank also had the requisite air of affluence to accompany his sophisticated manner. He took Ved out for an expensive dinner, plying him with wine and pumping him for information about his son. During the course of the meal, Frank confided in Ved that Dom's relationship with Henrietta was costing him thousands of pounds a year and causing Dom considerable harm. Frank said he was determined to break up the relationship and would cut off Dom without a penny if he continued to see her.

Chapter 7

The Smart Set *vs.* the Chelsea Set

In the 1950s bohemia was made up of overlapping social sets; its heartland was still Soho, but to the north was the Hampstead Set of 'intellectuals' and to the west the Chelsea Set. They didn't all mix with one another. Some were very territorial and stuck to their own patch, whilst others, like Henrietta, oscillated between all three. But the Chelsea Set had shifted on its axis when Elinor Bellingham-Smith closed her 155 Salon and ran off with John Minton's boyfriend to the Suffolk countryside. So, Henrietta gravitated to the poet Elizabeth Smart who'd recently moved back – in the other direction – from Suffolk to London.

But who was this much lauded new mother figure in Hen's life? Well, Elizabeth's story is a classic tortoise and hare race. She'd had four children with the poet George Barker, whom everyone (including Dom) considered a poetic genius. Nobody cared that Elizabeth wrote poetry too. When her 'poetic masterpiece' *By Grand Central Station I Sat Down and Wept* was first published in 1945 it sank without trace, but when reissued as a paperback in the 1960s Elizabeth finally stepped out from George Barker's shadow. When asked what he thought of her book, Barker replied: 'The best thing since *Wuthering Heights*. And I hate *Wuthering Heights*. Women don't have souls.' Barker fancied himself as a lady's man, and liked to live off them. He couldn't believe his luck when a rich debutante like Elizabeth Smart fell for him. But she found out to her cost that to George's long list of literary merits could be added: thief, swindler and habitual liar.

Unable to make a living from her poetry, Elizabeth became a copywriter at the highly influential Crawford's Advertising Agency in High Holborn. She worked in the fashion department, where her bohemian appearance caused quite a stir. Although she sometimes appeared out of kilter, her work was very organised and accurate. She thought of fashion design as an art form and helped the course of British fashion by writing copy for every major brand from Yardley's perfume to Mary Quant. A heavy drinker, Elizabeth started each new day with a 'stiffener' and could be spotted at her desk with her nose in a large jar of glue – predating the 'sniffin' glue' craze of the punk movement by two decades. Her professionalism and quick-witted nature also allowed her to clear her desk by 3 p.m. each day and head off to the Colony.

When she left Crawford's to join *Queen* magazine, Elizabeth became part of the 1960s revolution, helping to change the course of literary journalism in Britain. Using the 'hip' magazine to showcase young talent, she covered the posts of subeditor, fashion writer, literary editor and associate editor. One colleague remembered her arriving in the morning, taking a huge swig of gin, chain-smoking Gauloises cigarettes and popping the odd 'brilliancy pill'. She also used the pages of *Queen* to battle against the male establishment's lack of attention to female authors, reviewing up to fifteen books at a time as well as laying out fourteen pages of fashion, writing intros and captions. Long before famous feminists such as Germaine Greer began to articulate issues of femininity, Elizabeth Smart was discussing the difficulties facing female writers in her column *Queen's Counsel*. She also loved helping out fellow Soho barflies, she got Jeffrey Bernard his first job in journalism (at *Queen*) and landed Henrietta a plum job in an advertising agency.

Somehow, Henrietta had managed to weedle her way into Elizabeth's family nest and upset the order of things. Henrietta became one of Elizabeth's favourites, much to the annoyance of Elizabeth's own daughter, who after some time away returned to find London swinging to the sound of the Beatles and her role within the family somewhat usurped by Henrietta. She told me that Henrietta came into her life quite frequently during this period, Hen was everywhere, but she didn't like her very much because Hen treated her as if she were her personal servant.

They say attack is the best form of defence … and Hen would go for people, goad them incessantly, to see when they'd snap. She hurled abuse at Norman Bowler whenever their paths crossed and taunted Dom for being a 'twenty-four-hour poet'. To some, Henrietta was a tyrant, they'd run around the house hiding the liquor whenever they got wind of her descending upon them, but Elizabeth adored Henrietta and gave her daughter's beloved black overcoat to her. Of course, the first her daughter knew about it was when, to her horror, she saw Hen sporting it in the French. Then, on demanding it back, Hen point-blank refused, which went down like a cup of cold piss.

The artist Patrick (Paddy) Swift, who was nicknamed the 'Poet's Painter', lived in the flat beneath Elizabeth Smart's Westbourne Grove home. Paddy and the deaf poet David Wright set up a magazine called *X* – beautifully produced, with contributions from the artistic and literary worlds including Alberto Giacometti, Samuel Beckett, Stevie Smith, Frank Auerbach, Michael Andrews, etc. Elizabeth let them use her living room for their editorial meetings and would run around as a factotum for them, as Paddy's friend Tim Motion told me:

> Paddy would do very good Francis Bacon impressions and recount amusing stories of the Colony. He was very close to the painter, Michael Andrews … and then there was Henrietta, she was wild. She had a slightly gypsy aroma to her – a free person in whose company anything might happen. She wore very bright and colourful clothing long before the hippy craze happened. People talked about her and she was the subject of much gossip – she could be anywhere at any time and with anybody. She, better than anyone else I'd met, symbolised the divide between 'them' and 'us' in society. I came from an aristocratic background where there were stiff expectations and standards of dress. There was a strong social hierarchy in society back then, barriers of class, race etc. Henrietta cut through them all. My sister was a debutante, her youth was a series of swish dances and charity balls before finally entering

'society'. I myself, at this stage, was an upper-class twit and dressed like one.

After Elinor's 155 Salon had shut, Elizabeth Smart's home became the new bohemian party house on the block and her son, Christopher Barker, told me that coming home from school was like being beamed down from another planet. After shedding his starched school uniform, Christopher would slip into his Beatnik attire of a jumper and jeans so he could easily conform to the weird 'alien' life forms that followed Elizabeth around. Most of them formed the flotsam and jetsam that had washed up from the shores of Soho, such as Paul Potts and David Archer, since Elizabeth attracted literary outlaws like bees to honey.

Despite her role as the hostess, no one ever heard Elizabeth once voice an opinion at any of her parties. None of the women did, and no man asked their opinion either. Except for Henrietta: she had no problem holding forth whatsoever. According to Elizabeth's daughter, it was just before the women's liberation movement and debutantes, like her mother, had been raised and conditioned to never say anything in mixed company. Her children noticed that Elizabeth was conspicuously silent. Henrietta was the exact opposite, which tickled Elizabeth – perhaps she saw in Henrietta something she'd like to be but didn't dare. Hen frequently crops up in her diaries: 'Children dancing ... and Henrietta until 6 a.m. Me still in bed with a temperature.'

However, the striking thing about Elizabeth's parties was the breadth and diversity of the guests: Isabel Rawsthorne, Francis Wyndham, Fay Weldon, Merilyn Thorold, Muriel Belcher, Harry Diamond, John Deakin, Hetta and William Empson, Daniel Farson, Fenella Fielding, Doris Lessing, Olivia Manning, Frank Norman, Peter Owen, Paul Potts, Wally and Sandy Fawkes, Lady Rose McLaren, the Bernard Brothers (Oliver, Bruce and Jeffrey), the artists Craigie Aitchison, Frank Auerbach, Frank Bowling, Patrick Swift, Lucian Freud, Richard Chopping and Prunella Clough, the fashion designer Mary Quant and even Elinor Bellingham-Smith's son, John Moynihan, who, as we know, was a long-time admirer of Henrietta. Somehow, John had managed to combine his love for partying with his love of literature by becoming the gossip columnist for the *Evening Standard* newspaper ... in which he reported on Monday 5 December 1960:

> The Indian poet Dom Moraes looked into Chelsea Registry office this morning and married Mrs Henrietta Bowler. It was the most unusual wedding of the year. Mr Moraes wore a raincoat, dark shirt and grey slacks. His bride was more dressy in a black mohair coat and pearls. A few friends were there. Most of them following Mr Moraes example, didn't bother to dress up. Afterwards they all went round to the Queens Elm for a drink. 'We had known each other for about four and a half years' said Mrs Moraes afterwards. 'We decided to marry quite recently. We'll be having a party tonight to celebrate and later on we will go to India, where Dom has a television program to do.
>
> **Literary Lion ...**
> Witnesses were critic Francis Wyndham and publisher James McGibbon. Other guests included the poet Brian Higgins in a duffle coat and sweater ... Mrs Moraes was formerly married to the actor Norman Bowler. She is 27. Her husband is 22 and has already been a literary lion for two years – ever since his first slim volume of poems won the Hawthornden Prize.

Looking back on her third marriage, Henrietta admitted: 'We drank too much.' But it was the mention of 'the poet Brian Higgins in a duffle coat' in John Moynihan's gossip column that really piqued my interest, because, by all accounts, Higgins was not the sort of person you'd invite to a wedding. So, forgive me for a moment, dear reader, as I lift the lid on the dustbin of history to give you a pungent waft of their wedding guest ...

Brian Higgins was part of a new wave of young poets. Elizabeth Smart and George Barker were both struck by his poems and invited Higgins to London. He arrived from Batley in West Yorkshire carrying a small but promising reputation. He was to be published in *X* magazine and shocked Elizabeth's 'Smart Set' when they first met. Squat and bulky, with the visage of a large scruffy rodent,

Higgins was partially bald, with curly sideburns, pallid skin and rubbery lips from which emanated his thick Yorkshire accent. Dom said Higgins looked like Dr Johnson and certainly ate like Johnson, whose table manners Boswell had deplored. When offered a pie, Higgins began to perspire heavily in anticipation. Then, when the pie appeared, he seized it in both hands and with the veins standing out on his sweaty forehead, ate so noisily that Henrietta and Dom looked on in stunned amazement.

Higgins was not everyone's idea of a perfect house guest as he belched and farted quite a lot. He was a very complex character who provoked physical revulsion in people, which limited him in his search for love, since no girl would go near him. He certainly didn't help matters by telling all and sundry 'How quickly ah coom' in the presence of prostitutes.

He desperately wanted to be accepted into the Monster Club and thought the best way to endear himself to them was to play the clown, but he did not like this and suffered being the butt of other people's jokes. One night George Barker was at Elizabeth's, lording it over everyone with one foot on the fireguard and an elbow on the mantelpiece. Higgins gazed lovingly at George for a while before crawling across the floor on all fours and kissing his feet. George gave Higgins a swift kick, which caused him to roll over on his back and wail like a baby. It was, of course, a piece of pure theatre but Elizabeth's son, Christopher, was appalled by his father's behaviour and felt increasingly sorry for Higgins who, like Henrietta, had a homing instinct that could spot a tender and charitable heart from a mile away. Both Higgins and Henrietta exploited Elizabeth's generous nature, as her son Christopher clearly remembers:

> He came to Westbourne Terrace for tea once and among others there, was Henrietta … she was foul-mouthed but beautiful and totally uncompromising in her attitude. She had a cripplingly sardonic humour which she embellished with casual profanity. Higgins asked Mum, 'Hey, Luv, d'yer mind if I take a bath?' The room full of chattering people fell silent, then everybody roared with laughter. (Higgins and bath in the same sentence was almost

> unimaginable.) When Henrietta finally stopped honking and hooting, she said fondly: 'Hey cunty, mind you leave me some hot water. And if you piss in it, wipe the bath clean. I'm after you.' Higgins was a long time in the bathroom and returned looking scrubbed and polished. Up went Henrietta but she came back down seconds later. She sought Higgins out, who was sniffing around the kitchen, and gave him a savage kick in the shins: 'You dirty ... lazy ... faggot ... Go and clean the fucking bath. It's still full of your revolting pubic hairs which are so fucking springy they refuse to go down the plug hole!' And she pushed him out of the door as I squirmed in disbelief at her abuse. I made a mental note not to cross her. Higgins, who was used to being treated like this, leaned over and told me to close my mouth – it was only her convent education talking.

Tellingly, Paddy Swift painted a portrait of Higgins as an ape of a man and although Elizabeth used to invite him to dinner once a week, she confessed to Dom that she'd put Higgins dinner on the table and walk away because she couldn't bear to watch him eat. One day, finding the front door open, Higgins headed straight for the kitchen, where a huge leg of lamb was cooking in the oven. Elizabeth returned home to find a gnawed bone lying on the floor, with a note attached simply saying, 'Thanks for lunch ... back later', and Christopher soon realised his mother's kindness was wide open to abuse:

> Mum would prepare marvellous stews for us kids that she put on the slow-cook hob for hours. This almost solved the problem of continual food supply for us ... when she couldn't get home from work ... Almost solve, but not quite. The pot, while cooking, was vulnerable to hostile raids. It was like mother-leopard leaving a carcass out in the veldt for her pups, hoping the hyenas wouldn't get it.

Christopher would often come home from school hungry, to find his dinner gone and Higgins' mouth dripping – with his mother's stew – like a cathedral gargoyle after a thunderstorm.

One day Dom bumped into Higgins by Paddington station. He was squatting in a derelict house; there was no furniture, so Dom sat on the floor strewn with bits of discarded poems scrawled on lined paper as Higgins lamented, 'Ah've no family and no home.' There was no electricity either and as the daylight faded all Dom could make out of Higgins was a lumpy caveman-shaped hulk in the dark, emitting a peculiar primeval sound. It took Dom a while to realise Higgins was weeping. Some weeks later Higgins fell sick and Dom visited him in hospital. 'You'll be better soon,' declared Dom. 'Na, Dommie. Ah've been a bayd boy and now Ah'm for the 'igh joomp.' A few days later he died aged thirty-five of a rare heart disease with a tongue-twister of a name. When his *Collected Poems* were published several months later, one in particular seemed to sum up his own short life:

His life was crime, his death a gaffe.
A footnote was his epitaph.

When Christopher heard the news, he was upset but not surprised; he had grown fond of Higgins. Dom felt particularly guilty over Higgins' death. He haunted him in his dreams, emerging out of the rain, dripping and weeping. As he turned to go back to wherever he came from, he raised his hand as if to say 'goodbye', but the next night he returned again to haunt him. Like many in Henrietta and Dom's circle, including the author Anthony Carson and the artist Paddy Swift, Higgins has been dumped in the dustbin of history despite being a gifted mathematician, a professional rugby player and leaving behind three books of published poetry. Higgins' mistake was to head for London and mix with the Monster Club, which consumed him. Deep down Dom knew this; he didn't really fit in either. Dom wasn't a Monster, but Higgins' death certainly made him feel like one.

The Dustbin of History ...

Amidst all this, Dom's publisher, David Archer, had now embarked on a career as a full-time Soho scrounger. 'Tap, tap, tap,' declared Deakin. 'He's like a fucking woodpecker.' But considering the vast sums of money David Archer had given away over the years, who could blame him? He now engaged in a daily battle with one of his former beneficiaries, the poet Paul Potts, who, being a professional hustler, became a serious rival. From here on, whenever Elizabeth Smart walked down Dean Street with Henrietta, they'd be flanked by Paul Potts on one side asking for a loan and David Archer on the other. 'Fuck *off*, Archer,' hissed Potts. 'Oh, I say ... *really!*' protested Archer who'd come to the bitter conclusion that life had treated him unfairly. But Archer's constant requests for money stretched Elizabeth's patience to the point where she once threw her cheque-book at him and ran off to the bathroom, screaming.

But let's close the lid on the rancid dustbin of history for now and quickly return to the sweet-smelling bouquet of Hen and Dom's wedding on 5 December 1960. After they got hitched at Chelsea Registry Office, everyone headed back to Apollo Place for the wedding reception, which was rammed with members of the Chelsea Set. There was also a preponderance of poets, each of whom had written something for the happy couple. Peter Levi rose to the occasion with an atmospheric poem featuring noisy rain, boisterous wind and crumbling monuments, as Brian Higgins sung to the glory of Johnny Haynes, captain of the England football team, to whom Brian declared his undying love before passing out on the floor.

According to the artist Camilla Shivarg, her father Alexander had also written a special poem for the newlyweds because 'Dom was around our house a lot when I was a child, along with Henrietta.' Camilla's mother, Joan Wyndham, had been part of old bohemia, which featured the artists Augustus John and Nina Hamnett. Joan's father, Dick Wyndham, was central to the whole scene and her cousin, David Tennant, had opened the Gargoyle in 1925. Joan was bohemian aristocracy, a party girl through and through, so when the 1960s began to swing, she admitted she wasn't going to let anything like middle age get in her way:

> Luckily – and contrary to popular misconception – this was not just a time for the young: people of all ages could have a ball. We may have looked rather silly as we twisted and shook, but we had a bloody marvellous time. Our adrenalin was sky-high, and every day seemed like a new adventure … The King's Road was a wonderful place to be in then. It was full of friendly atmospheric cafes, bars, clubs and restaurants where you could always be sure to run into some member of that amorphous group dreamed up by journalists and known as the Chelsea Set.

At weekends Henrietta and Dom now frequented the Picasso Café on the King's Road for a late breakfast beside its fake Guernica mural. On a Saturday morning all the odd bods and bohemians gathered there – Joan Wyndham, Francis Bacon, George Melly, Quentin Crisp, etc. Saturday evenings were spent at the Arethusa nightclub, an amazing place catering for every walk of life, where anything could happen, and usually did. It was here that they first ran into Christine Keeler. 'A jolly, friendly girl with rabbity teeth – not exactly beautiful, but with great style and very sexy,' remembered Joan, 'I used her to distract the barman so that I could nip behind the bar and pinch us both drinks.'

Bring a Bottle …

Christine Keeler would later become an infamous femme fatale for almost bringing down the British government during the Profumo Affair. Another party girl was April Ashley, who'd been working as a female impersonator in a Parisian nightclub when she decided to undergo some pioneering but primitive 'sex change' surgery and transition from being a man to a woman. Upon her return to London, with her striking nubile physique, April soon became the preferred underwear model for *Vogue*. But both April and Christine

Keeler would soon be publicly ridiculed in the national newspapers and April lost her modelling career once her early life as a man had been exposed.

It was in the company of this new generation of femmes fatales that Henrietta now mixed. She and Dom became a regular fixture at Joan Wyndham's party house on Wellington Square. Every few weeks there would be a 'bring a bottle' party with very loud music. Here is a rundown of the build-up to a typical Joan Wyndham party, as told by the hostess herself:

> First … collect two large casks of scrumpy … Wash out large white dustbin and pour it in, ready to be laced with spirits brought by guests. Pile up bread and cheese on kitchen table. Hide valuables. Clean floor. Change into white mini dress with huge gilt apple earrings and insert contact lenses.
>
> 8 p.m. Switch on enormous secondhand tannoy speaker and line up tapes and records.
>
> 8.15 p.m. Arrival of Aziza the snake dancer, who is to be our cabaret, carrying a BOAC bag containing her python warmed by a hot water bottle.
>
> 9 p.m. Blast off with 'I Want to Hold Your Hand'. The room goes crazy.
>
> 9.30 p.m. First gatecrasher arrives without a bottle. He is thrown out by David Litvinoff who works for Rachmann, an evil property tycoon who puts rats painted with fluorescent paint through letter-boxes to flush out sitting tenants.
>
> 10 p.m. Aziza does snake dance.
>
> 11.30 p.m. Someone is locked in the lavatory with somebody else's wife.

> Midnight. Arrival of April Ashley, our beautiful sex change friend, in full evening dress with her train of pretty-boy acolytes. Upstairs, unknown to us, some of David Litvinoff's henchmen are 'doing the overcoats'.
>
> 3 a.m. Arrival of the fuzz, called by indignant neighbours – in fact only one rather small and pink-cheeked constable. April swoops down on him, bottle in hand, and bears him away.
>
> 4 a.m. The fuzz is trying to do the twist with April and feeling no pain. Christine Keeler is dancing on the bar wearing his helmet.
>
> 7 a.m. Arrival of Joe the milkman, friend and confidant to half the street and the last milkman to keep his horse. The hardcore lines up on the balcony to greet him. Some have swopped clothes, some are topless and all are legless ... by now the room smells like the inside of a very old wine cask, the carpet is sodden, cigarette ends are uncurling in half empty glasses; single earrings and empty bottles litter the floor ... somebody whom nobody knows is asleep on the sofa. The party is over.

Not surprisingly, Joan Wyndham gained a reputation for giving the grooviest parties in Chelsea, though not according to her daughter Camilla, who complained in her diary: 'Mummy and Daddy gave another of their *boring* parties, not a single man under thirty!' But now, looking back as an adult, Camilla has a different perspective:

> By 1960 everyone's social life seemed to revolve more around Chelsea than Soho. We lived on the King's Road, which was the place to be and people were always pounding on our door, it was a daily occurrence ... it was as if we were living under siege and we had to constantly watch out for bores and freeloaders. We'd look out of the windows quietly and carefully, to see who it was, before retreating away. Everyone came to the King's Road during the Swinging Sixties and our house was always full of people like Henrietta and Dom and Jeffrey Bernard – who had nothing better to do than get drunk during the daytime and bet on horses and

shout at one another. Although I was a child at the time, I noticed that all these people seemed a bit lost, they were all very bright but didn't do much and they all died of drink or killed themselves.

Henrietta was a real piece of work. If I had to write a book about them I'd call it 'Marvellous Monsters', their behaviour was appalling. Henrietta I knew well, she and Dom were friends of my father, Alexander. Henrietta would leave a party twice the size as when she arrived. My mother collected very beautiful 1930s silk scarves which Henrietta tied all around her legs and as she was leaving, they'd be hanging down peeking out of the bottom of her trousers. You had to keep an eye on Henrietta, she was a bit of a Kleptomaniac.

Brain Like a Bandsaw

But it wasn't just the parties that attracted Henrietta. Camilla's parents had lots of extraordinary lodgers staying in their house too, many of whom were old Soho friends of Hen's: the louche Jeffrey Bernard, the artist Michael Andrews, Soho's No. 1 detective the ever so eccentric Lady Marye Rous and the novelist Robin Cook, whose book *The Crust On Its Uppers* depicted Henrietta's Chelsea milieu of petty criminals, posh kids and bohemian bums. Robin Cook would later find fame under the pen name of Derek Raymond and become the 'Godfather of British Noir' (black novels) where the characters are killed and dismembered in the most hideous ways.

Finding himself at a loose end one evening, Robin Cook decided to pop down to the World's End and visit Henrietta. Upon arrival, Hen said, 'Hullo darling, how nice to see you. Do you see this poisonous-looking person here? It's a sort of writer, critic person bundled up in a suit to make it feel real ... Never mind, it's just going now that I've put the gin out of reach.' The person in question didn't speak, but stirred like a stiff curtain and left with a muffled resignation. 'Well, there was a seduction scenario that didn't work,' she cheerfully continued. 'Anyway, have a drink.'

Then, after a few drinks, Hen said: 'I think you'd better go now ... I've got a very strange lady coming round any minute. She is honestly the kind of person who could certainly not stand you, because you are the epitome of everything Veronica loathes and detests.' When Cook replied he couldn't wait to meet her, Henrietta said, 'Well it's your funeral, but don't say I didn't warn you,' then the doorbell rang.

Cook said Hen's friend walked in looking like the type of intellectual who resolutely balked at being one. Veronica Hull wore a grey two-piece suit, untidily, with black stockings and dusty high heels. Her white face bore a long thick mouth and sunglasses. When Cook enquired what she did, Veronica replied in a very long spaced-out laconic way that Cook could be 'taken for a cunt' before announcing that she was a novelist. Veronica lived at 94 Priory Road, West Hampstead and, like Henrietta in Apollo Place, had obtained her property via a circuitous route. The house belonged to her husband who was in the process of divorcing her and, like Hen, she let out various rooms to facilitate her bohemian lifestyle. The basement contained a Nigerian gentleman attired in an African tribal dress with 'Made in Birmingham' printed along the edges, the son of the Chilean Ambassador resided on the ground floor and a talented Turkish pianist on the first. Along with Henrietta, Robin Cook thought Veronica was the most extraordinary woman he'd ever met. She was a constant source of philosophical enquiry and was just as outspoken as Hen: 'You've got a good brain; trouble is you don't know how to use it. But we will soon put that straight.'

A few years earlier, in 1958, Veronica had published *The Monkey Puzzle*. It exposed the double-dealing and hypocrisy of British university life as seen by a philosophy student seduced and dumped by her head of department (the philosopher A.J. Ayer). The novel satirised the sexual side of university life and the female students' relationships with their tutors. The repercussions of writing the novel and the ensuing scandal broke Veronica. She cracked under the weight of the British establishment which seemed intent on crushing her for exposing Professor Ayer as a sexual predator. Henrietta knew Ayer from the Gargoyle – a favourite hunting-ground for fresh meat – which he'd attended with Francis Bacon's other muse, Isabel Rawsthorne.

The Monkey Puzzle became a cult novel with university undergraduates, but the book precipitated a series of mental breakdowns for Veronica – her brilliant mind went down and life let her fall. *The Monkey Puzzle* should have earnt her a place in British counter-culture – but she is now forgotten. Cook said being with Veronica was an education. She taught him and Henrietta a great deal of philosophy. He also described himself as one of Veronica's 'few survivors' because she 'had a brain like a bandsaw', which could cut through anyone or anything. Maybe that's why Henrietta liked Veronica so much, after all Hen could cut through any social occasion like a chainsaw.

They Wouldn't Dare Mess with Her!

Anyway, let's get back to the party … as we know, Henrietta first fell in with the Chelsea Set as part of Elinor Bellingham-Smith's circle. When Elinor moved to the countryside she left behind her son John, who mentions in his memoir Joan Wyndham's extraordinary party house blasting pop music to the thump of champagne corks wedging themselves in the ceiling and red wine running down the walls. Along with Robin Cook, John Moynihan became a lodger of Joan Wyndham's too, with his new wife Diana Melly who vividly recalls the period:

> Over time I got engaged to three different men one of whom was John Moynihan, a journalist with whom I shared the same friends. One of whom was Henrietta. Back then, Henrietta wasn't really known for anything apart from being outspoken and being married twice whereas Elinor Bellingham-Smith, who, for a brief period was my mother-in-law, was known as an artist in her own right and infamous for getting incredibly drunk.
>
> If the men were misogynistic then the young women were ageist. It never occurred to me that Elinor might be beautiful – we

didn't think that any woman over the age of forty was attractive or even had a sex life. I just considered her a drunken old woman, but Elinor was what we'd call nowadays a feminist. There were a few about then, like the photographer Lee Miller – they did exist but they weren't labelled as such back then. Perhaps, they were just considered difficult women!

One of the reasons I married Johnny was because he was so wonderful to his mother – coping with her 'eccentricities' (and drunken rages). I thought if he was such a wonderful son, he would make a wonderful husband and by this time I had run out of excuses not to marry him. When I first met him, he was working for the *Evening Standard* as a reporter on the gossip column, *In London Tonight*, in which he would mention who attended the glamorous parties in town. Johnny was a good writer and often very witty but was funny about money – he had a neurotic insecurity about it – maybe because of the way his parents brought him up. He would never let me have any – so I would have to go through his pockets to find the money to buy nappies etc. One day I lent Jeffrey Bernard 10 shillings on the condition that he gave it back to me later that same day as I was desperately short of cash. And when I saw him later at Muriel's I asked, 'Hello Jeffrey, have you got that 10 bob you owe me.' He took it out of his pocket and dropped it on the floor – forcing me to get down and pick it up. He did it in an attempt to humiliate me, but it didn't bother me. There were a few women who stood up for themselves and wouldn't be treated like that – Henrietta for example – they wouldn't dare mess with her!

I saw a great deal of Henrietta around 1960/61 when I was expecting my daughter, Candy. I needed to get a crib but what with Johnny being so careful with cash he wouldn't give me any money towards one. So, Henrietta took me off to Bonhams, the auctioneers in Lots Road, Chelsea. There we found a lovely battered white wickerwork crib for a pound. We bought it and Henrietta and I pushed it all the way home, up the King's Road. We always had little adventures and great fun together. She was a good friend to me.

We were vaguely left-wing Labour supporters and together we went on all the big protest marches and rallies of the time: CND

(Ban the Bomb), Reform of Homosexual Laws, Stop Capital Punishment (Ruth Ellis had been hanged a few years earlier for a crime of passion). Then there was an incident in the township of Sharpeville, South Africa. The police had fired on a crowd of black civilians protesting against apartheid, killing and wounding hundreds of them. We'd heard of the massacre and later, at a party Henrietta and I decided we'd go and protest outside the South African Embassy. So, we took a taxi to South Africa House where there was a huge crowd of people protesting outside the building and police guarding them. We were both dressed in our smart party clothes, unlike the other protestors in jeans and t-shirts – and so, as we got out of the taxi the police mistook us for dignitaries and parted the crowd of protestors to let us through. Henrietta and I smartly marched right up to the front of the Embassy and took the milk bottles out we had concealed on ourselves and threw them through the Embassy's windows. We were then promptly arrested by some very irate Policemen, slung in the back of a van and carted off to the cells. Frank Norman, the razor scarred author, came by, bailed Henrietta out of jail and paid her court fine the next day. But no one came to pay mine!

Chapter 8

The Honeymoon from Hell

After their wedding, Henrietta and Dom decided to honeymoon in Paris, much to the annoyance of Elizabeth Smart's daughter, who received an unexpected phone call from Hen saying she was staying in a hotel right next to the one she was in. Hen wanted something from the chemist and demanded Elizabeth's daughter fetch it for her. That's how it was – she'd sometimes use people – and to make matters worse she still hadn't given Elizabeth's daughter her lovely coat back. But Henrietta was powerfully persuasive, she was a strong character and people could be rather intimidated by her. Once she'd had enough of terrorising Elizabeth Smart's offspring, Henrietta decided to extend her honeymoon by taking the *Simplon-Orient-Express* from Paris to Athens, travelling in a mahogany panelled first-class Pullman compartment, trimmed with brass fittings. At night, pink silk-shaded lamps illuminated the room, which romantically unfolded into an undulating snow-sheeted bedroom. The journey took four days, with the restaurant car disappearing somewhere near Serbia. Henrietta thought there was no better way to travel and they arrived to find Athens covered in snow and Hen's old friend (and fellow Chelsea Girl) Suna Portman in residence.

Bambi ...

Dom nicknamed Suna 'Bambi', and depicted her in his memoir as having green eyes, long golden hair and being the daughter of a very rich aristocrat. The combination of which many men found irresistible. The London gossip columns had been full of Bambi's attempts to run away with one unsuitable lover after another. Each of these attempts at marriage had been foiled by her father, as Marianne Faithfull's former minder, Mim Scala, told me:

> Suna Portman was a fantastic, ethereal, man magnet. Serenely tall and drop dead gorgeous. All the boys thought she was untouchable – much to our dismay – because she was so utterly gorgeous and good fun. We all looked up to Suna; she was a class act. It was just at this period that things were changing socially – posh kids were trying to sound working class. Their parents were getting pissed off with their debutante daughters who were loving the 1960s social shuffle. These very strait-laced posh parents (whose alcohol consumption was horrendous) couldn't understand what the fuck was going on. They'd brought their daughters up to attend a ball at the Dorchester and come out into 'Society' and the next thing they knew they were hanging out in a Soho club with a bunch of scallywags.

In an attempt to keep her out of further trouble, Bambi's father had given her a large sum of money and sent her to Athens where she promptly shacked up with an unemployed American actor. In his memoir, Dom recalls Bambi being 'charming in her amiable stupidity', and when Hen and Dom went to breakfast in Bambi's flat the next day, Dom said they were offered homemade marijuana preserves. Bambi, who was trying to reinvent herself as a writer and artist, informed them that the poet Gregory Corso was in Athens. Henrietta should have known something was up when Corso excitedly told her he'd never been on a honeymoon before.

They hired a dumpy Fiat car, which proved to be not quite large enough for them all. As Bambi drove them through the deserted countryside to the sites of Ancient Greece, the twentieth century receded away behind them in the rear-view mirror. They stopped at Corinth, Epidaurus and Delphi and then, at one unscheduled pit stop, Corso decided to befriend a donkey and fed it a bottle of brandy. It then galloped drunkenly after the car – being driven by a wide-eyed Bambi – all the while braying like the Eddie Murphy character from *Shrek* as it enthusiastically shat itself and became incredibly randy on the brandy. The next morning they had to rescue Corso from the police station, where he (along with the donkey) had been taken into custody for indecent behaviour.

Once released from jail, Corso resumed his place beside Dom in the back of the car with another bottle of brandy and continued behaving like an excitable child: 'Look at all the flowers in that field. Let's all make love among the lovely flowers,' before Bambi dampened his ardour by pouring a bottle of wine over him. Henrietta said that when they arrived in Mycenae in the late afternoon the sky was full of dark purple clouds and the wind whistled ominously as they drove up to their hotel, La Belle Helene. As Hen signed the register, she skipped back a few pages and found it to be full of signatures of eminent Nazis like Hermann Goering and Heinrich Schliemann – the archaeologist who'd excavated Mycenae and brought the swastika to Germany.

Ignoring the ominous Nazi-starred omens, they climbed the hillside above Agamemnon's Tomb by moonlight and consumed a bottle of ouzo. Dom pressed his ear to the grass and swore he could hear the old king humming to himself in the beehive cavern beneath. Not yet having had their fill of the Greek ruins, the next day they decided to picnic in the dark at Olympia. Dom said ancient ruins can sometimes be eerie in full sunlight, but at midnight, amidst the deserted countryside in which owls and reptiles made spooky noises, it was terrifying … and Bambi fainted when Corso conjured up a ghost story.

On their way back, Bambi and her boyfriend parked the car on a beach, where it sank to the hubcaps. With the tide advancing they had to find a local farmer and a team of donkeys to pull it free. By the time they returned to Athens, Hen was exhausted and Dom had had enough of bumping along country roads with Bambi.

A Theatre of Cruelty

On 11 March they flew from Athens to Tel Aviv where Dom had been commissioned to cover the trial of the Nazi war criminal, Adolf Eichmann, for *The Times* of India. Upon arrival, they found Israel in a state of extreme tension over the trial of such a high-ranking Nazi. Hen and Dom were given a press car and travelled from the Sea of Galilee down to the port of Eilat, where Solomon had once received the Queen of Sheba.

It was still only thirteen years since Israel had received independence and, within this short period, it had fought two wars. The last, the Suez Affair of 1956, threatened its very existence. After spending a day being driven around it was not difficult for Henrietta and Dom to realise how small Israel was – hemmed in on three sides by its enemies, with nowhere to run except for the sea, Israel felt claustrophobic. They were introduced to a poet called Carmi, who invited them for a drink with a group of writers and painters on the beach. They ended up cruising to and fro between two artists' cafés and it descended into a riotous night with Henrietta and Dom meeting many people whose names they couldn't remember in the morning. Dom said he'd developed a spontaneous liking for the people they met because, unlike in London, there were no hangers-on. To Hen and Dom, they were kindred spirits – refugees and misfits who'd gathered from all over the world. They could empathise with them because they considered themselves to be in a similar situation back in Britain.

Tel Aviv soon became a media circus as journalists arrived from all over the world. As well as sociologists and historians, hordes of television and radio crews were coming, the whole city was prepared for this media invasion and accommodation was scarce. But Hen and Dom found a small and very pleasant flat on a hill, where Chaim Bialik, the father of modern Hebrew poetry, would often write. Passing a kiosk on 26 March 1961, Henrietta purchased a postcard depicting a mosaic of a heron and serpent from the Church of the Multiplication of the Loaves and the Fishes, on which she wrote to Peter Levi:

> Peter, look at this angry bird. It's very exciting here and nice. We had tea with a Bedouin Sheikh – real – and lunch with a Druze Mullah. Greece was lovely – but not Athens. Corso mad. Love Henrietta and Dom.

The next day they met Patrick O'Donovan, foreign correspondent for *The Observer* newspaper. Larger than life and one of the hardest drinkers they had ever known, Patrick had served previously in Palestine as a British Army Officer and had been around when Jerusalem's King David Hotel was blown up. He introduced Hen and Dom to Fink's Bar and the artistic community who frequented it. The painter, Yosl Bergner, explained to Hen that both the Jewish situation and the Jewish religion *demanded* the former Nazi Adolf Eichmann stand trial. He said their religion was a religion of vengeance, in which debts of blood had to be repaid and Eichmann was now required to repay.

Amongst the world's press, Dom stood out as the youngest correspondent at the trial, which began on 11 April 1961. Hen, Dom and Patrick formed a clutch and got together every night to share what information they had gathered about Eichmann – an obscure and rather bland angel of death who'd been a pen-pusher executing orders and prisoners with meticulous detachment. Eichmann had personally visited the camps where the Jews had been exterminated. The trial was designed to illustrate the magnitude of the Nazi crimes through the deeds of this one man who, along with many other Nazis, escaped with his family to South America. However, unlike his compatriots, who took large sums of money into exile with them, Eichmann had worked in Buenos Aires as an electrician for fifteen years and was probably contemplating an uneventful old age until the Israeli secret service kidnapped him.

Henrietta said the trial was not held in a courtroom but instead in a newly built theatre, Beit Ha'Am, 'house of the people'. Eichmann was placed in a bulletproof glass box on the stage, which reminded Hen of a Francis Bacon painting. Within his glass box, Eichmann sat at an oak table piled high with paperwork and sporting a pair of carpet slippers. The judges and the jury sat in the orchestra pit and each witness climbed the circular staircase to the edge of the stage, to give evidence from the wings. To Hen, if this was a piece of theatre, it was a theatre of cruelty. The first three days were spent establishing the legal precedent for the state of Israel to kidnap a foreign national. The charge was genocide.

In the glass box Hen witnessed Eichmann's lips move and heard for the first time his toneless flat voice eerily amplified through a metallic speaker system. Dom said the initial shock of being in the presence of a real live Nazi took time to wear off:

> The trouble was that Eichmann was so dull. His shoulders were slightly hunched, his scalp bald, his spectacles rimless, his clothes and face grey. He looked, talked and behaved like a clerk, a natural subordinate used to following orders. My attempts to imagine him in the uniform of a Gestapo … the black clothes, the boots, the sinister shoulder-flashes and cap, proved singularly unsuccessful. He continued to look like a clerk … he scribbled constant notes; sometimes he made objections. He must have been inhibited by the certainty that at the end of all this he would die, that there was no possibility whatever that the Israelis would ever allow him to escape the rope.

The early days of the trial proceeded at a snail's pace, as they tried to establish Eichmann's identity and outline the various places he'd been posted during the war. Hen found it all *very* dull. Outside the courtroom was a small bar where she and Dom used to lunch before the court recess to avoid the rush. It was manned by a solitary figure called Avram. One day Avram was cleaning the counter with his shirtsleeves rolled up when Henrietta noticed the indelible marks of a concentration camp tattoo. Avram confided in her that he had lost both his wife and son as well as sixty-two of his relatives in the Nazi concentration camps. Ironically part of his work was serving lunch to Eichmann in the courthouse. He admitted that he would like to poison Eichmann's food and kill him, but there was a difference between being a Jew and being an Israeli. As a Jew he wanted to kill him, but as an Israeli citizen he felt compelled to protect Eichmann until he was tried and sentenced.

From this point on, Henrietta began to notice that many Israeli citizens had concentration camp tattoos. She found it a surreal situation, chatting and laughing with people about life's trivialities at a party only to find out that they had been subjected to the horrors of the Holocaust. Henrietta discovered that most people wanted to forget about it, but some wrote books about it, which Dom said were pitched in a 'hysterical tone', and filled him with the horror at events 'so improbable, so lunatic, as to make any survivor hysterical'.

For once in her life, Henrietta did not want to make herself the centre of attention. She was quiet and sat in stony silence as witness after witness was called to give their horrifying testimony. She saw a row of otherwise hardened journalists in tears and, despite the outcries from the public gallery, Eichmann sat impassive. He denied every charge, he denied being Eichmann, he denied his signature was on the documents authorising the extermination of innocent civilians and admitted only to obeying orders from above.

Henrietta and Dom found it an exhausting and nerve-wracking experience as day by day the evidence became more and more harrowing in its content. They spent two days watching film footage which the Nazis themselves had shot in the camps. Much time was also devoted to when Eichmann found a small boy, a slave labourer, stealing cherries from his orchard and had beaten the child to death. Numerous witnesses testified to this particular incident. Henrietta met one after the court had adjourned for the day. The witness was in a very nervous state, anxiously pulling at the corners of his handkerchief, as he wept: 'How can I tell you what I feel about Eichmann ...? I knew the little boy he killed.'

Outside the court, crowds thronged daily around the theatre building. As the world's press attention slowly ebbed away from the long, drawn-out trial, Hen and Dom's attitude hardened ... they were determined to see it through. It was a hot summer and the courtroom was stifling, outside sporadic bursts of wild torrid rain fell on the theatre building to an operatic backdrop of thunder and lightning; it was as if the very spirit of Jehovah himself was bearing down on the proceedings. A mighty storm erupted and suddenly all the lights blinked out in the courtroom. Momentarily, a certain midsummer madness engulfed the pitch-black proceedings. When the lights finally flickered back on Eichmann was no longer in his glass box. There was no trace of him … except for the carpet slippers he'd once stood in.

The guards were just as shocked and alarmed as everyone else at Eichmann's sudden disappearance and began wildly wielding their guns, looking around frantically. Then Henrietta spotted Eichmann, climbing out from under the oak table. The balding German eagle stood up and adjusted his spectacles. He had obviously thought that an attempt was being made on his life and, seeing the nearest shelter, kicked his slippers off in haste.

Henrietta was convinced of his guilt and Dom remarked that, 'it was like watching the trial of a person already dead,' since the result was a foregone conclusion. The mountain of evidence that piled up against Eichmann day after day seemed irrelevant to Dom in the end. In no way could he connect the prisoner in the glass box with all the numerous crimes he had committed or any other human activity such as laughing, crying or sleeping:

> One could only connect him with the glass box. Even his flat voice, when he spoke in German, seemed unconnected with the speaker. It was equally impossible to feel anything for him. I could not feel pity, because of the evidence and because of his dehumanization by the glass box; for the same reasons I could not feel anger or hatred. The evidence might have caused those emotions; but the evidence had become unconnected with the man … I made intermittent trips to Jerusalem and dropped in at the trial, as one might drop in at a familiar club.

Then Dom applied to the prime minister, Ben-Gurion, 'the Lion of Judah' and co-founder of the state of Israel, for an interview. He and Hen had been introduced some months earlier at a concert. The interview, for some reason, was to be held in Tel Aviv at 6 a.m. They drove there the night before and hit the local bars until 4.30 a.m. So, their drunken 6 a.m. meeting with Ben-Gurion seemed to be a natural end to the trip. They only went back to Jerusalem once more for Eichmann's final speech, in his defence.

He seemed tired and his voice often faltered. He knew (as everyone else did) that the end was near …

A Certain Desolation …

By this time Dom had stopped filing reports to *The Times* and they were running out of money. Hen and Dom had just enough cash left to buy a ticket home on a cargo boat from the port of Haifa. For the angst-ridden poet, standing on the deck of the cargo boat as the shores of Israel receded, Dom felt a certain desolation and realised for the first time that he had a vocation, as a nomadic poet and writer, wandering all over the world. Whereas the non-poetic Henrietta told it as it was: 'a three-week voyage which took longer as the engine often broke down and drifted off course.' They were stuck on a cargo ship carrying cans of tomato juice and melons. Hardly the most romantic end to the eight-month honeymoon from hell. Later, at dinner, Henrietta noticed there was an odd assortment of thirteen passengers, all of whom were somewhat unstable. The ship's officers were all Scottish and enjoyed tearing strips off one another. Meals, which everyone took at the captain's table, were subject to violent arguments between the crew and punctuated by threats of suicide from a Jewish lady from Golders Green, which gave Hen and Dom uncontrollable fits of giggles.

Back in Blighty, Hen held court in the Colony Room. She recounted the Eichmann trial to Francis Bacon and Muriel Belcher: Eichmann in the glass box, the detached bland angel of death with his tinny metallic detached voice, and Francis undoubtedly hanging on her every word as Hen painted horrific pictures in his head.

Much Too Neurotic …

Upon her return from Israel a trail of bad luck had dogged Hen. Whilst visiting the cinema to watch Elvis Presley in *Jailhouse*

Rock, halfway through the film as Elvis began his pelvic thrusts and to gyrate his hips to the music, he literally brought the house down. A central chandelier, weighing a couple of tons, broke off its mooring and plummeted on to the audience below, exploding into shattered crystal, lacerating the audience and the screen in the process. Henrietta and Dom sat in stunned silence, as the dust began to settle. Beneath them, in the circle seats, the dead sat facing the image of Elvis ethereally flitting on a shredded screen. After the initial shock they thought it had been a terrorist bomb, until one cinemagoer pointed out in the chaos and confusion the mangled bodies in the front row. They exited through the foyer, picking their way past the wounded and headed straight to the nearest bar for several medicinal brandies.

By now, their drinking had reached epic proportions. Henrietta, by her own admission, had become 'much too neurotic' for Dom's delicate disposition. Her constant questioning made him evasive which fuelled her suspicions even more. During the Eichmann trial she had developed a penchant for amphetamines and the ups and downs of her pill-popping habit didn't help their relationship. They knew how to wound each other and how to dig deeply. Their marital bedroom now seemed remarkably like a prison cell. After one violent outburst, Hen remarked bitterly, 'I suppose you now want to leave me.' To which Dom murmured, 'Anyone who behaves like you do deserves to be left.' With that she fell silent and when he looked up he was shaken by the tears silently streaming down her face.

Then, one day, Hen got in a flap when Dom didn't come home. She began searching round town for him following false leads and dead ends until she tracked down her quarry to a bedsit in Pimlico, where our hawkish Hen swooped down on a dishevelled-looking Dom and, ignoring his protests, hauled him back home in a taxi with the help of Nana.

Ved said Dom often turned his sorrows into stories, as if they belonged to someone else; it was his way of finding solace. By this stage Dom had been dining out for some years on a long, convoluted story about the circumstances of his mother's death, but it wasn't until some years later, when Dom published his autobiography, his friends realised he'd invented the whole thing. Ved said Dom was prone to extraordinary fantasies and one never knew what was true and what wasn't. His creative imagination always tried to make everything more interesting than it actually was and it was this tenuous hold on reality that made him such a great poet.

However, Henrietta's dramatic behaviour and naked hostility had caused Dom's overactive imagination to forever entwine in his mind the image of Henrietta with that of his mother, Beryl. Once he'd made that connection maybe he realised that he hadn't been looking for a wife after all, but a replacement mother figure. His birth mother had been a doctor for the guru of modern India, Mahatma Gandhi, and a glamorous socialite until she started to suffer from depression, which made her acutely paranoic and violent. Her life had centred around Dom and when she realised he would be leaving her to study in England, her behaviour worsened and she was confined to a psychiatric hospital. Dom had suffered a great deal from her as a child. She had attacked him several times with knives and left permanent scars from her habit of stubbing her cigarettes out on him. He became party to wild and violent scenes, which no child should bear witness to.

Unsurprisingly, Dom was left mentally scarred by his hostile mother's bulging eyes, piercing screams and unnerving habit of laughing for several minutes at a time for no apparent reason. In adulthood the anxiety of seeing his mother made Dom nauseous, bile would begin to fill his mouth. Like Henrietta, she was possessive and overbearing and the pairing of them in his mind poisoned everything. His reaction to any emotional confrontation with a woman was always to retreat within himself. But whenever he withdrew and became silent, it would only provoke Henrietta even more because she wanted, she *needed* a reaction. Then a few weeks later, at Joan Wyndham's house, Dom made another desperate bid to break free from Henrietta's domestic abuse, as Joan's daughter Camilla told me:

> Everyone was sitting around drinking and Dom said, 'I'm just going out to buy a packet of cigarettes' and he never came back. That's

> how he left her. He walked out one afternoon when they were all having a jolly old time drinking at my parents' house, most bizarre!

In his memoir, Dom said it was during that summer of 1963 when he found himself standing morosely at the bar of the Queens Elm on the Fulham Road. Here he was, an established writer with only five shillings to his name, drumming his fingers on the bar and waiting for fate to intervene. He had achieved quite a lot of success: the Hawthornden Prize, scripting documentary films for television and reporting on the Eichmann trial. He had also blown a lot of money. He was bored and craved change; he was sick of discussing poetry in pubs but too restless to write and he'd had enough of being Hen-pecked.

The problem was, he was so terrified of Hen getting into a flap, he'd completely chickened out of telling her.

Chapter 9

Non-Dom

When Dom deserted her, Henrietta was bereft. To make sense of the situation, she put his disappearance down to certain misunderstandings that had arisen. But she just couldn't understand why Dom told so many lies, did he do it to *please* her she wondered? Even his friend Bernard Kops had to concede: 'Dom was an apparition from another age, another time, another class.' Somewhat guiltily, Hen began blaming herself, thinking she was just 'too neurotic' for Dom's nervous system. She wept on Nana's shoulder, who did her best to reassure her: 'He'll be back, Henrietta. You'll see.' She was grief-stricken, and like so many who have lost a loved one, she thought she heard his voice and caught glimpses of him everywhere she went. She didn't know if he was dead or alive but, like a ghost, Dom continued to flit in and out of her existence ...

Toying with Its Prey

When Henrietta went to the Chelsea Registry Office to obtain a copy of their marriage certificate she was informed it did not exist. That's when she seriously began to question her sanity and wondered if they were ever really married at all. Then, eighteen months later, sitting in a pub with her new boyfriend Hussein Shariffe, she spied Dom through the pub window ... and set off in hot pursuit. Tailing Dom through the winding streets of

Chelsea she was surprised to see him enter Joan Wyndham's house. Henrietta said Joan's husband, Alexander Shihwarg, was the most hospitable man she'd ever met, which came in rather handy as she forced her way into his home. There she cornered a dishevelled-looking Dom, who, like a condemned man, drank glass after glass of whisky as he sank deeper and deeper into his armchair in the vain hope it would swallow him up. Suddenly, out of the corner of her eye, Henrietta spied an old pistol lying on a sideboard and began wielding it at the petrified Dom, striking combat poses in the most cavalier way, deliberately designed to terrify him and his host, who appeared unsure as to whether or not the gun was loaded. Then, like a cat bored toying with its prey, she took one last swipe at Dom and slunk off home with Hussein.

As sure as night follows day, Hussein Shariffe inevitably replaced Dom in Apollo Place. Descended from Sudanese ruling stock, Hussein had an air of inner nobility about him. He'd studied at Cambridge University before attending the Slade School of Art where he had been tutored by Lucian Freud and went on to win the prestigious John Moores Painting Prize for young artists. During his lifetime, Hussein painted over 500 pictures, though few have been documented. Henrietta's friend, John Deakin, photographed him with his paintings and the athletically built African soon became a well-known face on the Soho scene.

Hussein exhibited at Gallery One, which resided on D'Arblay Street, Soho. Not only did it exhibit up-and-coming British painters such as Gillian Ayres, Craigie Aitchison and Bridget Riley it also championed members of the Indian avant-garde such as F.N. Souza. But it was Henrietta's new lover who became the gallery's most successful debutant, with *The Times* newspaper heralding Hussein as 'a painter in love with his medium'.

The sexy bohemian edge of Gallery One appealed to Hen as it was owned by Victor Musgrave whose wife Ida Kar was a well-known photographer. Musgrave and Kar had a very open marriage. His predilection for kinky fetishism with prostitutes led him to become such an authority on Soho's 'working girls' that he was commissioned to write a book on them. Meanwhile, his wife, Ida Kar, had developed a penchant for young men and her erotically charged photos of a half-naked Hussein, looking pensive with his paintings, now reside in London's National Portrait Gallery. Suffice to say, Musgrave and Kar's outré behaviour made Gallery One a magnet for bohemians. It was another meeting place where (rather like the Colony) painters, poets and authors rubbed shoulders with wealthy socialites: Francis Bacon, Lucian Freud, George Melly and Henrietta all frequented it.

But had Hussein Shariffe unwittingly introduced a sinister element to Henrietta's existence? She claimed her new boyfriend's presence at Apollo Place provoked a series of psychic phenomena: heavy footsteps in the night, a breathing sofa that behaved like a living creature, a spooky man sitting in her armchair and a decapitated head in a bucket of blood. Even Hen's nanny, the normally down-to-earth Nana began seeing ghosts in the hallway. Henrietta discovered that the house, being situated at the World's End, was built on the former site of a slave traders' warehouse and thought that Hussein's Sudanese heritage (she claimed his ancestors were great slave traders) had triggered the phenomena rather than the large amount of drink and drugs they both consumed on the premises.

But, in her defence, she did rent out a room to some Chinese students who complained about being kept awake all night by the loud party going on overhead in the studio. Hen was perplexed, as she'd been at home all night, quietly reading a book in bed and hadn't heard a peep. But the loud footsteps of an unseen presence rushing up and down the studio stairs soon became a common occurrence. One wonders if it ever occurred to Hen that if anyone was going to throw a spooky party in the afterlife it would surely be Johnny Minton? After all, he was condemned to walk the earth in limbo for eternity, having committed suicide on the premises, and he also had *the motive* to come back and haunt the woman who'd walked off with his boyfriend. Although, to be fair, Minton had made the mistake of telling Norman Bowler, 'You must choose between us.' 'My heart fell to my boots,' said Henrietta. 'I dreaded that he was going to choose me.' And he did.

But let's forget the ghosts for a minute, the elephant that really haunted the room (and which Henrietta never mentions in her memoir) is the racism that was then rife in wider society. At the time black and Asian immigrants genuinely believed the 'Mother' country would be happy to see them, but sadly the reality often fell short of expectations. Although Hen was half-Indian she was very pale-skinned compared to Dom's darker complexion, and she also now had an African boyfriend, Hussein, so she must have encountered prejudice in the public sphere, but never mentions it, although at that time intimate encounters across the 'colour bar' often provoked violence. White women who 'consorted' with black men were condemned as careless pleasure-seekers and whispering campaigns were conducted against interracial couples.

Yet, despite the tensions, it wasn't race relations that caused Henrietta and Hussein to split. Blind to both race and gender, bohemia itself tended to break up all sorts of couples who came crashing upon its rocky shores, and many Soho characters, such as Muriel Belcher, took great delight in these diverting melodramas. Hussein left Henrietta to go back to Sudan and marry his cousin, Diana Melly deserted her husband, John Moynihan, when she met the jazz singer George Melly by Muriel's piano and Henrietta's friend Merilyn Thorold hadn't got divorced over some other man, but rather over the amount of time she spent at the Colony. Merilyn was a wonderful and very beautiful part of that scene who stood out with her marvellous golden red hair, mustard yellow tunic dress and thick black stockings, which were quite outré at that time ... according to Viscountess Harriet Bridgeman:

> Merilyn was very much a free spirit. She came from a wealthy family and being raised a Catholic, she had a strong conscience and loved helping all those artistic down and outs, like Paul Potts. She was also amoral in the nicest possible way. She had a wide circle of friends from all walks of life. One was a prostitute and another was David Tennant of the Gargoyle club.

Along with Henrietta, Merilyn liked to hang out with the poets and the painters at Muriel's. Now they'd both become single mothers, Merilyn and Henrietta formed a mutual support network, as Merilyn's daughter, Emelia, explained:

We were the same age as Henrietta's children and we all spent a lot of time together in the early 1960s. When Mum and Dad broke up we went on holiday to the Greek island of Hydra for a long summer break to escape the fallout from their separation. On the way down, our train compartment doors didn't close properly so Mum and Henrietta took it in turns to sleep by the door so none of the children could wander off. Then, when we finally got there, we all had lice, so Henrietta and Mum took us all down to a petrol pump in the harbour and hosed our hair down in petrol, which killed the lice but meant we smelt of gasoline for days afterwards, despite rigorous hair washing. All the supplies were carried up the hill daily by donkey, up the main street known as 'Donkey shit lane'. It was a very trendy island to visit at the time, hip people like the singer Leonard Cohen had homes there. On the way back we sailed into Marseille by boat, at the same time as the 'Algerian Crisis' was unfolding and we ended up at the docks, penniless, where everyone assumed we were Algerian refugees.

Subsumed by Soho ...

When Henrietta's housekeeper, Nana, took Joshua and Caroline for their annual visit to Arklow in Ireland, to visit Nana's daughter, she took the unusual step of sending the children back without her. Then, as the months rolled by Nana still hadn't reappeared so Merilyn said to Hen, 'Don't you think we'd better go to Ireland?' They arrived in time to find Nana on her deathbed riddled with cancer. Henrietta wept copiously, her grief was palpable. A stabilising influence on her life had been extinguished. Nana was the loving maternal grandmother figure Henrietta never had and, from that point on, Hen's life began to slowly unravel. Upon her return to London, she became subsumed by Soho again. Early in 1963 Francis Bacon approached Henrietta in the French, which led to one particular incident that's now passed into legend:

> I used to see Francis [Bacon] every day, drinking in Soho with him. Francis said, 'I'd like to paint you,' so I said, 'Of course.' He said, 'Deakin can come and take some photos of you. I can't work from a live model because people are always so shocked and appalled by what I make of them.' So, I said, 'fine'. Then a week later I was at home and Deakin came round and started taking these photographs. He was very sure about the angles, but they didn't seem right to me. I asked him if he was sure, it seemed rather extreme, all these intimate shots. I didn't think Francis would want to paint me in those attitudes.

Did Deakin defile her with his lens? Hen admitted to feeling a little shy of stripping in front of a homosexual who didn't desire her and might be disgusted by the sight of so much female flesh. But the more Hen held back the more Deakin goaded her into opening her legs wide. According to Marianne, Hen had initially posed sat on the bed with her arms and legs crossed but Deakin demanded that she threw herself back on the bed with wild abandon:

> Deakin perversely took hundreds of close-up, wide-angle shots of her pussy … a few weeks after the first photo session with Deakin, Hen came across him in a Soho drinking club flogging them as dirty pictures to a bunch of sailors for ten bob a pop. At first, Henrietta was absolutely furious with Deakin for flogging pornographic pictures of her around the pubs but couldn't remain angry for long because she found it so damn funny … she merely said, 'I don't really give a damn about your selling pictures of my cunt, John, but at least you could buy me a drink. *Several* large drinks.

Marianne said that whenever Henrietta was reminded of the incident she would laugh and yell, 'Traitor! Toad!' And as Hen predicted, a week later, when Deakin presented Francis with the photographs in the French, the artist declared the images useless. They had been taken at the wrong angle and he certainly didn't want pornographic shots, so he asked Deakin to try again. But Henrietta wasn't keen to repeat the ordeal, so he bought her a large drink in the Colony before broaching the subject:

> Francis said, 'Look here, Henrietta, this blithering nitwit has reversed every single shot of you that I wanted.' 'Ho,' I said. 'You amaze and astonish me.' 'Well, look here, Henrietta' – Francis shot his cuffs, displaying enormously strong-looking wrists – 'would you mind letting him do the whole thing all over again, but the other way up this time?'

So, Hen submitted herself to a second shoot. After all, she couldn't help liking the duplicitous Deakin, who had plenty of enemies and was said to be as unreliable as Henrietta herself, which she claimed had eventually got him sacked from *Vogue*:

> He was a seriously good photographer. He took a photo of Johnny [Minton], which I think is brilliant. The old sailors he found with no teeth, have you seen them? He had a very good eye, but was an alcoholic and that tends to get in the way …

Hypnotically Warm and Witty

As well as Deakin's notorious sequence of photographs of her upside down on rumpled sheets, Henrietta was also one of the lucky few to have been painted by two of the greatest British painters of the twentieth century, Francis Bacon and Lucian Freud, who she claimed 'couldn't be more different from each other'. Hen was the type of person whom extraordinary things happened to without the need for moralising. Some models inspire artists by their looks, others with their personality. Hen was hypnotically warm and witty but confessed to picking up bad habits like iron filings:

> The pictures that [Francis] finally got painted from Deakin's photographs … the nudes, I like but found more mysterious because there was one with a hypodermic syringe with three drops of blood on the bed. And I'd never really heard of anything like hypodermic syringes or serious drugs at that point. It later caught

> up with me ... but that must have been something he'd just seen because it certainly did not exist in the flesh at all then.

Francis said that when he was painting Hen's portrait he realised he needed something on the right-hand side to balance the composition but couldn't think of what to do, so he stuck a hypodermic syringe in her arm, as a formal way of fixing the figure to the bed, and although the painting captured her forceful beauty it was not recognisable as Henrietta. But Francis was so taken by Deakin's photographs he went on to make twenty-three more paintings of her.

Francis appreciated the impact of painting on massive canvasses at a time when it was seldom done. The unpredictability inherent in his painting process revealed so much about Francis' psyche. He was a compulsive gambler and his gambling grew out of his awareness of the role that chance plays in our lives and our vulnerability to it. He utilised 'accidents' in his painting with the cold calculation of an experienced gambler. With the action of throwing paint and the chance movement of the brush, Francis often found he'd created a more interesting image than he had intended. His shocking use of brightly coloured backgrounds jarred with his smearing of paint, which looked like torn flesh. There was a buzz of excitement whenever Francis exhibited his new work. His paintings were shocking and his audience were both simultaneously seduced and repelled by them. His work was audacious. No one had seen such savage images of human beings before and they went on to inspire a whole host of horror films, macabre literature and artistic imitators who enjoyed butchering people with their paintbrushes.

By the time Francis began painting Henrietta, he had just been given a prestigious retrospective at the Tate Gallery in 1962, which coincided with the death of his lover and muse Peter Lacey. A former Colony Room pianist and fighter pilot, Lacey liked nothing more than destroying Francis' paintings and with his passing Francis required fresh meat, raw material for his unprimed canvas. He painted Henrietta as a triptych, three portrait paintings of her intended to be placed side by side, like a church altarpiece. It was an unusual choice for someone living such an unholy existence and

Hen's contorted facial features take on a demonic quality. Henrietta told her daughter that Francis admired her 'herculean body' which he found both curvaceous and muscular – but it was Henrietta's aura of danger, of walking on the precipice, that informed the mood of Francis' paintings. As John Moynihan put it:

> The rude, unabashed outburst of Henrietta, Lady Brett of the Gargoyle, lifted waiters on their heels as she mocked her party or destroyed an admirer with a sidelong glance. She was one of those versatile highly intelligent girls, who arrive one day and stay. Francis Bacon chose her as the subject for many of his paintings. In *Three Studies of Henrietta Moraes* (1963), the first shows her in an old Gargoyle mood, wild, haughty; the next two are more flexible Bacon torn images, her expression, in the first case smashed inwards, wounded and less menacing. The second is a defiant mother's face.

Comrades in Arms ...

It wasn't too long before another defiant mother arrived on the scene and collided with Henrietta at the Colony. Her name was Thea Porter and she would, over the next decade, become a fashion designer to stars such as Elizabeth Taylor and Joan Collins. Thea lived on the top two floors of a house in Bolton Street, Mayfair, where for many years these dark small-roomed eighteenth-century houses were mostly inhabited by retired butlers who kept lodgers. As Thea's friend Ros Baronio Archer told me:

> Thea had landed in London with no money. Someone suggested that she should make cushions with the Lebanese fabric she had and it grew from there. Her boutique was at the top end of Greek Street, Soho, in an interesting row of shops such as Patisserie Valerie where you'd see Eric Clapton having a coffee on a Saturday morning.
>
> Thea had deserted her husband in Lebanon to come to London with her baby daughter. It couldn't have been an easy relationship being Thea's daughter because of her posturing. She was like a Noël

> Coward character poised with her cigarette and glass of Pernod, all beautifully theatrical but very disconcerting if you wanted to just have a casual conversation with her; if you asked, 'Do you need some coffee?' she'd be rather haughty. She didn't want to deal with anything domestic like that.
>
> Then curiously, I was talking to my uncle and aunt about this fantastic woman I'd met called Thea Porter and their ears pricked up: 'Thea? Thea Porter? Goodness, we know Thea!' My uncle had been First Secretary at the British Embassy in Beirut and they knew Thea socially. My aunt Marion, who was a dreadful snob, said: 'Oh, Thea, honestly. The whole Embassy would go for a picnic up in the hills behind Beirut and Thea would appear tottering on her high heels and long silk scarves. It was ridiculous, just ridiculous!' But to me it sounded wonderful, this image of Thea tottering around in her high heels – high above Beirut!

As if to prove the general rule that Henrietta Moraes was almost always once removed from every major scandal that rocked the British Establishment, Thea Porter's brother, the author Patrick Seale, was the Middle East correspondent for *The Observer* newspaper and had been friends with the British diplomat Kim Philby. No one realised Philby was a double agent working for the Russians until he defected to the Soviet Union in 1963. The funny thing was … Patrick's sister, Thea, was now hanging out in the same Soho places (such as the Colony and the Gargoyle), in which Philby's fellow double agents Guy Burgess and Donald Maclean had once partied with Henrietta, just before they too had defected to Russia. Rather like the spies themselves, Thea Porter's own persona was somewhat fabricated, as Ros confided in me:

> She was not a naturally beautiful woman, so she created a style for herself and a way of being that made her incredibly beautiful. It was in the way she dressed and carried herself … she had integrity as a designer. When she talked about life in the Middle East it was all about how women lived and their relationship to men. There was a sensual aspect running through it all and that got expressed with her fine eye for detail. She was never going to be 'middle of the road'.

Thea had fallen in with the Colony Room crowd and became a fan of Francis Bacon. Thea knew that it was good for business to get Henrietta and Muriel Belcher to wear her clothes. She gave them things to wear and, on the flip side, Muriel wanted Thea in the club entertaining her wealthy clients. However, although Thea was a brilliant designer, she was a terrible businesswoman and often teetered on the edge of insolvency. Muriel's former barman, David Marrion, told me he had been given the job of saying to her: 'Thea you've reached the end of your credit.' Well, that really pissed Thea off and, as a fully paid-up member of the Monster Club, if Thea took umbrage at something it was *terrible* and according to David Marrion she enjoyed making his life hell:

> She'd often give Muriel clothes she had designed … kaftans and flowing scarves but I didn't want any of that shit, 'Oh, David I must give you something.' But I didn't want it and neither did Francis, it was far too effeminate … Thea enjoyed hanging around Francis. She once borrowed an invitation for Francis' exhibition, and had it copied on the exact same paper so she could gate-crash the reception. Thea sucked up to Muriel for Francis' exhibition in Paris – 'Oh, Muriel, you must come with me, I'll take you there.' She only did that to make sure she got a good seat next to Francis, that's all there was to it. I never saw Francis being overly friendly or affectionate to her, I just saw her as the 'Evil Little Dwarf'.

But try as she might to ingratiate herself into Francis' circle, even a woman as versatile and feisty as Thea Porter had to admit she couldn't get the better of experienced hands like Henrietta:

> The first time I saw Henrietta Moraes at the Colony, I recognised her from Bacon's and Lucian Freud's paintings. She was sitting on the banquette below the window, and looked dark and powerful. I was wearing a turquoise ring from Aleppo that she admired; she said she had had a turquoise but had lost it. Before I knew what had happened, she'd magicked the ring off my finger.

Shocked by the audacity of the theft, Thea soon discovered to her cost that Henrietta lived by the law of the jungle: survival of the fittest. Forever foraging and liberating other people's possessions, Henrietta was about to take it to a completely new level: as a cat burglar.

Chapter 10

The Cat Bungler of Bohemia

By now drugs had become a major problem and Henrietta was on a downward spiral, as tragically witnessed by her son, Joshua. She had smoked her first joint at the age of twenty-two, but Henrietta said it was whilst she was at the Eichmann trial that she first experimented with drugs and became addicted to those little pills that knocked the 'edge off life'. As Marianne remembers it:

> Henrietta had a brief and disastrous career as a cat burglar and a somewhat longer career as a methedrine addict. She would shoot liquid meth (a terrifying drug sometimes used to resuscitate the dead and Hitler's favourite pick-me-up) which made her as high as a kite.

And Hen being Hen, she was quite open about it:

> You inject it. It's the stuff they gave the troops during the war when they were going to do something incredibly brave. It swept London. It makes you want to go and be a soldier, kill people or burgle. I really liked it.

Hen had a fine mind when she chose to apply it; she was not the foul-mouthed thieving drunk that Francis Bacon's biographers often portray her as. Ironically, Henrietta had just written an eloquent piece for the then prestigious *Sunday Times Colour Magazine* about drug addiction:

> It is an odd paradox that it is against the law to smoke marijuana in this country ... yet it may be perfectly legal to get your doctor to prescribe you several grains of heroin and cocaine per day. The difference between smoking marijuana and taking heroin and cocaine is enormous, and the latter is a far more serious business. Those who use it say marijuana is laughter-making, appetite-increasing and, with some people anyway, enhances their love life. There are, however, side effects and smoking it to excess can be damaging. Heroin will certainly cut you off from the company of anybody save fellow junkies, make you more or less impotent, stop you from working unless your character is sterling, and if taken in conjunction with cocaine will shorten your life ... a real interest in *something* other than drugs seems to be a preventative, for a junkie literally does not have time to do anything else in his life except fix.

Henrietta began to retreat from the world, jacking in the job Elizabeth Smart had got her at the copywriters' and taking to her bed for several weeks. She acquired a new beau called Joe, a registered drug addict who legally obtained drugs from his doctor. Back then, the doctors' surgeries were full of scruffy impatient young people suffering from severe bouts of involuntary shivering and runny noses. 'One of the fundamental causes of addiction seems to be the failure to communicate with other human beings,' observed Henrietta, whose home soon became Junkie Central.

There were two addicts whom Hen talked to the most and got to know quite well; to her they typified the 'sadness and futility of a junkie's life'. Like Hen, they were both young and 'orphaned'. One of them had been in and out of various institutions, including prison, since he was two years old. They got very little pleasure from the drugs but found themselves unable to stop taking them; they held back from forming attachments or relationships with anyone as they had no faith in humanity. Their whole life focused around scoring drugs and they enjoyed the ritual around the injections: the preparations, over which they took a lot of time and effort, were a type of foreplay, a kind of preliminary to lovemaking. As Marianne Faithfull's first husband, the artist John Dunbar, told me:

> You can sum up the early Sixties as before drugs and after drugs – our parents' generation were all drinkers; alcohol was their drug whereas we were into new drugs. They were all pre-war and the younger generation were all post-war. We stayed away from drink in general because we had discovered new drugs. I remember the first time I met John Lennon I was with Marianne smoking dope in the Ad-Lib club, 'Is that drugs?' enquired John. Then the Beatles went to America and *whoa!* Drugs were alright.

For that pre-war generation of bohemians, especially those femmes fatales of the 1920s, in whose footsteps Henrietta unwittingly walked, drug addiction was not perceived as deviant but rather the result of overwork or medical treatment gone awry. It was only later on that drugs began to be associated with moral deviancy and criminality. Users were no longer perceived as aristocratic hedonists but as working-class criminals and there was a racist element that scapegoated immigrant communities as drug pushers. In this way, drug use had developed a new set of meanings by the 1960s, and the press whipped up a moral panic surrounding their use. Heroin is a highly addictive derivative of morphine, producing a state of unusual well-being, and is highly effective in suppressing emotional and physical pain. As John Dunbar told me:

> By 1962 Doctors were allowed to prescribe heroin and it didn't take long to seep into the culture. People could get heroin on prescription from their doctor, so there would be queues of junkies outside the 24 hour Boots the chemist in Piccadilly Circus. When the repeat prescription came through every Friday, they'd all be off to Boots in Piccadilly, ready for the stroke of midnight …

Needless to say, Henrietta became quite a connoisseur of the scene in the public lavatories at Piccadilly Circus underground station. Obscene graffiti decorated this gloomy sanctum … a tomb for the living dead where, with the bang of cast iron, a cistern would gargle empty, as yet again another bolt on a cubicle loudly slammed back. There was an unpleasant odour. A rubbish bin was filled to the brim on the urine-streaked floor, which complemented the broken cubicle door. Vera Vomit had left her mark on the toilet seat along with feckless faeces smeared on the walls and some bold dried blobs of blood. Here men engaged in ill-lit liaisons, their mouths pouting in the twilight as they loosened their office ties as well as their sexual inhibitions. The toilets were frequented by rent boys who plied their trade there and at the railings nearby, known as the 'meat rack'.

Then, just after midnight came the first fix of the day. Having handed in their prescriptions at 11.30 p.m., they'd collect them half an hour later and in the subterranean world of the public lavatories Henrietta witnessed a man (having got the water from the lavatory pan) boiling up drugs in a bottle with a lighted match before using a piece of string as a tourniquet around his upper arm to make the blood vessels stand out, then loosening the string and injecting straight into the vein. He gets a 'hit' at once and vomits. The scars on his arm are called 'tracks'.

According to Henrietta, before 1945 there were only a handful of known heroin and cocaine addicts in Britain, apart from therapeutic addicts, i.e., cancer sufferers. In 1959 there were no known addicts under the age of twenty, but by 1963 there were 635 registered addicts – fifteen of whom were under twenty – mainly due to an influx of North Americans. Between 1959 and 1965 the rate of increase in drug addiction became so disturbing that one West End pharmacist Henrietta talked to compared it to a typhoid epidemic. As John Dunbar explained, the Americans had arrived because:

> They could get smack on prescription from the National Health Service. Whereas in New York, needles were super rare. That's why the Beats were all hanging out in London, William Burroughs lived next door to my gallery in Mason's Yard, Mayfair. When Henrietta met Burroughs, he showed her the tracks on his body.

Fence the Loot ...

The public, in general, were naive about drug use. Most of London was not 'Swinging' in the Sixties; it's something of a myth since it was mainly rich kids and aristocrats who could really afford to 'drop out' of society and the hip youth of Swinging London swung only in 'select' areas. As the former art student Jo Reed Turner told me:

> It never occurred to me that Henrietta had developed a drug habit. I wasn't aware of drug use. I thought people behaved the way they did because they'd drunk too much. Rose Barnicoat dealt with the copyright for Orbis books. She had recently married the author, Robin Cook with whom she used to have terrible public fights. Her father was Mr Reckitt, of Reckitt & Colman [who manufactured Britain's most famous household brands like Harpic toilet cleaner and Durex condoms] … Rosie was one of those rare women who would 'oil the wheels' for others. She had a house in Chelsea and liked to collect 'oddities' and invite them for Sunday lunch and for some reason Rosie would sometimes invite me along too. Then, one lunchtime, she turned to me and said, 'I've got this beautiful ring for you', and presented it to me. I was astonished, 'How wonderful thank you'. – 'Actually', continued Rosie, 'I've got a lot of jewellery' and produced this bag of wonderful trinkets. 'Would you like it?' – 'Yes, how marvellous! That's very kind of you'. The bag was full of beautiful Victorian gold jewellery. I was overjoyed. Then I found out, years later that Henrietta had committed a burglary but lost her nerve and didn't know what to do with her spoils, which were somehow ferried over to Rosie to distribute and disperse to 'innocents' rather than attempting to 'fence' the loot.

However, Henrietta's drug-addled lifestyle could not go on without repercussions. Her home life suffered and in all probability her children did too. When she failed to keep up with the household bills she lost Apollo Place and ironically (considering her love of prescription drugs) sold it to a doctor. She then fled from the World's End to a flat south of the Thames, on Prince of Wales Drive, Battersea. It was here that she welcomed countless addict friends who dossed down with her. One day Hen's young son found an addict known as Dustbin Joyce dying in his bed. She'd got the nickname because she used to live in a dustbin, conveniently placed halfway between her doctor and the chemist …

A 'Soho Mystery'

Henrietta now surveyed the Hogarthian scene on Prince of Wales Drive with some relish as she upped her pill intake and fooled herself into thinking she was immune from any form of addiction whatsoever.

Another regular visitor to Henrietta's drugs den was a sixteen-year-old girl who claimed she had been an addict for a year after taking cocaine and heroin at a party in the suburbs. She thought it was fantastic and was soon hooked, despite being extremely sick every time she had a fix. She wasn't a registered drug addict and, with no doctor's prescription, she was forced to buy her drugs from other junkies outside the all-night chemist at Piccadilly Circus. Her dose was still quite small, so she shakily managed to hold down a job as a hostess, chatting up businessmen in a Soho clip-joint. These were hostess bars where they'd charge an extortionate amount for a beer and even more for fake champagne. You had to keep buying the hostess drinks with the end goal of wooing her into having sex with you, which of course you never achieved – what you did achieve though, at the end of the night, was a ruinous bill and the feeling you'd been well and truly fleeced. The teenage girl hated her work and although she didn't sleep with anyone she admitted to Henrietta that pretty soon she'd probably become a prostitute, after all she had already become a 'Soho Mystery', a label given to young girls, runaways, who were both homeless and friendless, no one knew their names or where they came from hence the 'Mystery'. She'd had a happy suburban childhood, but now hardly ever saw her parents because she didn't want them to know what she had become.

Amidst all this, Henrietta slowly descended into a state of acute amphetamine psychosis – a type of severe mental derangement – brought on by the habitual use of amphetamines. She became a human jackdaw – attracted to acquiring nice things that did not belong to her, she got a buzz from liberating them from their owners. It was the kick of the adrenaline rush from climbing up the drainpipe and padding over rooftops, the thrill of it all became addictive, she'd become a cat burglar who lived on the edge. She laughed in the face of danger and always fell on her feet (or so she liked to think). Unfortunately, unlike nine out of ten cats, she was not blessed with nine lives. An acquaintance of her junkie boyfriend Joe, named Stan, became her partner in crime. Like all good comic book villains, they operated in a nocturnal world of shadows and, as the old joke goes, 'They say crime doesn't pay, but it's a living, you know.'

After one late-night drinking session topped off with hashish and a lot of pill-popping action, they were making their way back from Henrietta's friend's (Sandy Fawkes) house in Hampstead when they took a shine to one particular mansion which they proceeded to rob of its Meissen china, pausing only to partake of cocktails from the victim's drinks cabinet. Later in life the very memory of these far-off days would make Hen wince and howl:

> Don't say it, I know. I've just always refused to grow up and let go, life was one long party. I didn't really have what are called 'role models', no father, and a family that didn't care. I'm a Gemini, for god's sake, and you know what they're like … eternally stupid.

It was gone 4 a.m. in the morning as Hen and her sidekick, Stan, made their way past the comedian Peter Cook's house on Church Row towards Hampstead underground station. That's when Stan spotted some nosh through a window – breakfast! – and despite her protests, Stan forced entry to the premises, only to reappear at the front door moments later yelling 'Run!', as he whooshed past her hotly pursued by someone in stripy pyjamas yelling, '*Stop Thief!*'. Henrietta was so laden down with bags of swag that she found it hard to gain any momentum at all. The milkman, who was doing his early morning delivery, took in the scene and joined the chase, swiftly followed by the paperboy. It soon descended into something resembling a slapstick comedy as the conga line of pursuers grew longer and longer, until an exhausted Hen was finally nabbed and escorted to the police station. 'You don't know what time of day it is do you darling?' observed a patronising policeman to a heroically amphetamine-riddled Hen, who was so high she felt like she was living in a Marvel comic and had convinced herself she was Superwoman on speed.

And so, our heroic Hen turned out to be not so much a cat burglar as a cat bungler. When questioned by police she refused to name her accomplice, but they had already nabbed him whilst he was trying to break into Henrietta's place on Prince of Wales Drive. Hen was then promptly sent to Holloway prison in a Black Maria, strip-searched, combed for crabs and presented with a prison uniform replete with a 'shameful' pair of knickers as rough as sandpaper.

Playing to the Gallery

Eventually, she was brought before the judge and used the trial as an opportunity to play to her friends in the public gallery to much hilarity. Not for a single moment did Hen take the court seriously and it certainly never occurred to her that she'd be found guilty. So, she played the questions pitched at her by the prosecution for laughs. Unfortunately, the judge didn't share Hen's sense of humour and remanded her in custody for two weeks for a medical report. She was put in Holloway Prison's hospital wing. 'Full of nutters,' observed Henrietta who, according to Diana Melly, could have just as easily been talking about the Colony Room:

> Henrietta drank too much, but then again, we all did back then – there was no heroin around perhaps some Purple Hearts (amphetamines). Then Henrietta began taking serious drugs and money became a problem. There were dark rumours swirling around Soho about her. Her children, Joshua and Caroline, eventually came to live with us for a while after Henrietta was arrested.

In the French: Gaston Berlemont behind the bar and Henrietta Moraes by John Deakin. (© John Deakin Archive)

French fables: Henrietta and Francis Bacon by John Deakin.
(© John Deakin Archive)

There goes lunch: Tony Hubbard by John Deakin. (© John Deakin Archive)

Into the lion's den: Muriel Belcher and Anthony Carson by John Deakin.

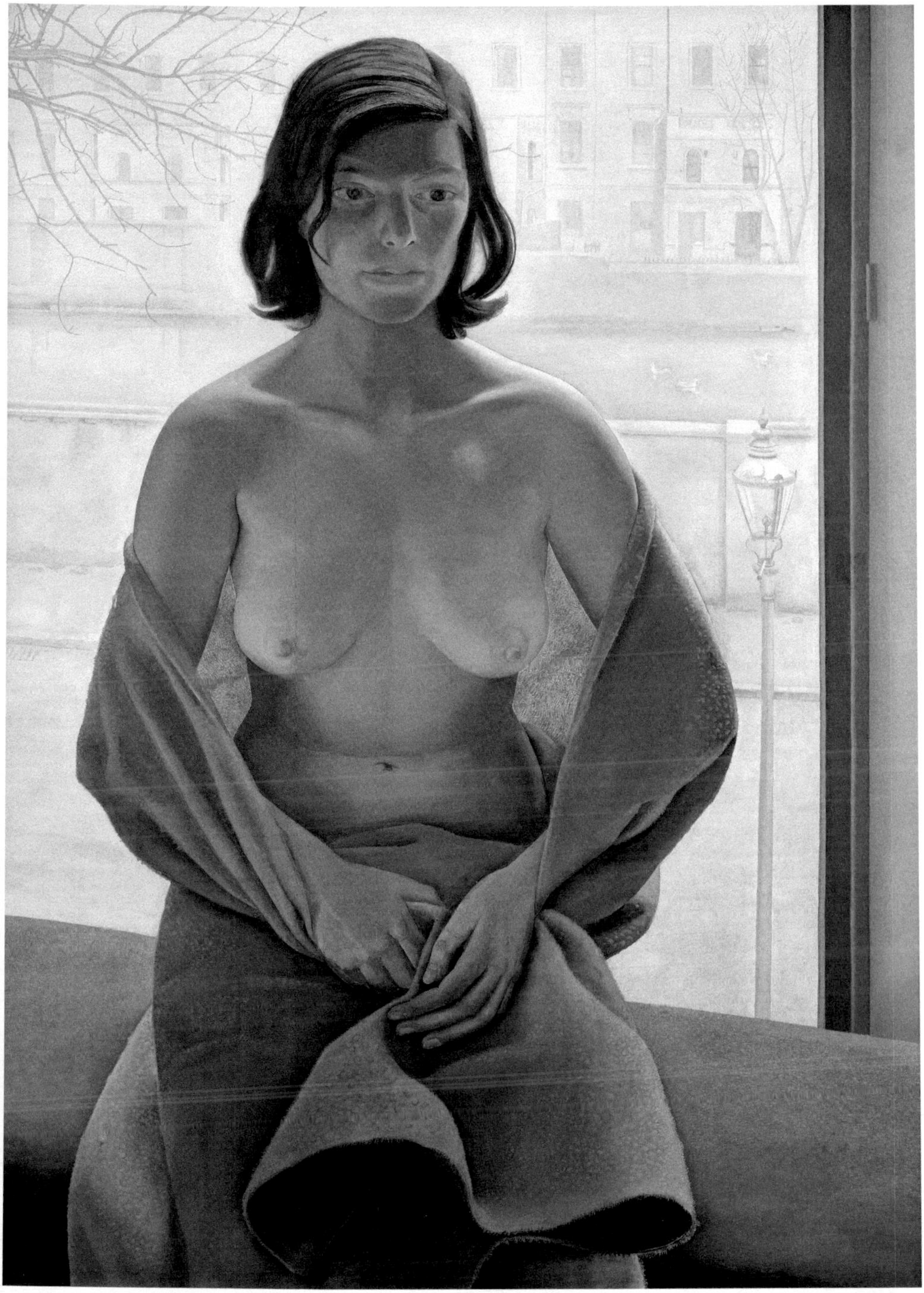

Henrietta is the *Girl in a Blanket*, 1953, by Lucian Freud. (© The Lucian Freud Archive. All Rights Reserved 2025/Bridgeman Images)

Top: Michael Law. *Below:* 'Minton's Circus' circa 1953: John Minton, Charlotte Jennings, Norman Bowler, the Singe-Headed Sailor and Olive Oil. (© Leo Moynihan)

Chelsea Girl: Elinor Bellingham-Smith. (© Leo Moynihan)

Prince Charmings? Norman Bowler and Dom Moraes by John Deakin.
(© John Deakin Archive)

Top: David Archer, patron saint of poets. *Below:* David Archer and Dom Moraes in the French by John Deakin. (© John Deakin Archive)

97.

married but very pregnant. At the same time I was very touched : it seemed to me that K. was willing to sacrifice herself to me because she knew I loved her. This generous gesture of hers I resolved to answer with one of my own : "I couldn't possibly," I said. She looked simultaneously annoyed and amused : then shrugged her shoulders and said, "Well, let's go ~~on~~ and have a drink."

The doomed quality of the shop not only continued, but increased. The day before I was due to leave for Oxford, K. became very ill, and it was discovered that she was one of the handful of people in the British Isles who had typhoid. She had contracted this through eating a bad oyster at lunch with me. If I had believed in portents, this would have made me think very hard. As it was, I half believed in them, and I felt a kind of apprehension : about K., about the shop, about my book. Archer was very worried : the Health authorities had called, and told him that the premises might have to be closed for the quarantine period. Through my worry about K., I found time to worry about him : he turned a pile of bills over ruefully, and said, "Dear, dear. Dotty me, really, I shan't be able to pay these."

Top: Original typescript of Dom Moraes' memoir in which he refers to Henrietta as 'K'. (© The Colony Room Archive™). *Below:* Dom, Henrietta and Quentin Stevenson at Oxford, 1958. (© Estate of Peter Levi)

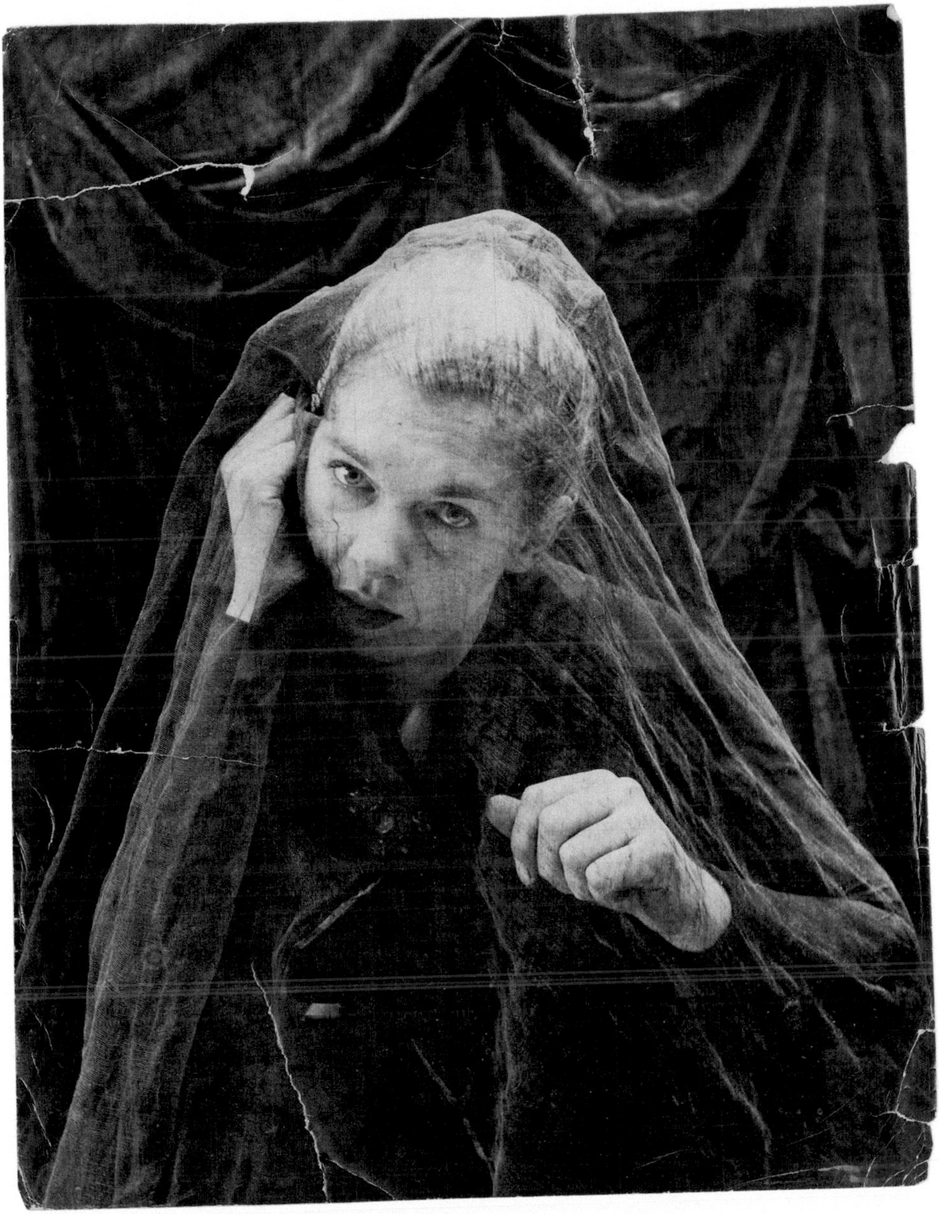

The Smart Set: Elizabeth Smart by John Deakin. (© John Deakin Archive)

24-hour party people. *Clockwise from top left:* April Ashley; Alexander Shihwarg and Joan Wyndham; Dom and Henrietta on Joan Wyndham's sofa. (© Camilla Shivarg)

Clockwise from top left: Merilyn Thorold (© Marcus Thorold); Christine Keeler; and 'Bambi'. (© The Colony Room Archive™)

Topsy-turvy lovers: Hussein Shariffe and Lucian Freud by John Deakin. (© John Deakin Archive)

Bringing home the Bacon: Tony Hubbard by John Deakin. (© John Deakin Archive)

As nature intended: Henrietta by John Deakin. (© John Deakin Archive)

12 **Lying figure with hypodermic syringe** 1963

Oil on canvas
78 × 57 inches (198 × 145 cm.) illustrated in colour

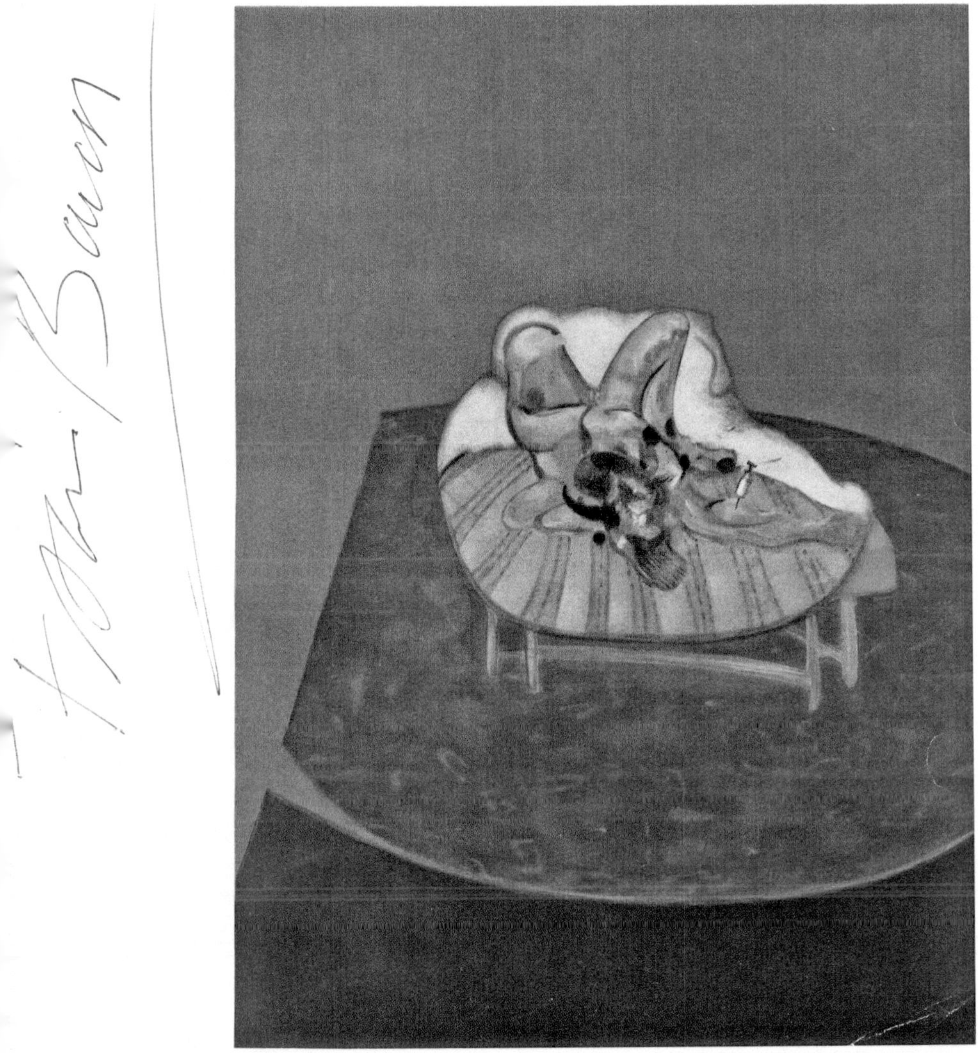

Signed and torn page from a 1963 exhibition catalogue, featuring Francis Bacon's painting of Henrietta. (© The Colony Room Archive™)

Dangerous muse: Henrietta by John Deakin. (© John Deakin Archive)

Torn page from *Derrière Le Miroir*, 1966, featuring another of Francis Bacon's paintings of Henrietta, signed by the sitter. (© The Colony Room Archive™)

Top: Sympathy for the devil? The Process Church becomes a house of cards. *Below:* Henrietta, Jane Rainey and Suki Potier dining in Hong Kong. (Collection of Darren Coffield)

The Cat Burglar by Sally Ducksbury, inspired by the exploits of Henrietta, with whom Sally had once formed part of 'Minton's Circus'. (Collection of Darren Coffield)

On the wagon? Hen and hound. (© Matthew Connolly)

Through a glass darkly: Henrietta returns to drink by Maggi Hambling. (© Maggi Hambling)

Top: Queens of Bohemia: Marianne holds court. (© John Dunbar). *Below:* Maggi Hambling and Henrietta at a John Minton exhibition, May 1991. (© Dafydd Jones)

The prototype punk pensioner: Henrietta by Maggi Hambling. (© Maggi Hambling)

Henrietta and skull by Maggi Hambling. (© Maggi Hambling)

12 June 1998: 'I have become Henrietta's subject, rather than she mine.' (© Maggi Hambling)

Henrietta at the Accident and Emergency Department of Chelsea and Westminster Hospital on the afternoon of her death by Maggi Hambling. (© Maggi Hambling)

Henrietta lying in her coffin by Maggi Hambling. (© Maggi Hambling)

Henrietta's grave at Brompton Cemetery, created by Maggi Hambling
(Photo © The Colony Room Archive™)

Henrietta Eating a Meringue, 2001 by Maggi Hambling: 'When Henrietta was told she had diabetes, she tucked into cream cakes in a big way. It was part of her defiance.' (© Maggi Hambling)

While on remand in prison, Hen held court with a motley crew of maimers, larcenists, dog-stealers, bestialists, embezzlers and prostitutes. She wrongly assumed that she wouldn't get sentenced for her first misdemeanour and was convinced she would soon be out, but Diana knew that if there was to be any hope of Hen and her children being reunited the gas and electricity bills had to be paid and the utilities reconnected. More importantly, the heroin addicts living in Henrietta's home had to be rehoused. Diana and her new husband, George Melly, drove over to Battersea and found a young couple in bed having sex, which was surprising as Henrietta always maintained that heroin addicts had no libido. They left them to it and cleaned the rest of the squalid flat, where dirty crockery rose precariously from the sink and mould sprouted proudly from the saucepans. Diana carefully disposed of the hypodermic syringes and other drugs paraphernalia that littered the place. George gave the junkies an old leather suitcase of his father's into which he doled their few belongings. He then sat and scratched away at the luggage label which had his and Diana's address on it … before driving them to their new abode, a suburban house with bright floral wallpaper and a respectably neat landlady, whilst Diana drew up an action plan:

> We needed to get them out and raise £1000 to settle the bills and other outstanding debts on Henrietta's flat. I made a list of friends who might help – Francis Bacon, Sonia Orwell, Lady Rose McLaren, Muriel Belcher etc. They all loved her and were very generous. We raised enough money to clear all her debts and have £100 left over for Henrietta. However, upon release she was outraged that we had 'wasted' so much money paying her bills – she'd rather have spent it on getting high.

In fact, Henrietta was so furious with Diana and George that she cut them from her personal history and never mentioned them in her memoir. Instead, Hen praised Muriel for it all, informing a television documentary that upon her prison release: 'there was £1,000 waiting for me at the Colony, which was amazing.' Yes, but not quite true, but then – as Henrietta stated in her *Sunday*

Times article – each addict is an individual with a different set of problems: 'Each person will tell you a different story ... the problem about giving up the habit is that you must have something to put in its place.'

The 'Help Hen' Fund ...

Once Henrietta got out of jail, her children, Caroline and Josh, didn't automatically go back home because Hen had indeed disappeared somewhere to spend the £100 left over from the 'Help Hen' fund on getting high. In her memoir, Diana Melly describes Hen as: 'Formidable, dark, attractive, clever, cruel, witty and often quite overpowering.' But once the cash had run out, Hen inevitably reappeared and went to stay with Diana, whom she'd follow around the house armed with a mug of coffee, which she would liberally top up as she went from room to room: a drop of vodka from the dining room drinks cabinet, a splash of cooking wine in the kitchen, etc. Then, once comfortably numb in the sitting room, Hen would sit cross-legged with her caffeine-based cocktail endlessly playing *Beatles* records and demanding that Diana locate her spider-like false eyelashes, which would mysteriously go to ground and take refuge in the shagpile carpet.

Before long, the funfair arrived in Battersea Park and whilst wandering through with the children Hen's eye was caught by a burly black boy operating the brake on the Big Dipper ride. She met him again in a young girl's bedsit-cum-drugs-den, with a dozen or so cold turkeys eagerly clucking to score. Hen got high and injected the black boy too before taking him home with her. His name was Rebel and he'd escaped from South Africa's racially segregated Cape Town. He originated from District Six where all the black folk were herded together and his earliest memory was of having his head kicked in by a white policeman at the age of four. Massively built and as muscular as a bull, Rebel stood resplendent in his silver-studded black leathers and winkle-picker shoes. He lived every inch up to his name and soon moved in with Hen. He made her clothes; black leather short skirts trimmed with white fur. When they sauntered down the street together, the pavement cleared in front of them. Everyone scattered at the sight of the pair – she in her leather miniskirt and he in his sharp-toed winkle-pickers – they appeared outrageous, and the more genteel residents of Chelsea may have mistaken them for a gangster and his moll. He certainly knew how to handle himself and had admitted to killing two men whilst boasting of his knife skills. According to Hen, her children yelled, 'Yippee – teach us how to fight with a knife!' Hardly the ideal role model for young children.

Like Hen, Rebel was a drug addict. In her memoir Henrietta says she went out for dinner one night, only to return and find Rebel stone-dead. Although a friend of Henrietta's told me another version of events, which involved one of the children waking up to get ready for school only to find they couldn't get into the bathroom, so they forced their way in and discovered the obstruction, a dead African. Rebel had died of heart failure – despite being built like an ox, the drugs had done for him, which begs the almost rhetorical question: was Henrietta unlucky in love? Well, another bohemian woman on the scene, Fiona Green, seems to think so:

> John Moynihan threw a party back in 1964; Henrietta Moraes and I were both invited. She was in another room and my husband, Martin Green, kept us apart. She'd been a huge iconic female figure on the scene, but I never got to know her because Martin had previously been engaged to her and did his utmost to keep us from meeting one another. Martin and Henrietta had originally met through David Archer's bookshop where they both worked. It was a whirlwind romance and before they knew it, they were engaged to marry. Francis Bacon was so overjoyed at the news he paid for them to go on a pre-nuptial honeymoon in Ireland before they tied the knot. However, when Martin met Henrietta's two children the enormity of what he was taking on dawned on him. He realised he'd made a big mistake and got cold feet. Her poor kids. Imagine being told this is your new father, then him disappearing the next day.

When the summer holidays finally came, Henrietta disappeared again, and Diana decided to take the children to Wales. At some point, Henrietta came up for a few days and astonished the locals by blowing up horses' nostrils and explaining that was the best way to communicate with them. Then, drunkenly abandoning a cigarette, Henrietta accidentally set fire to the large Edwardian wooden cot she'd previously helped to buy and nearly burned the house down too. Realising that Hen wasn't in full control of her faculties and wondering what to do with the children, Diana turned for advice to her friend Sonia Orwell, widow of the *Nineteen Eighty-Four* author George Orwell:

> Sonia suggested approaching Caroline's godmother, the writer Caroline Blackwood, for help. Little Caroline had been named after her godmother, who was rich and had been a good friend of Henrietta's. She was willing to pay for Caroline to go to Frensham Heights, a progressive boarding school, but on two conditions: Henrietta must never be told that she was footing the bill and I was to get little Caroline assessed by an educational psychologist to confirm that boarding school was right for her. Uneasily I found one and took Caroline along for the interview. Understandably Henrietta was furious and I couldn't tell her that it wasn't my idea. Nevertheless, Caroline went to Frensham and so did her brother, Josh.

Unfortunately, Josh had made friends with a thirty-year-old American called Ted, whom he and Hen had met in Hyde Park. Ted liked to take Josh to football matches and although George Melly made jokes about Ted liking Josh, neither George nor Diana realised until it was far too late that Ted was sexually grooming and raping little Josh. In those days people hadn't heard of paedophile rings and no one had any idea of what Josh was being subjected to. At the end of August, just before her children's departure to boarding school, Henrietta informed Diana that she no longer trusted her and that she was not to see her children again.

The loss of her dear friend Henrietta and that of the children was a bitter blow to Diana, who began to feel guilty and couldn't shake the nagging doubt, 'Was Henrietta right in accusing me of trying to steal her children's love?'

Chapter 11

Hen the Heroine

As I began to piece together a portrait of Henrietta, it soon became apparent that the circle of friends she drew upon were as extraordinary as the woman herself. While she floated around the World's End it was the height of the Cold War, the threat of nuclear Armageddon hung in the air with the Cuban Missile Crisis, and so it was only natural that Hen should have a Russian connection too. This came in the unlikely shape of the Fentons: Margaret and West de Wend Fenton who lived a bohemian existence, cheek by jowl with a livestock of lodgers that included pot-bellied pigs, goats, chickens, deer, llamas, peacocks and a turkey called Henry. Their unusual lifestyle and their bohemian friends like Hen soon became the talk of the village, as their daughter Rose told me:

> We lived in what is known as the smallest stately home in England and it was always in danger of falling down. There were a few acres of arable land where my parents kept sheep and cows. To supplement the farming in the 1960s my father (West) used to take tours across Eastern Europe in an old Bedford van. He would advertise in *The Times* newspaper 'Moscow and back £50' and gather an extraordinary group of people – a kind of ship of fools: artists, journalists and some military people (probably spies) – to take behind the Iron Curtain. They would visit cities, museums, and churches en route … they even happened to be in Berlin the night the wall went up.

> My father used the services of an agency called 'Progressive Tours' set up to organise travel to communist Eastern Europe and the Soviet Union. It was run by an extraordinary woman, Sofka Skipwith, also known as The Red Princess. On the eve of the Russian Revolution, she had fled the country for Britain with her family who were leading members of the Russian nobility. In later years she became an active member of the British Communist Party and was passionate for people to see what communism had achieved and encouraged as many people as possible to see for themselves. My father would visit her office just off Marble Arch with his travel itinerary to Moscow together with the list of people travelling with him and she would organise visas, notifying the relevant authorities of the date of arrival and departure for each country – how many days in Hungary, when they were expected in Poland etc … at the height of the Cold War when travel to Eastern Europe was highly suspect and very difficult.

The word 'bohemian' might have been invented to describe Sofka's unconventional life. Born into a life of luxury and privilege in Imperial Russia before the First World War, she claimed descent on her mother's side from Catherine the Great. Her grandmother nicknamed her the 'little Bolshevik!' Sofka may have ended her days in a humble Devon cottage, living a quiet life with a trade union activist, but in between she ran a literary salon and was a powerful propaganda tool for the Communist Party. As secretary for the bohemian Chelsea branch, Sofka was also to play a major role in the Communist Party's tourism agency, Progressive Tours. A passionate woman, Sofka embarked on a series of casual affairs. She claimed to have had more than 100 lovers in a dozen different countries. To some she led a fascinating dramatic life fighting against oppression, but to others she was a hard-hearted selfish nymphomaniac and a lousy mother. She was spied upon for decades by the British Secret Service and her MI5 file describes her as a 'flamboyant creature … looks a typical Chelsea bohemian type', rather like Henrietta Moraes herself. Everyone would gather at Hen's home before heading off behind the Iron Curtain, as Rose Fenton recalls:

> Henrietta was an extraordinary woman. My father, West, would often stay at Henrietta's home in Battersea before setting off on one of his trips, 'Oh good, West, you've got the van,' said Henrietta one day, 'Someone has given me a dining room table up in Hampstead. Could we drive up there and pick it up?' – 'Yes of course'. So, my father drove her up to Hampstead where they arrived at a rather grand house. Henrietta jumped out and knocked at the door which was answered by the housekeeper, 'Hello! I've come to pick up the dining room table.' – 'Oh' replied the bemused housekeeper, 'I didn't know it was being collected. Please come this way.' So, Henrietta and West carried the dining room table out into the van and then drove back to Henrietta's home in Battersea. Once the table was safely installed, she remarked: 'That was easy, wasn't it?' She then told my father that she'd been to a dinner party in the house a few weeks earlier – she didn't really know the hosts – but had heard they were going away for a month. She took a fancy to their dining room table and, as bold as brass, decided to go and pick it up. When my father remarked, 'We ought to take it back', Henrietta replied: 'They're rich, they can afford it.'

Henrietta's other friend was West de Wend Fenton's wife, Margaret, who had been born into the aristocratic Lygon family. Her father was the former Deputy Mayor of Chelsea and Evelyn Waugh had based his best-selling novel *Brideshead Revisited* upon the peculiar ups and downs of Margaret's family. Margaret herself was a rather genteel lady who found Henrietta's directness and approach to life rather invigorating, as Rose remembers it:

> My mother rather admired Henrietta, she thought there was something heroic about her and used to cite the time she landed in prison for throwing a brick through the South African Embassy window during an anti-apartheid demonstration. However, on another occasion my mother had accidentally left a very valuable book of illustrations at Henrietta's home. The illustrations were by my mother's great, great Grandmother Eleanor Vere Boyle, a pre-Raphaelite artist, admired by many of the important painters of her day, including Burne-Jones. My mother realised to her dismay

what had happened when she got back to Yorkshire (and rather worriedly) contacted Henrietta but received no reply. Then, about six months later, back in London, Henrietta casually handed over the book, 'Isn't that good of me? I could easily have sold it and taken the money.' She expected, rather amusingly, to be praised for handing it back.

However, my most abiding memory of Henrietta as a child is of a spectacular multi-coloured trifle she had made for a children's tea party. Henrietta caught me eyeing it longingly and said, 'Rose, would you like some trifle.' And I was so embarrassed to be caught looking greedily at it I said, 'No', even though I wanted it so much. Thirty years later, when I told Henrietta that story, she was very touched that I had remembered her trifle!

It was now 1966 and change was afoot as long-haired Apollo-addled youths floated up and down London's fashion capital, the King's Road, which had become the meeting point between high society and mass culture. The strip owes its name to King Charles II who had it constructed as a private road in 1694 to guarantee a smooth journey between his palaces. Although some believe it was built in order for the king to visit his mistress, Nell Gwyn, and the area has a long and colourful history. Beau Brummell, the great dandy of his age, frequented the district and dyed his hair green some two hundred years before the punk icon Johnny Rotten.

Until the 1960s, the King's Road was a local high street selling basic goods and services to the community with numerous residents listed as artists, such as Augustus John and Elinor Bellingham-Smith, but for a brief moment, in 1966, the King's Road was the most fashionable place on the planet. *Time* magazine titled it 'Swinging London' – as *Vogue*'s former fashion editor Geoffrey Aquilina Ross explained:

People came to the Kings Road because it was cool. It was a very small world, you knew everyone because there was such a small pool of talent. When the boutiques came the King's Road really took off and all the locals avoided the road on a Saturday because it didn't attract the right sort of person! Clare Rendlesham who was

> the fashion editor of *Queen* magazine was a rather grand lady who sniffed, 'I don't know how you can live there, I wouldn't be seen dead on the King's Road.' And where did she die? In her car at the traffic lights outside Chelsea Town Hall, on *the Kings Road*!

Walk down the King's Road today and you wouldn't believe it used to be the sexiest, grooviest street on earth with fabulous-looking people and outrageously beautiful clothes. But back then all types of 'Swinging' females could be found concentrated on the strip. Every Saturday afternoon flocks of young women could be witnessed window-shopping, catwalking or seductively sitting in traffic in their convertible cars – 3.30 p.m. was the peak time when everyone was out on display – it both reflected the best and worst of youthful taste, a heady mixture of vivid beauty and vulgar exhibitionism. Those on parade were interspersed with tourists and thrill-seekers – all out for a gay old time – and Henrietta and her friend Jeffrey Bernard were determined to make the most of it.

The April 1967 edition of *Town* magazine contained a feature by Jeffrey on 'How to Chat Up Birds', the magazine cover featuring the strapline: 'That's a nice dog you've got there, did you knit it yourself?' Among Jeff's top tips of where to pick up girls was 'The au pairs pram parking lot at Peter Jones' department store on the King's Road'. Another edition of *Town* magazine featured a guide to London's 'Young Pubs', and recommended a couple of King's Road hostelries – the Chelsea Potter and the Markham Arms, next door to Mary Quant's Bazaar, which was apparently 'full of talent', like Henrietta.

The hot summer encouraged everyone out into London's parks and squares with young optimistic youths strumming guitars, smoking joints and having picnics. These youths were collectively labelled 'hippies', in America being a 'hippy' (or hippie) was political, but in Britain it was largely social and the American hipster had been translated into the happily innocent British 'hippy', who believed money was the root of all evil.

It was at this time that Hen's friend Bill introduced her to a new pharmaceutical drug called lysergic acid or LSD. Bill had just brought it back from a laboratory in Switzerland where it was being used by doctors to work on the psyche of their patients. 'It's pure acid baby,' purred Bill who put some drops on Hen's tongue. Suddenly she experienced a spiritual revelation as she tripped headlong through Aldous Huxley's *Doors of Perception*. Everything seemed so vital and alive as the carpet's patterned colours and textures began re-forming themselves into entertaining new displays. The art dealer Robert Fraser (soon to become headline news for a drugs bust) entered the room and grew a pair of horns topped off with a halo which spat sparks. He also, rather worryingly, had a tail whiplashing to and fro around his cloven feet. Undeterred, Hen went with him to a discotheque where everything seemed amazing as her awareness became heightened and her fantasies ran riot. The LSD let Hen's brain off the leash and her cerebral connectivity exploded. As her friend George Melly explained:

> Acid changed you ... there is a conservative streak in the British, even among the rebellious young, which made them hesitate. Pot [marijuana] of course was different. Pot had been around for years ... Pills? Everybody took pills, including cabinet ministers – but acid was something else ... what distinguished plastic flower power from the hard-core pop-hippies was 'the experience'.

An apartment on Pont Street, by the borders of Chelsea, became the focus of this new fascinating sensation. Operating under the name of the 'World Psychedelic Centre' it was run by Michael Hollingshead, a type of acid evangelist from America whose visitors included Paul McCartney, Robert Fraser, Eric Clapton, William S. Burroughs, Roman Polanski and Henrietta. For some the effects of LSD were confusing and frightening but for Hen it seemed the perfect cure. She had been plagued with depression and bleak suicidal episodes for years, all of which the hallucinogenic drug swept away. It is now recognised as a medical treatment for those suffering from long-term depression, and Hen was an early success story.

The Dark Side of the 1960s ...

But there was a dark side to it all. Among the beautiful young people that began to congregate outside Chelsea's Picasso Café was Claudie Delbarre, an eighteen-year-old French au pair and model who was photographed there by the street photographer John Bignell on 19 February 1967. She had just been sent to *Penthouse* magazine by her model agency, but within forty-eight hours of her photograph being taken outside the café she was murdered by Bobby Lipman. Rather than getting a life sentence for cold-blooded murder Lipman got off on a manslaughter charge as he claimed he did not know what he was doing whilst tripping on LSD.

With the arrival of LSD, the excesses of Swinging London got into full swing. In retrospect Marianne Faithfull thought it was odd that so few of her friends didn't see *anything* negative about the 1960s. They'd tell her it was wonderful, which Marianne found deeply unsettling:

> When I hear things like that I question myself, wondering if I got it all wrong ... am I mad? But I think I have been completely sane all along. Back in the Sixties I certainly did seem to attract the most dreadful people: fringe types, cranks, weirdos ... it was all so creepy ... which reminds me about the time when dear Henrietta wrote an article about L. Ron Hubbard, the founder of the Scientology religion. She infiltrated meetings in order to write her piece, which went into great detail about what she saw as the dark rotten core of what Hubbard did ... so of course he was furious when Hen's article was published. She became convinced that people were following her around and got so terrified that she eventually went to the police.

The dark side of the 1960s revolves around the sinister religious cults that seemingly sprang up from nowhere during the 'Summer of Love'. Coming to terms with one's identity is part of adolescence, the difficulties of which seemed compounded by the cultural and social upheavals of Swinging London. Many young people were looking for answers to their questions concerning identity and spirituality. The alienation of youth from society and the disenchantment with the establishment led some to immerse themselves in drugs, radical politics and Eastern mysticism, all of which helped fuel alternative lifestyles and value systems.

When Hen began investigating some of these esoteric cults both *The Times* and the *Daily Telegraph* were too timid to publish her findings. It was one of Hen's drinking companions from the Colony Room, the Australian author Jill Neville, who came to the rescue. Now largely forgotten, Jill was a bohemian protégé of Elizabeth Smart. She had a younger brother called Richard Neville, who'd recently arrived from Australia and had caused quite a stir by publishing an anti-establishment magazine … a beacon of 1960s counter-culture called *OZ*.

It was in issue 4 of June 1967 that Henrietta's article about 'The Process' (a sub-species of Scientology) appeared in *OZ* magazine. The latest of the mystic quasi-religions sweeping the Western world, 'The Process' maintained two properties in London's expensive Mayfair district, a yacht in Greece and a club in Mexico. It had also made the headlines when a group of high-flying lawyers flew out to Mexico to rescue some of the cult's aristocratic followers, and their families' inheritance to boot. The *Sunday Telegraph* nicknamed the cult 'The Mind Benders of Mayfair', but they referred to themselves as 'The Process'. The King's Road was now suddenly 'aflutter' with 'Process' teenagers thrusting the organisation's magazine at unsuspecting shoppers. 'Marianne Faithfull Tells All!' shouted the cover's headline, used to hook and reel them in … and hippy legend also has it that the Rolling Stones' 'Sympathy for the Devil' was inspired by Mick Jagger's flirtation with the cult.

Henrietta's audacious piece of investigative journalism centred on Mr and Mrs de Grimston, or rather Bob and Mary Ann, as they liked to be known. They were the innovators of the hybrid psychological treatment the 'Process', which they said was to help people suffering from debilitating neuroses, but it gradually evolved into a quasi-religion and a way of life for their followers. Henrietta realised that Mr de Grimston liked to play the messiah, claiming that their movement 'was the last hope for mankind'. Of course, the de Grimstons' disciples had to pay substantial sums of money in order to participate in their salvation as it was considered necessary to undergo at least sixty hours of therapy to discover the patient's chronic neurosis. Then, having reached their bleak nadir, the 'patient' would be in a state of emotional dependence on their 'Process' therapist and be open to all kinds of suggestions.

To her horror, Hen discovered that the de Grimstons had no recognised medical or sociological training. Their methods and much of their jargon were derived from L. Ron Hubbard, a writer of pulp science fiction. Being an author is a hard way to earn a living and Hubbard had once reportedly turned to a fellow author at a science fiction convention and stated that the only way to make money in this world was 'to form your own religion'. Today, Hubbard's religious cult has thousands of members worldwide but when Bob and Mary Ann de Grimston met at the Hubbard Institute of Scientology in Fitzroy Street, London, they found that they had much in common. So, they married and left the Institute after a few months to spread their own evangelical 'Truth'.

During the 'Summer of Love', the de Grimstons were to become plucky Hen's most feared Nemesis. The 'Process' messiah, Robert de Grimston, was a thirty-year-old former Winchester School boy – over six foot tall and powerfully built with Aryan blue eyes and blonde hair. A sharp dresser, he was hailed by his followers as 'the Christ of Carnaby Street'. In sharp contrast to his self-assured posh schoolboy persona, his wife, Mary Ann, was a thirty-six-year-old working-class lass with a searing Scottish accent, long talon-like fingernails and wiry copper-coloured hair forced into a bun.

In Mary Ann, Henrietta had met her match. She had a domineering personality and the ability to project it forcefully. She was raised by foster-parents just outside Glasgow and missed a lot of school due to having to nurse her foster-mother, who died when Mary Ann was just thirteen years old. When her foster-father remarried and turfed her out, she came to London and worked as a waitress before deciding to educate herself by taking numerous courses she found advertised in magazines: numerology, hypnosis, palmistry, spiritualism, occultism, yoga, reading tea leaves and modelling. Before being sucked into Scientology, she'd also found time to become a partner in a dry-cleaning firm.

When Mary Ann's husband stated that 'mankind is heading for destruction', and that he was 'sent to instruct', an incredulous Henrietta asked Robert de Grimston if he believed himself to be the Son of God. At first he did not reply, then a few minutes later he agreed with Mary Ann that 'Evangelist' would be a more suitable description. Hen found out that their followers weren't allowed to question the 'Process' procedures, let alone stray from them. The de Grimstons had a very strict interpretation of the concept of free will. They believed that the individual was responsible for their subconscious motivations and actions. These beliefs extended to a point where they alleged, at a public meeting attended by Henrietta, that a child born with a hereditary disease (e.g., cystic fibrosis) had chosen to be born in this condition and that it was the sole responsibility of the child. A horrified Hen realised this regressive thinking was a form of extremism that led to the abuse and persecution of the individual; particularly the vulnerable. When Mary Ann said that 'All the Jews in Hitler's Germany walked into the gas ovens because they chose to do so', Hen's hackles began to rise.

For those anxious about where the human race was heading, the attraction of the Process Church was that it not only seemed to provide firm answers but also gave reassurance that you too could reach happiness. But they claimed that nobody could achieve such a state of spiritual well-being without undertaking a course of their 'Process' sessions, which they used to create converts through therapy, and fund their church. Confident of their ability to achieve success with everyone they met (despite their lack of medical training), the de Grimstons' sessions were a much more demanding ordeal than any treatment by a qualified psychiatrist or analyst. A 'Process' patient was allowed to book their six separate sessions in one long six-hour block. But when dredging the subconscious, highly unpleasant aspects of anyone's personality can surface and cause intense anguish. Few can digest too much, too soon, without being mentally scarred.

Hen thought that the techniques used by 'Process' therapists were curiously similar to brainwashing. The questions would begin benignly enough at the start but soon the guilt which exists in us all would be exposed and, through group pressures, all past values destroyed. When Hen questioned them on the advisability of this 'blitzkrieg' upon the brain, the de Grimstons gave her repeated assurances that they had never had a case they couldn't handle. But, as she reported in *OZ* magazine, Hen was far from reassured:

> It should be clear that the 'Process' and Scientology, from which it stems, possess all the characteristics found in an authoritarian regime. They demand complete dedication and unswerving obedience from their followers. They punish deviators by ostracism, ridicule and expulsion. They are positively anti-intellectual, though many of their theories appear to be gained from the written word, this is seldom acknowledged. They use a fabricated jargon to bolster their dogmas and to weaken the accepted meaning of the language: it also helps to preserve a sense of mystery and exclusiveness. They KNOW that they alone are The Truth.

To the Process Church, Hen was a negative force, a troublemaker spreading wild stories and propaganda. Persecution, real or imagined, enhances a disciple's commitment, unifying those who gain strength through their sense of persecution and now they had received bad press – journalists, parents and concerned members of the public, such as Hen, were considered 'instruments of Satan'.

The Process Church's techniques bear an uncanny resemblance to the highly sophisticated and effective brainwashing methods used in China and North Korea today, robbing the individual of their freedom in all things and reducing them to a near zombie-like state of subjection. But through her exposé, Hen had unwittingly poked a tiger. These cults could be dangerous. 'The Process' later established a base of operations in America and prosecutors investigating the Los Angeles murders committed by the Manson Family in 1969 suggested that there were links between Charles Manson and the Process Church. Despite the connection being unproven, the allegations stuck and subsequently damaged the church's reputation.

Over the passing decades, the Process Church has become legendary – in the annals of both hippy and satanic lore. It has often been cited as part of a wider satanic conspiracy indulging in blood sacrifices. However, there was also a great deal of money involved and they had the fervour of religious maniacs when it came to protecting their financial interests, i.e. their disciples. Hen became paranoid that she was being tailed by the de Grimstons' henchmen. But no one, including the police, took her fears seriously until the night she came home to find two thugs in tightly belted beige rain macs bent over her typewriter reading her manuscript. They swung round as she entered the front room and one of them raised his hand menacingly as he pointed at her and yelled: '*You will never write again!*'

Chapter 12

Paint Your Wagon

Some consider the Chelsea Set a bunch of wealthy partygoers who frittered away their time in expensive restaurants and boutiques, but that's not all they did … on the following pages you will witness how difficult it was to maintain one's position in the Chelsea Set. This is a modest record of Hen's achievements, perhaps not comparable to the fashion designer Mary Quant or the iconic Marianne Faithfull, but I like to think Hen did her bit and inadvertently helped us get to where we are today …

Ever since she'd stopped injecting methedrine Hen's life had changed. She kept away from her junkie friends and now that her children were away at boarding school her flat, which harboured so many unhappy memories, felt empty. She also, rather wisely, dropped the Monster Club and its associated venues: the French, the Colony, etc. As hippy chic kicked in, Hen's life shifted gear and she made a whole new set of friends: aristocratic, wealthy, young and beautiful, she 'latched on' to them all. The two she spent most time with were the antique dealer Christopher Gibbs and the interior designer David Mlinaric, who numbered Mick Jagger among his clients and whom Hen had nicknamed 'Monster' – since it takes one to know one.

With this new aristocratic crowd, Hen took to enjoying long canal holidays and miraculously morphed into a beautiful hippy. She looked resplendent dressed in her Afghan robes from the King's Road boutique Hung on You, London's most hip clothes store, where the emerging rock 'n' roll royalty mixed with old-school aristocracy to a point where it was almost too scarily cool to enter.

Hen also sported a pair of boots from Granny Takes a Trip, which laced up to the knee. However, they hilariously proved almost impossible to do up when stoned so she bought some bright red zip-up suede boots covered in gold-coloured stars, which made her look like a comic book superhero.

Granny Takes a Trip emanated a kind of camp nostalgia for frilly satin and velvet Victorian garments. It attracted all the big pop bands: the Beatles, the Stones and even Pink Floyd wore clothes from Granny's. It was at the opposite end of the spectrum to Mary Quant's boutique. Granny's brought into full visibility the counter-cultural style with the most exotic and androgynous clothing. As *Vogue*'s former fashion editor Geoffrey Aquilina Ross told me:

> It was one of those upmarket shops where you could buy garments you felt expressed yourself. Granny Takes a Trip was enormous fun because no one had any money and all the fabrics they bought for their clothes were fabulous but didn't last long. Someone would be wearing a pair of velvet trousers and you'd suddenly notice a split appearing up the side of their leg.

The boutique was suitably situated at the World's End, which had a great deal of notoriety attached to it. In the eighteenth century it was a den of vice and had a louche reputation, it was the dead end of the King's Road, but Granny's was more than a boutique, it was as infamous for its druggy reputation as it was for its clothes and became a major hub for the psychedelic counter-culture. The front of the shop was painted with a cartoon of the Hollywood actress Jean Harlow which covered the whole front of the building, with her mouth left open as an aperture so you could peer into the shop. There was also an old American Dodge car which had been cut in half with its front protruding from the shop, as if it were driving through the wall.

On 12 February 1967, Marianne Faithfull, Mick Jagger, Robert Fraser and Christopher Gibbs were busted for drugs at Keith Richards' house. From then on, the Metropolitan Police's infamous Chelsea Drug Squad became suspicious of anyone in the area who was looking too 'groovy'. They would harass young men around the King's Road and if your hair was too long you got stopped all the time. Then the notorious Sergeant Pilcher began raiding all the King's Road boutiques and was given the nickname 'The Gardener', because he was always planting drugs on people.

Not easily deterred, dropping acid and smoking joints now became a spiritual exercise for Hen. She floated around Chelsea, from Christopher Gibbs' flat in Cheyne Walk (which was used for a BBC programme about psychedelic drugs) to David Mlinaric's on Tite Street, and took to making chocolate hashish cakes so strong they'd paralyse everyone in sight, so her social circle would just sit there completely stoned to the sounds of the Rolling Stones. Everyone was wearing flower prints or ice cream-coloured suits, as frilly shirts with laced ruffles and crushed velvet became *de rigueur*.

Baghdad House

Now she'd left Soho's Monster Club behind, Hen's favourite place to meet was Baghdad House, a Persian restaurant on the Fulham Road where she sat on cushions and drank yoghurt. Here the crème de la crème of hip London Society hung out and smoked marijuana, dropped Mandrax and swallowed acid while eating kebabs. It was the first public place where people openly smoked dope in London and became a popular spot with the Beatles, the Rolling Stones and their aristocratic circle of friends. The photographer Cecil Beaton could be found there dining with Christopher Gibbs, the Hung on You boutique owner, Michael Rainey and his wife Jane Ormsby-Gore and their little baby, Saffron, lying asleep in a shopping basket, oblivious to the flashing lights and the jukebox belting out the latest hits. Close by sat Mick Jagger in a gold brocade coat with tight brown trousers and beside him sat his girlfriend Marianne Faithfull. With her beautiful blonde hair and slightly smudged eyes, Marianne would be making groovy conversation with exiled European royalty like Prince Stanisław Radziwiłł of Poland. According to Cecil Beaton the most intelligent one there was the art dealer Robert Fraser, but in the club-like atmosphere of the Baghdad's basement sat a beautiful young man who was about to become very important in Henrietta Moraes' life – Sir Mark Palmer.

Despite the cultural, social and sexual revolution going on all around, this was still mainly a patriarchal clique. Cecil Beaton who had recently returned from working on the Hollywood film version of *My Fair Lady* didn't offer to play Henry Higgins to Henrietta's Eliza Doolittle, although there were plenty who would, but Hen was too much of a tomboy to play the damsel in distress. Then, Mick Jagger turned to Cecil Beaton and enquired, 'Have you ever taken LSD? Oh, I should ... it would mean so much to you; you'd never forget those colours.'

Although the psychedelic in-crowd of the mid-1960s were not a part of the proletariat, they liked to mingle with working class folk like the Rolling Stones, as the *Daily Express* gossip column reported:

> There's no harm these days in knowing a Rolling Stone ... and pop people do not seem to mind who they mix with. Some of their best friends, in fact, are fledglings from the upper classes.

Despite her obvious baggage, Hen managed to throw away her shackles and enter the more progressive ranks. She was embraced in aristocratic circles as if she were a long-lost sister returning from a spiritual voyage to La-La Land and attended wacky parties in Chelsea where people performed DIY frontal lobotomies on each other with power tools.

By now the social mobility Hen had enjoyed for years in bohemian Soho had become much more widespread – these young aristocrats were much, much younger than her and she loved the attention. Hen had at first entered these posh social circles by befriending the Ormsby-Gore sisters, Jane, Victoria and Alice. The people who hung around Hen's favourite boutique, Granny Takes a Trip, were rich kids, beautiful people, hippies that made things happen. Other friends in this circle included Lady Beatrix, the eldest daughter of Lord Lambton, who had four sisters – Lucinda, Rose Diana, Anne Mary and Isabella. Their father was Lord

Lambton, an MP who became caught up in a political scandal after he was found in bed with two prostitutes and a stash of drugs. Hen probably only knew the two older sisters, Beatrix and Lucinda, as the others were far too young. Decades later, the family sued each other over the £12 million estate of their deceased father, in a most un-hippy like way …

Flower Power …

But the 'Summer of Love' was slowly coming to an end and the fun days were over. Rather than a statement of individualism, hippy and flower-power fashions became a high-street style, sporting flowers in your hair became passé and many hippy boutiques like Hung on You closed down. Though London has no Disneyland there are many parks in the city where the kids can get their kicks and legend has it that Baghdad House regular Sir Mark Palmer was sitting in Hyde Park when an idea popped into his head, which went something along the lines of this: 'Why don't we drop out, leave London and go to the country? Why don't we buy a horse and cart and travel all over the place, all over England … and be free?'

But before we get to the fun bit, folks, let's get the name-dropping out of the way first. Sir Mark Palmer's godmother was Queen Elizabeth II and he had recently opened the English Boy modelling agency with Trisha Locke, who had been working for the infamous pop group The Who, doing their PR and dealing with the ensuing chaos they caused:

> I left The Who and set up the English Boy model agency with Mark Palmer in 1967. Mark, who came from an aristocratic family (and was a real hippy) decided that there should be a model agency that specialised in pretty boys. So, one day he approached me and said, 'I'm going to open this agency for beautiful men will you run it for me?' – 'Yes, of course' and that's what it was like in the 1960s, you just fell into things. We had a little office on Radnor Walk, above the Quorum boutique where the fashion designers Alice Pollock and Ossie Clark worked. I booked all the boys. On another floor

of the same building was where Brian Jones of the Rolling Stones lived with his girlfriend, the model Suki Potier.

Everyone would go upstairs and smoke dope, but I was quite straight. The male models then were beef cake types with rippling muscles and big chests whereas our models were all rather skinny and beautiful. They included Christopher Gibbs' boyfriend Peter Hinwood, Julian Ormsby-Gore, Nigel Waymouth of Granny Takes a Trip and Brian Jones of the Rolling Stones.

Sir Mark was quoted in the press as saying: 'My boys represent the new English male – the new hero.' But it wasn't just boys. On the 20 August 1967, the *Daily Express* ran with the headline 'Christine Keeler Makes a Comeback', and reported:

Christine Keeler may soon be back in the public eye. She has joined the 'English Boy' model agency, run in Chelsea by Sir Mark Palmer, 25. 'I asked her because she's very pretty,' says Sir Mark an Old Etonian baronet and former page to the Queen. We are going to be her agents – not just for the photographic modelling only but films and television as well.

Trisha Locke told me that although Christine Keeler was on their books, she didn't get much work modelling:

It was all just taking off. It was a very exciting time, but it was very laid back, we were having fun and getting a lot of press, thanks to me. We ran it for about three years from a tiny office. Jimi Hendrix was always around; he was a friend of Brian Jones and had this thing with Suki Potier who was also with Brian. There wasn't much money in modelling in those days and we were terribly inexperienced. People would ring up and book a model for a shoot for £10. We had unaccounted for petty cash which we'd spend on clothes in boutiques like Hung on You, which sold the most amazing clothes. It was run by one of our models, Mike Rainey, husband of Jane Ormsby-Gore (the 'Lady Jane' from the Rolling Stones song), then a very aristocratic fashion writer and now an interior designer. She was pregnant at the time with her first child

> and said, 'I'm going to give birth to my child on **** with all my friends around.' Can you imagine? She also wanted to give it one of those flowery hippy names, which were in fashion at the time. At the agency, Jane's brother Julian would float in stoned and I'd say, 'You've got a photo shoot at Vogue House, 10 a.m. tomorrow' and tell him what to do. None of the models took it seriously, they all lived rather precariously. One of them, Bill Chenail, got done for drugs and I had to go and bail him out. It was all very disorganised, chaotic and great fun. I don't think Mark made any money out of it, he had financed it all from his inheritance, then went off on the hippy trail.

Life speeds up in an urban setting – summer in the city: perspiration, pollution and pedestrians choked by exhaust fumes. It now dawned on them that they were the right people in the wrong place at the wrong time. Sir Mark Palmer shouldn't be in London. He longed for the pleasant land – that green one they promised in all those ancient books – not this car cemetery of a city.

So, when Sir Mark decided he wanted to go and find the Holy Grail (the cup used by Jesus at the Last Supper and sought after by the Knights of King Arthur), he inadvertently dressed like the druid from the *Asterix the Gaul* cartoons and travelled across Britain in a horse-drawn gypsy caravan. Along the way Sir Mark took with him some kindred spirits like David Tomlin from the Giant Sun Trolley band who played at the legendary 14 Hour Technicolor Dream and Maldwyn Thomas, an English Boy model who was there right from the start:

> We bought a dung-cart, a sort of tipper cart. We put a tilt on it and wrapped it in canvas and it was very, very primitive. Mark bought this horse, a huge black and white mare. That was the start – and we set off.

It was far from luxurious, but the idea appealed to many people, although some just visited the caravan trail at weekends, like Brian Jones and his girlfriend Suki, whom Sir Mark had met in a club when she was seventeen. The fashion designer Michael Rainey closed his Hung on You boutique and went with his wife Jane on the trail too. He announced to the press that Merlin the magician was alive and living in Somerset, that flying saucers did exist (he'd just seen one the previous week) and that all human beings were reincarnated.

Acid Apostles ...

Another of Hen's new friends was Iggy the Eskimo – a Zelig-like presence on London's music scene, who also mingled with the aristocratic in-crowd. Iggy came from a posh family who'd raised her to be a ladylike debutante, but being a stubborn kid with a mind of her own she ran away from home aged fourteen. Freedom was much more important to Iggy than living in a gilded cage and, somehow, she fell in with Brian Jones and found herself being chauffeured around town in Brian's Bentley with its pop art cushions, scarlet fur rugs and pornographic magazines strewn across the floor.

Brian Jones was a twenty-seven-year-old musical prodigy, living the edgy rock 'n' roll life ... 'an evil genius' with a bad boy image. He took drugs, slept with more women than any other Rolling Stone and became a delinquent dandy. Brian claimed to have been the original leader of the Stones, but was soon to be sacked from the band in June 1969. A month later he was found mysteriously drowned, floating face down in his swimming pool.

Marianne said Brian's death was 'a relief' in that it had solved a terrible predicament for Mick Jagger and Keith Richards whom she said 'had a real vendetta' against their former bandmate. Henrietta, of course, knew Brian quite well as her friend Suki Potier had been his girlfriend. So, our heroine decided to go to Hyde Park with Suki and 20,000 other people to attend the Rolling Stones Memorial Concert for Brian. Hen spent all of the day and night before the concert with her acid apostles, wrapping up trips in silver paper to distribute at the concert. Once satisfied, Hen stuffed hundreds of them into her boots and headed for the park. Arriving as vast crowds began collecting in front of the stage, Hen made her way to the front, reached into her boots and threw handfuls of little silver packets into the sky where they glittered in the summer sky like fairy dust as she chanted: '*Acid, acid, acid!*'

Behind her, Mick Jagger walked onto stage in a white lace tunic dress and read a short poem by Shelley in honour of Brian, before the band struck up and, for two and a half hours, played their hearts out. Then, as the acid kicked in, Mick Jagger morphed from a white messiah into a praying mantis with a microphone … before shapeshifting into a magic mushroom … moving around the stage, Mick slowly blinked in and out of existence as the band's bass line built into beautiful bars of shimmering blue.

A tingling euphoria filled Hen's senses as musical notes materialised in the air and hung there for a few seconds before a long cascading series of echoing replicas trailed behind, like a stroboscopic photograph. As Aldous Huxley's doors of perception swung open and unhinged the audience, a constellation of visual distortions emanated from the Stones' speaker stacks. Guitars shimmered sparkles and flashed bright bolts of light, which were interrupted by the transparent blobs of colour floating around.

Hen noticed that everyone else in the audience had developed a halo around their heads – as a multitude of new neural pathways connected in her brain – the stereotypical, but incredibly real sensations of mystical enlightenment and the interconnectedness of all things began to take hold.

Then, as they floated higher and higher above the park, a high-pitched noise began to exceed the threshold. What happened next was a blur … the visuals got ramped up and they began going through an emotional rollercoaster. Finally, they spiralled down, down and down headlong into the park below. Many crashed and burned whilst others, oblivious to the acid casualties all around them, tripped the light fantastic.

A Travelling Circus

It was in that very same park where a Knight of the Realm, Sir Mark Palmer, had had his Holy Grail brainwave and, several months later, Henrietta bumped into him on the King's Road. 'Hello, hello! Are you coming to the country with us?' asked Sir Mark. Well, how could she refuse?

Henrietta joined the band of wanderers around Easter of 1970, but it would take Hen and Mark's happy band of travellers four years to reach their destination. The adventure began with Henrietta and several others climbing into a white car and heading for Cornwall. They arrived after midnight – cold and wet – and walked miles in the pitch black with Mark leading the way and Hen repeatedly tripping over her hippy robes until at last they came upon a clearing with a silhouetted little gypsy wagon lit by lanterns. Beside this romantic scene stood a tripod with a large cooking pot hanging from it and the glowing remnants of a fire. Hen thought, 'This is the life for me.' Mark then pointed over yonder, to a dilapidated building, and told them they could all sleep in the old shed over there for the night. The following morning Hen awoke feeling damp but not down as she lit her first joint of the day and looked in wonder at the pastoral picture postcard view all around her. She then walked downstream to wash and get dressed and, by her own admission, she felt like a new woman.

They decided to make an expedition to the nearby settlement of Launceston because Sir Mark felt it was likely to be Sir Lancelot of Arthurian legend's hometown. Everything took an enormous amount of practical preparation before they could move off – dealing with the horses and attaching them to the wagons seemed to take forever. When they finally arrived at the town, they were mistaken for a travelling circus by the locals who tried to buy tickets from Henrietta. There were all kinds of people staring at them and, for a while, Hen stupidly stared back. But these hippy travellers still showed signs that they were not quite yet prepared to completely drop out of modern society when Sir Mark purchased some Mars bars and Henrietta a copy of the *Daily Mail* from the local corner shop. But as Marianne recalls, that's not all ... they also bought:

> A barrel-top gypsy wagon and a brown and white horse they dubbed Rizla ... and off they went in search of the unfindable. How they came into a quest for the Holy Grail was ... oh, never mind. It was a motley crew. A lot of people joined Mark's endless parade: Michael and Jane Rainey, Christopher Sykes, Christopher Gibbs, Catherine Tennant and Penny Cuthbertson ... all sorts of people went looking for the Holy Grail, but it was Mark's *mission*.

Not everyone lasted the course. Some of them just came and went like Marianne's ex-husband, the artist John Dunbar, who explained that dropping in and dropping out was all part of the scene:

> I spent a couple of weeks with them, but I didn't go on the road with them. I hung out when they'd parked their caravans at some aristocrat's joint. Mark Palmer was really into horses – he had lots of aristocratic friends and they travelled from place to place in their caravans hanging out with them. It wasn't travelling in that gypsy sense, apart from the caravans – it was big in the 1920s as well, before the war, with artists like Augustus John. There was a romanticism about leading a life outside of society – a simpler existence closer to nature, but it was a lot easier before the invention of the motor car!

This was the Age of Aquarius and Hen gravitated towards the many youngsters looking for an alternative lifestyle, an alternative philosophy and an alternative religion. In some cases, this meant throwing Christian traditions overboard and replacing them with equally restricting oriental ones whilst still claiming they were liberating. But not everyone looked to the subcontinent, some aristocrats sought spiritual salvation closer to home, as the Rolling Stones guitarist Keith Richards remembers in his autobiography *Life*:

> There were a lot of Pre-Raphaelites running around in velvet with scarves tied to their knees, like the Ormsby-Gores, looking for the Holy Grail, the Lost Court of King Arthur, UFOs and ley lines.

Yes, and that's the point, they were into ley lines, flying saucers and other esoteric interests which cut across class barriers; the quest became a sort of caravan trail travelling along ley lines to Wales with motorcycle outriders, exuding the sort of exceptional eccentricity you've come to expect from English aristocrats, who are stereotyped as being slightly cuckoo.

But old habits die hard and when Hen walked into a village chemist shop to buy something for the weekend, the chemist had to go downstairs to fetch it. Whilst waiting she spied on the counter a large tin of her favourite drug, Drinamyl, popularly known as Purple Hearts. After a respectable lapse of time, curiosity got the better of Hen; after all, it was as if they'd been handed to her on a silver plate. Not believing her luck she emptied hundreds of the pills into her bag and hotfooted it out into the village lanes before the chemist could catch her. That little chemical brother never knew what hit him as Hen hurried off, feeling radiant …

In her memoir, Henrietta remembers riding Sagittarius, an Arab stallion, bareback since Sir Mark didn't believe in saddles. Not believing in saddles is one thing, but he was also convinced that real travellers on the road didn't need to bathe either, as he patiently pointed out to Henrietta during her vain attempts at personal hygiene. Should anyone enquire 'Would you like to have a bath?', Hen's running joke was to reply, 'No, it's alright. I had onc two months ago.' Sir Mark may have been born an aristocrat, but he really was very serious about living an alternative life. On the first leg of their journey, they visited places of Arthurian legend: Boscastle (where the wizard Merlin lived), Camelot (site of King Arthur's castle) and Tintagel (where King Arthur was conceived). It was during one of these forays that they said they had spotted their first flying saucer, which convinced them even more that they were on the right path to whatever it was they were looking for.

Another of Hen's fellow travellers was John Michell. Jokingly referred to as the counter-culture's 'New Merlin', Michell had written the book *The Flying Saucer Vision: The Holy Grail Restored* and firmly believed that UFOs were connected to the ancient Tales of King Arthur and the Holy Grail, although many complained he never really explained how. For Michell, flying saucers were *not* aliens. They could be seen as 'emanations of the human psyche', earthly machines, from the lost city of Atlantis perhaps. Like Henrietta, Michell witnessed strange lights in the sky, experienced new 'psychedelic' music, took a lot of hallucinogenic drugs and warned Hen that the world was about to flip over on its axis so that 'heresy will become orthodoxy and an entirely new world order will shortly be revealed'.

The mixture of getting back to nature, becoming part of a travelling community, caring for animals (especially horses), taking acid and smoking marijuana proved extremely cathartic for Hen and her fellow band of travellers. Their first winter was spent together at Stargroves in Berkshire, an estate belonging to Mick Jagger, but conveniently sold to him by UFO freak John Michell.

This Moveable Feast

Every person has their favourite winter sport. Some like skiing, others take to ice skating and the truly fearless love to bobsleigh. Hen's favourite winter sport was social climbing (and heaven knows she needed the exercise). Ever since the 1966 'Summer of Love' Henrietta had been hacking away at the diamond peaks of British society, planting her flag on the Afghan coats and thick skulls of some of the most important people in Swinging London. Whilst Hen scaled the heady social peaks at Stargroves, it was discovered that Sir Mark needed urgent medical treatment, as he'd become malnourished from living on an unbalanced macrobiotic diet. Marianne said that, at first, he refused to see a doctor, convinced that his body was just getting rid of all the toxins of the modern world:

> They all went along with this very strict hippy rule book about only eating macrobiotic food, avoiding anything edible that was white (bread, sugar), not taking baths and not using any medicine – which caused some very funny things to happen, you know. If anyone got the clap or crabs … they never got rid of them.

Along with Henrietta, Iggy the Eskimo joined this moveable feast, looking for the Holy Grail and sighting UFOs all over the place. Iggy remembers Henrietta being one of the people in the Port Eliot convoy. Although Henrietta was approaching middle age and Iggy was only twenty-one, Hen was still an important counter-culture figure to be reckoned with. Perhaps they both felt they had something in common. Just like Iggy, Henrietta was born in India. Their fathers had both been military men and Henrietta had also traded Soho for the psychedelic underground, taking every drug imaginable with her promiscuous lifestyle. Together, she and Iggy visited the castle at Port Eliot in Cornwall, and Iggy definitely remembers someone saying:

> There's a place in Cornwall called Port Eliot. A bloke I knew called Peregrine has a castle there. For the May Day celebrations, a party of his friends would gather round the village, which upset the Morris dancers. Peregrine's beautiful ladies were sitting astride the horses that were adorned with flower garlands, dressed as dames from King Arthur's Court.

The master of the Port Eliot estate was Peregrine Eliot, later the tenth Earl of St Germans. He was a partner in Seltaeb, the Beatles merchandising company, and was married to Jacquetta Lampson, who'd also been a model and lover of Lucian Freud. Her sister Roxana 'Bunty' Lampson was married to Ian Ross, who was co-founder of the groovy pirate radio station Radio Caroline, which famously broadcast all the pop music banned on the British mainland.

Peregrine Eliot happily opened his estate to Sir Mark's community of hippies who sought an alternative way of life by pooling resources and giving up traditional living in the pursuit of harmony, freedom and self-sufficiency. It all sounds very idyllic, but many of these unwashed hippies weren't hippies at all to begin with …

The 'wagon trail' became a magnet for underprivileged posh folk. Since they were not necessarily better educated, cleaner or richer than anyone else, the one way you could distinguish the upper classes was by their language. All you had to do was listen to someone and you could immediately tell exactly where they belonged on the social ladder, by the way they'd say 'Hey man, *groovy!*'

Cheque-Book Hippies ...

One of their number was Henrietta Garnett, an acclaimed author and a great beauty who had been painted by Duncan Grant and photographed by Cecil Beaton. Born with blue ink in her veins, her family's literary lineage stretched back generations. She was in fact a third-generation member of the Bloomsbury Group; a loose assembly of artists, intellectuals and writers. Suffice to say, Henrietta Garnett was bohemian royalty. Her father, David Garnett, was a publisher and author of *Aspects of Love*, which later became a famous musical, and *Dope Darling: A Story of Cocaine* which was based upon the life of the artist's model and muse Betty May, better known as the *Tiger Woman*.

Henrietta Garnett's parents had created a promiscuous scene long before the permissive society of Swinging London. Her mother, Angelica Bell, was also a writer and artist. She was not the daughter of her 'legal' father, but the daughter of the painter Duncan Grant. Added to this complex web, her 'legal' father was bisexual, and had once had a fling with her biological father. At seventeen, a pregnant Henrietta Garnett married the twenty-seven-year-old Burgo Partridge, author of *A History of Orgies*, who suddenly died of an aneurism three weeks after the birth of their daughter. So, Henrietta fled into London's underground club scene and led a bohemian life. Enjoying the Swinging Sixties, she eventually joined this band of aristocratic dropouts and travellers but wasn't really that impressed by what she saw and labelled them a bunch of 'Cheque-book Hippies', as she considered many of them to be rich kids who simply enjoyed 'slumming it'.

So, this hippy cavalcade really became the story of two Henriettas, both described as deeply affectionate, droll, mischievous, uninhibited and intensely loyal. They also both had a reputation for being exasperating and something of a menace, after a glass or two too many … I wonder if they ever really got on?

Psychedelic Pilgrims

According to Henrietta Moraes, eight people could travel in her horse-driven cart. But the Caravan Set was also accompanied by various cars and motorcycles, especially at the weekends when the part-time hippies travelled from London to wherever the convoy was, crawling along at the snail's pace speed of four miles a day. Hen identified several beautiful people as her fellow travellers and her list reads like a who's who of Swinging London: Derek Fitzgerald, member of London's flower-power intelligentsia; Greg Ridley, bass player of the pop group Humble Pie; John Michell, author of *The Flying Saucer Vision*; John Pearse, tailor for Granny Takes a Trip; Maldwyn Thomas, English Boy model; Nicky Kramer, perennially penniless 'hanger-on' and dandy dopehead; and Vashti Bunyan, a folk singer who'd gravitated to Hen's hippy circle.

Vashti had already released a couple of singles, under the guidance of Rolling Stones manager Andrew Loog Oldham, but the plan to make her into a second Marianne Faithfull had failed along with her idea of living a nomadic life and earning money by singing songs at rural marketplaces. This fell flat because the rural communities were not hospitable towards strangers; they were afraid that Vashti would either kidnap their children or steal their chickens.

A Day Trip to Hell …

One of Henrietta Garnett's 'Cheque-book Hippies' was Penny Cuthbertson who, like Henrietta Garnett, was also descended from bohemian royalty. Her mother was Teresa Jungman, one of Evelyn Waugh's Bright Young People famous for their excesses and exploits, which scandalised 1920s British society. Penny, another former model of Lucian Freud, had made the mistake of lending Henrietta her cosy little gypsy wagon for the weekend. Furnished with exquisite Afghan rugs, sensual earthenware ceramics and a cute little wood-burning stove, that night Hen felt like she was in heaven as she settled in and lit a candle before undressing for bed. Lost in the luxury of a vivid dream she was rudely awoken by a sea of blue flame and clouds of billowing smoke. Somehow, she managed to drag her drug-addled body out of the wagon, where – from her new vantage point outside – it had morphed into something resembling a medieval dragon breathing fire and smoke. Poor Penny returned to find her beloved wagon wrecked, reduced to a blackened charred shell, like a remnant from a day trip to hell.

Afterwards, a repentant Hen returned to London and sold her home on Prince of Wales Drive in the drug-induced belief that soon no one would ever need money again. This muddled thinking seemingly arose from Hen foolishly forgetting that her new circle of friends never kept any fiddling small change on their person because almost every one of them was a trust fund millionaire. Hen's warped logic was that her children, being at boarding school, no longer needed a family home. She thought they would enjoy the travelling life and brought them down to join her during the school holidays.

When she had first visited her children at boarding school Hen noticed that their existence was more like something out of *Lord of the Flies* than a traditional educational establishment. The children had built shelters and little houses in the shrubbery where they smoked cannabis. The fact that the kids were stoned out of their heads didn't seem to bother Hen who considered it to be the sign of an 'enlightened school'. Some years later, her son, Joshua, told *The Times*:

> My mother was charismatic and beautiful but quite chaotic … She loved me but she could disappear. One never knew where she was and if, or when, she was coming back.

Hen often complained she'd had no role models in her life, but she did not always moderate her own behaviour around children, as most adults tend to. One day, when her daughter was down for the holidays, they were passing the local vet's when Hen suddenly stopped, found the key to the surgery and helped herself to a large box of pethidine (an opioid painkiller) from the storeroom. Later that evening Hen lined up her friends and injected them with it, one by one. What her daughter made of all the adults wandering around as high as a kite that night on the campsite one can only wonder.

Chapter 13

Making Hay

In her memoir, Marianne Faithfull dismisses Sir Mark Palmer's quest to find the Holy Grail as 'childish'. This I cannot confirm, but there was certainly something comical about it all. The constant switching between the legend of King Arthur and the modern day as Sir Mark and his happy band of travellers did in their day-to-day lives would soon be used to great comedic effect in the movie *Monty Python and the Holy Grail*. The film almost appears to be a parody of what had been happening in real life. For although Sir Mark, resplendently dressed like a druid, didn't have a man galloping behind him, banging two halves of a coconut together whilst pretending to be a horse, the whole quest had accrued a somewhat surreal edge to it.

So, after four fruitless years, Sir Mark decided to end his quest for the Holy Grail, get married and settle down in a house in Hay-on-Wye, which left Hen feeling somewhat left behind. He had purchased the house in Hay from Hen's friend Suki Potier and her new boyfriend Bob, who were in a bit of a hurry to sell up due to a misunderstanding with the police over a cache of illegal drugs. The artist Nigel Waymouth remembered Suki as being very sweet but very stoned, 'Every time I saw her she was out of it'.

But if you thought the quest for the Holy Grail was daft, dear reader, things were about to get decidedly sillier because Hay-on-Wye was home to a British eccentric of the most authentic kind, Richard Booth, who turned this small market town on the Welsh borders into the world's second-hand bookselling capital and, in doing so, laid the foundations for the world-famous Hay Festival. Nowadays, it attracts 70,000 visitors and you read about it in everything from *The Times* newspaper to *Vogue* magazine, but back then no one had really heard of it.

The Sound of Bacchanalian Revelry ...

Feeling sad and lonely on her own, Hen decided to follow Sir Mark and give the second-hand book trade in Hay a go. So, off she went, alighting on some unsuspecting friends, whose good nature as her unwilling hosts was stretched to the limit. Never backward at coming forward, Hen telephoned Richard Booth to arrange a job interview with him during which he informed Hen that her friend Marianne was staying with him up at Hay Castle.

Like Hen, Richard Booth absolutely loved parties and Hay Castle was the perfect venue to indulge his passion. In the 1960s and 1970s, its castellated walls frequently reverberated to the sound of bacchanalian revelry, orgies and pop stars. He had declared Hay-on-Wye an Independent State and proclaimed himself King; with a crown created from tinfoil and an orb and sceptre made from a discarded toilet cistern. To declare a small market town an independent sovereign state back then was as visionary as it was bonkers. As well as wooing tourists, Richard Booth's anarchic spirit also attracted a wave of like-minded settlers such as Henrietta, Marianne, Sir Mark and his wife, Catherine Tennant.

The newcomers made superb courtiers, rejoicing in the King's whims, celebrating his eccentricities and (as far as Richard was concerned) the more bonkers they were the better. Many ended up working for him and almost all got inebriated with him. So, Hen headed to the centre of town to meet the self-appointed 'King of Second-Hand Books' and was surprised to find his castle (a large Norman pile looming over the town) a bit of a ruin, but still just about habitable. Part of the appeal for Marianne and the courtiers was that Good King Richard liked to throw riotous parties there ... and halfway through her job interview, when Marianne walked in, Hen guessed she'd got the job. Or, as Hay-on-Wye's very own Maid Marianne tells it:

> There comes a point even for talented layabouts where you say to yourself, 'Right, I've got to find something to do!' Write a book, make a record, sell drugs, you know, *something*. But if you haven't got an aptitude for any of these things, then you just get a job! I mean, I never said anything, but I always thought she'd be really happy as a barmaid, and very good at it, but she didn't want that – or anything remotely like it. There was something so sort of *twisted* about her attitude – not in a bad way – but, to be honest, her approach to work was practically sociopathic.

Richard thought Hen would be a suitable employee because he'd heard all about her husband, the poet Dom Moraes, and David Archer's bookshop. So, Richard took Hen to the Cinema, the biggest bookshop in his empire, but, sadly, Hen did not live up to expectations. She found selling books rather boring and endlessly rearranging shelves tedious.

Depending on her mood Henrietta had the uncanny ability to curdle milk, raise storms, plague people, dance with the devil (after all, he had the best tunes) and cause furniture to suddenly levitate and fly across the room. She also rode horses bareback and conversed with them by blowing up their noses. To some she was a witch imbued with mysticism, a type of magic realism, and although incredibly well read she mostly lived by intuition. Hen had an intensity which seemed other worldly to some, but to those who craved respectability she was both decadent and diabolical. It didn't take long for her to corrupt the bookshop's manager, William, who became an ardent lunchtime drinking companion and, as there were even more pubs than bookshops in Hay-on-Wye, they were both perpetually pie-eyed.

The King of Hay ...

To this day, Hay-on-Wye is a pretty but otherwise unremarkable border town that still thrives thanks to the remarkable legacy of its self-appointed monarch. In the narrow streets of the so-called Town of Books, you can still follow in Hen's footsteps and embark on an epic pub crawl amidst the tidal waves of tourists. Richard Booth had established his first bookshop in Hay in 1962 and, with his aristocratic bluster, succeeded in picking up the household libraries of the rapidly fading landed gentry before moving on to set up many more bookshops in the town. To keep his extensive miles of shelving well stocked he also bought books by the tonne from American institutions. It was during one of his buying trips to America that Richard saw in America's soulless shopping malls the shape of things to come and became determined to battle against the corporate world of chain stores. Others followed his lead and, at its peak, Hay-on-Wye with a population of less than 2,000 had more than thirty second-hand bookshops.

Despite his full title being 'Richard Coeur de Livre (Bookheart)', Richard Booth was never much of a businessman and was commonly known among his creditors as King Richard Rubbercheque. But the King of Hay was aware of the power of publicity and never reined in his passion for the wacky and the wonderful. Not only did Richard proclaim himself King, he appointed his horse as prime minister, printed his own passports and issued local banknotes. Edible currency was an early innovation, printed on rice paper so that people could put their money where their mouth was. Under his benign reign, Richard made Hay a haven for those once-successful people who'd somehow become casualties of the Swinging Sixties – whose lives had been put through the shredder – and either wanted to drop out, dig in or get their shit together. Despite specialising in defrocked priests, Hay was full of other eccentric and exotic characters such as the former model April Ashley, recently divorced and sporting a wardrobe of dresses designed by Monster Club habitué Thea Porter. April became a close friend of King Richard's (who promptly elevated her to a peerage), as she recalled in her memoir:

> He conferred on me the title of First Lady, Duchess of Hay and Offa's Dyke. Mind you, there is no denying that he is a man of some dottiness, given to falling off horses and inadvertently backing *his* car into other people's sitting rooms. When his castle burned down, he said that what woke him was the sound of applause. He got out of bed to see why his subjects should be demanding *his* presence at the ceremonial window in the early hours of the morning. Only then did he realise that it wasn't applause at all, but the sound of crackling beams.

Henrietta and April had much in common. Not only had they both reinvented themselves but they had once shared a similar circle of friends and loved living off the bones of the landed gentry. Since they'd last met on the Chelsea Set circuit, April's life had been as colourful and hair-raising as Henrietta's, or as April liked to dramatically put it: 'I was a *Vogue* model who was living a secret that was about to shake the world!'

Being a 'Lady' …

Some years earlier, April's day job had been as an underwear model for various luxury goods brands until a tabloid newspaper paid someone to 'out' her in an exposé. April knew something was up when a shady man in a rain mac knocked on her door and tried to barge in, but she somehow managed to shove him back out and slam the door. He claimed he was a reporter: 'We know all about you! We're going to publish the story anyway,' he shouted through the letterbox. The story appeared the following Sunday with the banner headline: 'The Extraordinary Case of Top Model April Ashley – Her Secret Is Out!' It revealed that April had been born a boy and had secretly undergone some pioneering 'sex change' surgery, which made a sensational news story because she was among the very first to do so …

The following morning the model agency informed April that all her bookings had been cancelled and they had received a lot of abusive phone calls from her former clients. Wondering what to do, April went home to find solace at the bottom of a bottle. That's when the dirty phone calls started. She became the focus of ridicule, terrible insults and unspeakable cruelty. As the phone rang off the hook, April was made to feel like a freak.

She was then wooed by a cross-dressing aristocrat, the 'dishonourable' Arthur Corbett, 3rd Baron Rowallan, who became so besotted with April that he deserted his wife and kids for her. Arthur invited April to go to Marbella with him and run a nightclub. That's when April's alcohol consumption escalated to epic proportions. Despite Arthur's penchant for dressing like 'Martha', with high heels, make-up and an effeminately shrill manner (and the fact that by her own admission she didn't fancy him one bit), April still married him. Perhaps the lure for a working-class Liverpudlian like April was not only to undertake the transition from man to woman but to move up the social scale too? Once she married Arthur she became 'Lady April Corbett'. She'd gone from being George Jamieson, a boy raised in a Liverpool slum, to being a 'Lady' in every sense of the word. It was printed on all her cheques and ... *oh!* ... how she loved waving that cheque-book about.

Like Henrietta, April had ended up in Hay-on-Wye via a circuitous route. Richard Booth had met her through his aunt, Viva King, one of the original Chelsea Girls who ran a famous London literary salon. According to April, Viva was the forerunner to Henrietta's rock 'n' roll wild child persona and enjoyed breaking all the female taboos:

> Viva ... was one of the grand eccentrics of the last century; a truly historical figure in bohemian legend ... the Hollywood image of the elderly English lady: white hair, china-blue eyes, the skin of a young girl, the house with 18th-century furniture, the stick, the memories, the sharp tongue that would suddenly melt into intimacies and good nature. From 1964 to 1974, Viva's birthday present to me was a party in her house. At one of them, I met her nephew Richard Booth.

That's how April became the Duchess of Hay and although he'd made April a duchess, King Richard had no intention of elevating poor Henrietta whom he was content to let languish as a serf. Henrietta spent her evenings in the pub with April, listening to her telling tall tales about her life. Henrietta found April camp, witty and kind and listened in as she recalled with relish the time Richard's aunt, Viva King, took her on holiday …

During the flight, a nice elderly English couple struck up a conversation with April and Viva, about how they were going abroad to retire. Then, the woman turned to April and said, 'I'm sure I know your face. Do you mind my asking your name?' – 'Ada Brown,' April lied nonchalantly. But knowing full well that her face had been plastered all over the front of every British newspaper, she conceded, 'I used to be quite a *well-known* model.'

When the plane broke down in Rome, April and Viva had to spend the night at a local hotel, where the retired couple appeared again and asked to join them for dinner. Well, how could April say no? True to form, the woman didn't stop playing with her pearls throughout the meal. 'I know … it's nagging me, but I can't help feeling that I know you … it really is driving me mad.' Throughout all this, Viva was tenaciously twitching with *her* own pearls too, itching to tell all to the innocent couple.

The following morning, when they went down for breakfast, the room was full except for one table, which Viva and April grabbed … and who should follow them in, with nowhere to sit except at their table? The nice retired middle-class couple. The woman started up again: 'I *hate* to be a bore but you know … I really can't get over the feeling that I know you.' Unable to contain herself anymore, Viva blurted out loud, 'Can I tell them?' – 'You say one word, madam,' April admonished her acidly, 'And you'll regret it!' By now, the couple looked agog, their jaws were on the floor, 'Oh, please! Do tell us, do!' The woman's pearls twisted up hard in anticipation. 'I'm sorry. I'm on holiday with my friend, Mrs King, who keeps opening her big mouth,' as Viva victoriously announced, 'She's the famous sex-change!'

At which point, the couple *died* of embarrassment, simply died. The woman was choking on her necklace so hard, the pearls snapped and shot all over the restaurant floor.

A Shell-Shocked Survivor

Although Henrietta and April had many similar attributes, they differed in one significant way … or as Viva put it, April's chief weakness was an 'excessive pride'. It was this that had partly led to her downfall and her washing up penniless with Henrietta in Hay-on-Wye. It was when April seemed to have life going the way she wanted that everything began to go wrong. It started when she tried to lay claim on her abandoned husband Arthur Corbett's house in Spain. She insisted that the house had been given to her by him, which seemed unlikely as it was the only place he could afford to live after losing his multi-million pound inheritance and being cut off without a penny for marrying her. Then, to add insult to injury, April tried to claim maintenance from him. It now seemed to Arthur that April had only married him for his title and wealth, and in an attempt to save what little he had left, he decided to seek an annulment of the marriage on the grounds that it was 'null and void and of no effect because the respondent at the time of the ceremony was a person of the male sex' and that the marriage was never consummated.

But as we all know, April had been having so much sex during the Swinging Sixties that she'd been practically swinging from the chandelier, but just not with her cross-dressing husband whom she'd dumped some weeks after their wedding. The fact that Arthur preferred to be Martha and that April was not attracted to what she called 'chicks with dicks' really meant their relationship was somewhat doomed from the start. But whatever spark their relationship lacked, legally the divorce was going to be dynamite. A sensational, heartbreaking and utterly humiliating experience for them both and it is said that the court case not only put back the cause of trans rights for many years but somewhat ironically made April: 'The Most Talked About Woman in the World.'

So, there they were, together again – stuck out in the sticks – Henrietta and April living off good King Richard's largesse. To pay for their board and lodgings, Hen unpacked boxes of books and stacked shelves all day whilst the Duchess of Hay doubled as its ambassador. With her high media profile, April did the King's bidding and secured an interview for Richard with *The New York Times* as well as doing lots of other public relations stunts for him. April had moved into a flat above one of Richard's shops and the address seemed rather apt considering her love of getting drop-down drunk with Henrietta on thirty-two dry Martinis a day … she now lived at No. 1, The Pavement.

Although the evenings of revelry in the local hostelries with April were fun, Henrietta found the daytimes quite dull. To alleviate the boredom of second-hand bookselling, Hen took to having wild sex amidst the shelves with her co-worker Bill Ripley. Banging away amongst the newly stocked American Civil War section, Hen regularly ravaged Ripley, who would emerge looking like a shell-shocked survivor from the Battle of Gettysburg.

Good King Richard could be rather amorous himself, but everyone has their breaking point and, despite his love of the absurd, Richard was aghast at Henrietta's cavalier treatment of his Civil War section and yet, according to Marianne, it wasn't necessarily all Hen's fault:

> Working for Richard wasn't exactly like a straight job – in fact it was quite mad; one of her co-workers was a defrocked ex-Bishop who had been caught in a dalliance with a chorus girl. Hen *tried* to do the Richard Booth thing, shelving tattered, musty, esoteric books as they came out of the packing crates at a frenetic rate, cataloguing them: D for Dickens … T for Thackeray … that lasted for about six months, then Hen had had it. She began dreaming about books, books parading down the High Street, talking to her – given the number of pink gins and Watson's Ales she was consuming on the job, it's hardly surprising. Eventually, Richard couldn't take her anymore and, with the same exasperated tone that Henry II must've used about Thomas Becket, he confessed to me: 'I'd fire her except that I can't think of anyone in their right mind who would employ Henrietta.' As quick as two shakes of a lamb's tail, I said, 'I will.'

Chapter 14

Faithfull Friends

During their time at Hay-on-Wye, Marianne had noticed that Hen was very well read and that she had an intellectual side to her, which many people were not aware of. Henrietta was somewhat older than her, so although they grew up in the same area, Marianne didn't know Hen back then. Henrietta had gone to Queen Anne's School in Caversham just outside the town of Reading, where the girls wore smart red cloaks and were very posh indeed – much posher than Saint Joseph's where Marianne went – or at least she thought so. Hen's first crush at Queen Anne's School was Valerie Fletcher, a girl who slept with a copy of T.S. Eliot's poems under her pillow and amazingly married the poet after he'd dumped his first wife in a 'loony bin'.

Marianne considered Henrietta to be part of an elite intellectual milieu that dreamt in manuscript form on soft sepia-coloured pages with beautifully flowing pen-lines. Compared to some of the other Hay-on-Wye newcomers, Marianne found Hen very erudite in a way that, say, Sir Mark was not. To her, Mark was much more interested in riding than reading, he was 'one of the beautiful people'. Marianne thought that Mark never got the intellectual side of Henrietta and so she somewhat naively took Hen on, who, needless to say, parachuted into Marianne's life with such a tremendous thud that it shook the very foundations of her existence.

Strangely, they had both found a common point of reference in the artist Francis Bacon. Henrietta began her search for the Holy Grail in 1970, just as the years of drug addiction began to take hold of Marianne, and her four-year relationship with Mick Jagger came to an end. As she later admitted: 'I could've stayed with Mick, and he did love me, but I couldn't bear it, that world. I just felt not good enough. Low self-esteem. All the things a drug addict feels.'

Marianne quite simply lost her way and slid down the social scale from being a sex symbol to a Soho bum – or perhaps, more precisely, a 'Soho Mystery', one of those homeless, rootless girls hanging around the streets, looking to score. A favourite spot of hers was the bombsite opposite the French on Dean Street, a former haunt of Henrietta's, where a dishevelled Marianne first caught Francis Bacon's eye:

> Yes, I used to hang out near a pub called The French … and Francis would come out and seeing me sitting there, he would take me to Wheeler's to feed me. In a strange way he knew what I was doing, Francis knew a lot about pain … whenever I bumped into him, he treated me as a long-lost friend. I don't know why … maybe he saw a kindred spirit. The people who crossed my path when I was a junkie were all gay men. Francis couldn't understand why in the world I wouldn't want to live with Mick Jagger! To him, living with Mick Jagger would have been heaven … Francis didn't try to stop me or tell me that I was making a big mistake, or any of that shit. My plan was to disappear for a while. Even the people I knew on the street didn't know my name. They didn't know who I was, or care … I thought I was invisible. But Francis Bacon, the man with X-ray eyes, could see me.

The Faerie Queen

By this point in our tale, Marianne has stopped living on the streets and is slowly getting her life back together. In fact, she was now living in a rather bijou little mews flat, which belonged to a friend of her mother's and Hen loved it. It was right by London's Regent's Park. Do you know those big Georgian mansions off Regent's Park? Well, there are little mews flats at the back of them, converted former horse-stables, and this particular one had a magnificent view of the park and of Queen Mary's rose garden. Being somewhat broke, Marianne couldn't pay Hen anything so all she could do was offer her what she had – which was her 'little bit of nothing'. Initially, Hen considered life with Marianne as a fairly desultory affair: two beds, a kitchen, a tiny sitting room and a bathroom. But after escaping the boredom of bookselling at Hay, Henrietta realised she'd landed on her feet and at the beginning was on her very best behaviour. No one had treated Marianne as nicely as Hen did. She would get up and make Marianne's breakfast and bring it to her in bed. Like the Faerie Queen (in Marianne's song), Henrietta enchanted and wove her spell around Marianne whilst exhibiting her charming I'm-taking-care-of-you side, so much so that Marianne considered Hen's arrival a great, wonderful gift ... until she met her horrific boyfriend.

As we know, Hen had a penchant for some truly dodgy characters and things soon began 'disappearing' from Marianne's mews. One day she returned to find that her beautiful Persian silk prayer rug (one of her most precious possessions from the time she lived with Mick Jagger) was missing and that Henrietta had hocked the museum-quality carpet for a couple of hours of hedonism. Marianne was annoyed that she'd lost her beautiful rug but, being pragmatic, she soon realised that Henrietta was far more valuable to her than any old rug. In fact, in the long run Hen proved to be a real lifesaver. For one thing, she got all their drugs sorted out. Hen had got some doctor so under her thumb that he was writing prescriptions for amphetamines: black bombers, Mandrax, etc. Hen and Marianne mostly lived on Green Groovers – a mixture of speed and barbiturates. Hen used to go to the doctor once a week with a group of speed freaks she'd met in the chemist's whilst collecting her drugs. Afterwards, they'd go off together, browsing through skips, rubbish dumps and empty houses, scavenging and lifting all *sorts* of things.

Marianne found Hen's high-octane amphetamine-fuelled antics fun for a while. Life had become an Alice in Wonderland-like non-stop Mad Hatter's tea party held in a minuscule little mews apartment that you felt you might suddenly outgrow and stick your head through the roof of at any moment. But few could keep up with Hen's heroic ability to indulge in every intoxicating substance known to medical science. Like Alice in Wonderland herself, everything that Hen came across seemed to be compelling her to 'Drink Me' or 'Eat Me' and, at some point, Marianne started to wonder if it wasn't all too much, even for her.

Amidst all the mayhem, somehow Henrietta went back to writing. This time for *Bananas Literary Magazine*, which was said to be the incubator for some of the most exciting writing talent of the decade: J.G. Ballard, Angela Carter and Ian McEwan, to name a few. It was edited by the author Emma Tennant, half-sister of Henrietta's ex-lover Colin Tennant, Lord Glenconner. Hen's piece appeared in issue 10, 1978. The magazine was achingly hip and everyone attended Emma Tennant's 'Bananas' dinner parties including her lover, the poet Ted Hughes; the pop artist Andy Warhol; the pop singer Marianne Faithfull; and, of course, Henrietta. That summer Hen and Marianne's mutual friend, Caroline Blackwood's seventeen-year-old daughter Natalya, attended one of Emma Tennant's parties and scored heroin off Colin Tennant's son Charlie. After the party she returned home, ran a bath and was found dead the following day – her head underwater, syringe floating next to her.

Over time Henrietta became Marianne's de facto minder, a necessary and somewhat vital part of her 'pop idol' entourage. For her musical comeback, Marianne decided to tour Ireland where her record 'Dreamin' My Dreams' had reached No. 1 in the charts. She took Hen along as a trusted companion and they set off from London for Dublin, via Richard Booth's Hay Castle, where they spent a riotous night wallowing in a lake of wine.

Once settled in Dublin, Marianne chose a backing band and got down to rehearsing. They were assigned a driver/henchman known as Rentokil (after a famous brand of pest control), for whom Hen established a grudging respect. With bohemian bravado, Hen would negotiate rat-runs around town with Rentokil, picking up pills and settling drug debts along the way. Marianne's very first gig was at the ominously sounding Snake Pit. Suffice to say, the venue lived up to its name and even a hard-nosed Hen admitted that she was glad she didn't have to go out and face *that* audience. Unfortunately, Marianne didn't want to go on either. Then, as if to confirm her inability to perform that night, her nerves got the better of her and she was violently sick all over Henrietta. Yet, despite the best efforts of Vera Vomit, our plucky Hen wasn't having any of it and spun Marianne around to face the stage and shoved her out there so hard she stumbled on stage with her right hand raised, trying to break her fall, but for all the world looking like she was giving a Nazi salute, which went down well with the rather rowdy audience.

Such episodes give us a real flavour of some of the fun they had together and why Hen was such a great sidekick for Marianne. However, having Hen as her minder wasn't all that helpful in dampening things down … like the infamous pork-chop incident when Marianne was a bit out of control (she was rather wild and unpredictable on that tour) and, as she sauntered on stage drunk, someone in the audience threw a pork chop at her, so she ducked and her guitarist got *chopped* on the head instead.

After such a debauched tour a magnanimous Marianne decided that she and her minder needed to relax and so they spent a wonderful time together – six months in fact – in Jamaica. They stayed at the Runaway Bay Hotel, which Marianne renamed the Runaway Bill Hotel, having the wildest time. Henrietta took to drinking zombies made with four different types of rum whilst Marianne tried to absorb all the vodka and grapefruit juice available on the island. They were hanging out with some very flamboyant and highly strung gay guys who were not the kind of clients the hotel was trying to cultivate. So, after a month they were asked to leave – or rather ejected – as the hotel management simply couldn't stomach Marianne and Hen's mayhem any longer.

Broken English …

Enter Marianne's record producer and legendary founder of Island Records, Chris Blackwell, who had the responsibility for trying to go and sort out the hotel bill, which was as long as the Bible and twice as difficult to study. The hotel had piled it on and Chris was obviously annoyed about having to pay such an over-inflated bill. Like two admonished schoolchildren, Marianne and Hen hung their heads in shame, but being philosophical about it Marianne had to admit: 'fucking hell I had a good time.' Anyway, she ended up paying for it all out of her royalties, although at the time she naively believed Chris Blackwell was chivalrously picking up the tab out of his selfless love for these two damsels in distress, but Chris was no Sir Mark Palmer and he certainly wasn't riding to their rescue on a white charger.

When Marianne went on a tour of America to promote her new album, Henrietta had to be left behind as she couldn't get a visa to visit America with her criminal record. So, with no money and no job our ever-resourceful Hen took to stealing Marianne's neighbours' groceries from their doorsteps and, Hen being Hen, she convinced herself that no one had noticed that all their deliveries were disappearing.

Then, an old flame, a former barman from Hay-on-Wye who'd long been besotted with her, arrived in town and, much to her annoyance, tracked her down. She found him tedious, boring and dull but he had a large wad of banknotes on him, so what was a girl supposed to *do*? Our heroine selflessly marched him straight to the nearest pub and began drinking the bar dry, with the kind of heroic abandon only Hen could muster. After three days of him telling her how *marvellous* she was and how much he loved her (to Hen's mounting boredom and fury), she left the pub and locked herself into Marianne's mews home.

When her doe-eyed drunken suitor followed her back, Henrietta told him to go away – to go *home*, in fact, to *fuck off* back to Hay-on-Wye. But the resourceful wretch found a wire coat hanger lying in the gutter and bent it about a bit before picking the lock with it and (to Hen's astonishment and dismay) the horny barman of Hay came bounding through the front door. She met him halfway down the stairs and kicked him as hard as she could, square in the chest. He somersaulted down and lay at an awkward angle, lifeless and broken, at the foot of the stairs, 'Oh God, I've killed him!'

Now panicking, she checked his heartbeat, but there was none … '*Bugger!*' So, she rushed to the bathroom, grabbed a compact mirror and held it in front of his mouth. When it failed to mist over, she wondered, 'What do you do when you've just killed someone?' So, she phoned Sir Mark Palmer's wife, the ever-resourceful Catherine Tennant, 'Hello Catherine, how are you? Yes, I'm well thank you … by the way … I think I've just killed someone and I don't know what to do?' To which the canny Catherine replied, 'Ring the police and your solicitor in that order.'

Hen put the phone down and stared at the bloody nuisance lying crumpled on the hallway floor. Seething with anger as the thought flashed through her head that she'd never wanted the bastard there in the first place, she couldn't resist giving the corpse a sharp kick in the chest. Then, as if by magic, the dead body spluttered back to life and slowly picked itself up: 'Now, will you *go*?' hollered Hen, triumphantly.

Her Reputation for Mayhem …

After exhibiting an apparent supernatural ability to raise the dead, a few months later Hen woke up one morning and heard a detached ethereal voice in her head instructing her to 'Go to Ireland'. So, off she went. She ended up at Roundwood House, an eighteenth-century Georgian mansion owned by the Irish Georgian Society, which had been set up by Desmond Guinness, husband of Hen's friend Penny Cuthbertson, whose beautiful wagon she'd previously burned down. As a preservation society, one would have thought the Irish Georgian Society were tempting fate letting Hen, with her reputation for mayhem, on the premises. Hen said the enormous mansion looked like a huge doll's house. The man responsible for restoring it was Brian Molloy. He took a shine to Hen, who well and truly got her feet under the table and soon became a resident. It was here she met the teenage tearaway Lord Patrick Conyngham, a tall birdlike creature who was considered a bit of a handful. But being kindred spirits, he and Hen hit it off immediately. They were supposed to be helping with the restoration of Roundwood House but, true to form, they spent an inordinate amount of time in the local pub where, according to Lucian Freud: 'She didn't wear any knickers, sat at a table, put up her legs and the pub owner came by and didn't really like what he saw and barred her.'

Life then took an unexpected turn when Hen's old friend and former Rolling Stones flame Suki Potier (who, you may recall, had previously sold up and left Hay after a drugs bust) phoned from Hong Kong. Heavily pregnant, Suki wanted Hen to stay with her until her baby was born. She said she needed an old friend around to keep her company whilst her husband, Bob, was out at work all day and Hen fitted the bill. Of course, Hen was only too happy to help since air travel brought out her inner child – and like most children Hen loved to fly. She enjoyed the excitement of boarding the big plane and watching the clouds go by the window before her attention naturally turned to the drinks trolley, which to every overgrown child is by far the most interesting part of the plane. Aeronautical engineers, realising this, have designed the drinks trolley so that the hard liquor is difficult to reach without the supervision of a trained adult member of staff. Undaunted by this, there is no doubt that travelling on a plane with Hen was a memorable experience – that every other passenger on board would like to forget.

As she flew high in the sky to Hong Kong, the yellow fever shot still tingled in her arm, her eyes remained glassy from the typhoid serum and her hands were shaking from the effects of the quinine pills. Sharp pains started running up her legs, but they didn't stay there for long. Suddenly they hit her in the stomach as she found the descent into Hong Kong's Kai Tak Airport to be the most terrifying experience of her life. The airport was located in the built-up city area, with an unusually steep and dramatic approach path. During their descent, Hen became convinced that the runway was too short and that they were going to crash into the mountains.

When Hen stumbled off the plane the first thing she noticed at Kai Tak Airport was the stench of the nullah, or storm-water channel, which oozed alongside the runway. Amazed at having survived her ordeal with Kamikaze Airways, she was met at the airport by Suki and Bob who whisked her away in a chauffeur-driven limo to their beautiful house by the South China Sea. Here, Hen was somewhat taken aback by the tight security. A seven-metre-high wire fence with barbed wire surrounded the house and locks were fitted on every window and door. Bob's father was the billionaire Stanley Ho, who owned nineteen casinos and was nicknamed 'The Godfather of Gambling'. With such wealthy (and possibly risky) relatives Suki and Bob were worried about being kidnapped and ransomed by the Chinese mafia, which was then a common occurrence.

Hen was also struck by some peculiarly surreal sights, such as the British policemen, with their distinctive uniforms and helmets, on the beat, looking completely out of context in their South Asian surroundings. But all was not well in paradise. Anti-British slogans had been daubed on the walls of the Supreme Court building and on the pedestal of Queen Victoria's statue someone had scrawled: 'Long live the invincible thought of Mao Tse-tung!' There had also been a terror campaign with both real and hoax bombs planted around town, during which fifty-one people, including eleven police officers, were killed.

Despite Bob and Suki's severe security measures, Hen soon acclimatised to living in a gilded cage. She and Bob smoked heroin around a pregnant Suki and together they ate in the best hotels and restaurants: oysters flown in from Australia, Aberdeen Angus from Scotland, excellent French wine and liqueurs. Hen also liked to eat in the local village café where, she pondered, 'there were lots of chow-like dogs wandering about ... I wonder if we ever ate them?' In the village she was assaulted by a fearless riot of smells, from fish drying in the sun to bean curd frying in great open woks on the streets. Added to this was the peculiar, cloying base note of vaguely rotting vegetation that underlined all the other smells when the humidity began to climb.

Soon the typhoon season was upon them, trees collapsed and buildings were blown away as Suki's waters inevitably broke and her baby decided to arrive early. The fact that the hospital was fourteen miles away and the roads had become impassable got Hen into a flap. Then, just as the contractions were getting so close together that everyone was really panicking, an ambulance arrived and Suki was stretchered out, followed by a heroic Hen crawling along the ground on her stomach, commando-style, so as not to get blown away by the typhoon.

To Hen's delight, Suki gave birth to a little girl at the hospital. But Hen's elation soon turned from sweet to sour due to the Chinese nurse's attitude: 'Girls no good, girls not go into business.' So, Bob had no heir for his family's gambling empire. It was then Hen realised Suki and her baby were now a long way away from the women's liberation movement and those hippy ideals of fraternity and equality, which they had once both championed back in London.

So, with her mission completed, a rather defeated Hen headed back to Ireland to take up residence once again at Roundwood House. During her absence, one of Hen's well-heeled friends had decided that an old master painting hanging in an Irish stately home 'was in the wrong hands'. Hen suggested that she was a good thief, so they roped her in to commit the heist, which was planned with military precision. It involved a great many people and the whereabouts of the old master painting is still shrouded in mystery.

As you may know, there is nothing the Irish like more than pulling an English person's leg, it's something of a sporting pastime to see how far they can egg the English on. One night, at the local pub, no sooner had Hen cadged a drink than someone introduced himself and said, 'You're English aren't you?' – 'Yes' – 'Then you'd be interested to know that we're only a few yards from where the great poet Oscar Wilde was born.' – 'Was he?' – 'Aye he won the Derby with a horse named Ulysses and when he died in 1900 he was buried standing up under the front door of this building.' – 'That's not true,' someone else piped up, 'I've heard it from Paddy McGuinness that he was buried horizontally under the front door.' Then another barfly butted in, 'Mrs O'Toole was invited to the funeral and said his ashes were buried in a biscuit tin in the backyard.' Not to be outdone, the pub landlord joined in, 'it was the front door and he was buried standing up. When the previous tenants, the Kildaires, moved in, Mrs Kildaire couldn't stand the thought of Oscar Wilde standing in the doorway every time she went by. So, they finally took the whole door off and buried him in the cemetery.'

The question of which direction Oscar Wilde had been buried in was kicked back and forth for at least an hour. Then when everyone in the pub thought Henrietta was getting bored with Oscar Wilde they said, 'Would you like to hear about Yeats?' But Henrietta said no, she didn't plan to leave the pub until she got to the bottom of Oscar Wilde's burial and although Henrietta had had her leg pulled all evening, she didn't feel the need for crutches when she staggered back to Roundwood House at closing time.

At the time, homosexuals were treated as figures of fun or, as in the case of Oscar Wilde, criminals. Late one night, Roundwood House's guardian, Brian Molloy, confessed to Henrietta that he was a homosexual. Of course, she didn't care, many of her friends in London were gay, but at that time in Catholic Ireland the state, the church and the family were all against it, which may have reminded Hen of being back at Oxford with Dom. Some years earlier, the publication of the Wolfenden Report had allowed many to live their lives to suit their own sexual preferences and led to the decriminalisation of homosexuality in Britain, but there was a terrible irony. Lord Wolfenden's son, who was up at Oxford with Hen and Dom, was overtly homosexual. He had a brilliant career ahead of him but ended up committing suicide in mysterious circumstances.

Brian Molloy took his own life too and left Hen a suicide note. It had been written in an agitated state, full of crossings-out and misspellings. It was an apologetic and loving letter from a man whose spirit had been snapped by a failed love affair with a young man from Dublin. Hen was heartbroken and the arrival of Brian's angry and aggressive family for the funeral did nothing to help matters. They resented Henrietta and all of Brian's friends whom they scapegoated for his homosexuality. Hen writes about the tragedy of Brian's death touchingly in her memoir and it is clear from her account that it affected her deeply.

Forever Lonely ...

After the funeral Hen stayed on at Roundwood, but despite all the people coming and going after Brian's suicide she felt forever lonely. So, when Suki fell pregnant again and summoned Hen back to Hong Kong, she was only too happy to go. By now Hong Kong had consolidated its position as the commercial centre of Asia. It also functioned as Britain's manufacturing sweatshop producing cheap plastic household items and toys bearing the legend 'Made in Hong Kong'. Long before it was superseded and absorbed by mainland China, Hong Kong became synonymous with mass production and kitsch plastic products.

So, it really shouldn't have been such a surprise for Henrietta to find – to her horror – that, as in the 1970s cult thriller *The Stepford Wives* (a film about free-thinking, intelligent women being brainwashed into being compliant housewives), Suki had been assimilated into the world of her shallow rich neighbours who made it perfectly clear they despised Henrietta because she was poor. That, combined with Suki's selling out of all the hippy ideals that they had once shared, made Hen realise that she was now superfluous to Suki and off she went back to Ireland.

Like Hen, Suki had also been unlucky in love. Before she hooked up with the ill-fated Stone, Brian Jones, she had been seeing the socialite and heir to the Guinness fortune Tara Browne, whose life encapsulated the glamour, excess and indulgence that defined the 1960s. Suki was in a sports car with Tara when he drunkenly drove it through a red light at over 100mph and straight into a parked lorry; somehow Suki survived. His death is eerily described in the Beatles song 'A Day in The Life'. Marianne said Suki suffered from 'survivor's karma' as the tragedy brought Tara's girlfriend and his best friend, Brian Jones, together. However, Hen's trip to Hong Kong would be the last time she saw Suki alive – whether it was a case of karma delayed or an ironic twist of fate – as a few years later, in 1981, Suki died in a car crash whilst on holiday with her husband.

Never one to be outdone by her friends, Hen was soon to suffer a near fatal collision with the grim reaper too. The Irish love horses and hunting, especially fox hunting. Oscar Wilde said that fox hunting was the 'pursuit of the inedible by the unspeakable'. Back in Ireland, Hen came off her horse and broke her collarbone, shattered her shoulder and broke her arm too. Immobilised in hospital, she drank Special Brew (a strong alcoholic type of beer once associated with homeless bums) and chain-smoked fags to her heart's content. When she was discharged just before Christmas, an old friend from the Chelsea Set, the 'Monster' David Mlinaric, came to the rescue and paid for Hen to return to London, where she took up residence at the Chelsea Arts Club, a few doors down from Elinor Bellingham-Smith's 155 Salon where Hen had partied hard back in the 1950s.

Penniless, homeless, down but definitely not out, our heroic Hen threw herself at the mercy of the state and began ringing around the local housing associations desperate to find somewhere to live. One such housing association was based at 11 Apollo Place, opposite the house she'd once inherited from John Minton and rather stupidly sold. Apollo Place had lost none of its glamour; the house next door was now occupied by Simon Le Bon of the pop group Duran Duran, and his model wife Yasmin.

The World's End ...

Hen was eventually offered a small room in a house on the corner of Edith Grove, Chelsea. Like some inescapable location in a recurring dream, she was back where she started, at the World's End ... some say that those dreams where you find yourself in the same place again and again are an allusion to falling back into old habits or committing the same mistakes. As if stuck in some terrible self-fulfilling prophecy, Henrietta appeared to be locked in a loop, unable to break free from her own inevitable world's end.

Although having never worked or paid any taxes for years, she was given unemployment benefit and a room on the condition she attended Alcoholics Anonymous (A.A.) and gave up drinking. Hen had never heard of A.A. before and thought it was something to do with automobiles, but keeping her side of the bargain she attended the meetings in the company of other old Colony Room habitués such as the former *Sunday Times* fashion editor Molly Parkin.

After the opulent Georgian splendour of Roundwood House, Hen found it difficult to live in one room on state benefits and a period of readjustment followed. Her new home was a housing association property full of old ladies. Trudie ruled the top floor with her knitting needles, below her lived a couple of former nurses who'd fallen on hard times and in the basement resided the stately Eve, who was pushing 100 and would regale Hen with tall tales of old Edith Grove.

For many the World's End deserved its name … a church encircled by rusted corrugated iron, a fly-ridden newsagent, a pissy old pub and a very greasy chip shop. The World's End also had a methedrine clinic for heroin users. The 1960s scene all came flooding back to her as Henrietta remembered blacking out three times between the World's End and Park Walk, at which point she decided to ditch the hard drugs.

Being true to its name, the World's End contained various venues for illness and death: St Stephen's Hospital, The Royal Marsden Hospital and The Royal Brompton Hospital, where the famous 'Brompton Cocktail', a mixture of morphine, gin and cocaine, was developed and administered to relieve the pain of dying patients and, to top it all, there's a few burial plots dotted around the area too.

In search of things past, Hen also recalled that in the 1960s the Rolling Stones had moved into a shabby abode at 102 Edith Grove where the local kids would taunt them and shout, 'Get your hair cut,' as the long-haired Apollo-like musical gods ran the gauntlet up the King's Road. In true World's End style, their dwelling was heroically bohemian – truly chaotic – dirty plates and glasses littered the floor, every conceivable surface was strewn with discarded cigarette butts and the place stank of a never-ending fry-up.

But the World's End skyline had been transformed since Hen had last lived there. By the early 1970s it had become a condemned playground and almost redeveloped beyond recognition as the Victorian streets east of Cremorne Road were pulled down and replaced by the imposing brutalist red-brick towers of the World's

End Estate. These monoliths to 1970s social housing became home to destitute Chelsea Girls such as Christine Keeler and Molly Parkin. Two damsels in distress (or two distressing damsels looking for redress) who'd once partied like mad at Muriel's Colony Room but for whom the frolics had fizzled out. Like party-ravaged Rapunzels they gazed down from the brutalist towers, surveying their end of the world … waiting for Prince Charming.

And so, just as it was in the 1960s, Hen's life became a daily routine of walking up and down the King's Road. She also became addicted to daytime television, especially soap operas such as *Emmerdale Farm*, which starred her second husband, Norman Bowler, playing a feuding businessman. And through some well-meaning friends, Hen picked up a few gardening jobs: tidying up and weeding at first, but she slowly built from there and began to design and plant too. Inspired by a visit to the Chelsea Flower Show she found gardening cathartic and pursued it for many years as old friends once more reappeared in her life, like the hardy perennials they were, and Marianne noticed that Hen had taken to gardening with the same satanic zeal with which she had once embraced cat burglary.

Chapter 15

Hen Today, Gone Tomorrow

So here we are, dear reader, in the 1980s ... sometimes labelled 'Thatcher's Britain' after the country's first female prime minister, Margaret Thatcher, who indelibly stamped her identity on the decade – so much so, in fact, that up in the Colony Room Francis Bacon had developed a rather kinky fascination for the 'Iron Lady' and her handbags which, inevitably, became the subject of much camp conversation.

By now, the flower-power generation of well-heeled hippies had been weeded out of Chelsea and a new breed of smarmy conservatives known as 'Sloane Rangers' (named after the 4x4 Range Rovers they liked to be seen driving around Sloane Square in) had replaced them. Sloane Ranger was a term made famous by the style columnist Peter York, who had noticed a tribe of young, privileged people unashamedly flaunting old-fashioned upper-class attire and espousing their class identity, all of which would have been unacceptable to the aristocrats Hen had hung out with during the 1960s. The Sloane Ranger represented the emergence of a newer, younger, more confident ruling class who would eventually end up running the country. Elsewhere in the city, the hippy was supplanted by the yuppie: venal, money-obsessed materialistic types who were into the ostentatious, tacky trappings of wealth and despised the poor.

Once Hen had reached the pinnacle of social climbing in the 1970s, the only way to go in the 1980s was down, which turned out to be something of a black ski run. By now, Henrietta's children had grown up and left school and through them she would meet the new generation swarming on the London art scene. Her son, Joshua Bowler, had gravitated to the bohemian world of Soho which his mother had once inhabited and drank in all her old haunts such as the French, the Coach & Horses and the Colony. Here he mingled with the remnants of the Monster Club and witnessed their drinking game. The rules, as such, were governed by the law of the jungle, which categorically states that: 'Under all circumstances and all conditions, a Monster has the right of way and a Monster should always come out on top.' I suspect there are one or two readers who don't know what their drinking game is but are too embarrassed to admit it. There really is no need to be because many of the Monsters who have been playing it for years don't understand the rules of the game either.

Of course, the best part of Monster-hunting was camping out under the serious moonlight of a Soho night, warming yourself beside a large roaring Monster, with the heady companionship of a few two-legged rats and malaria-ridden barflies feeding copiously on the carcass of someone else's bank balance – it was here, decades before her son, that Hen had once felt at peace with the world.

Although Monsters enjoyed snubbing tourists, they were often camera-shy and had an almost communist hatred of visiting Americans; they also had a deep love for corrupting the children of others and robbing them of their innocence. No one warned their offspring that it was not a good idea to hang out with the Monster Club. For instance, Henrietta's best friend Merilyn's son, Daniel Thorold (a childhood friend of Joshua Bowler), was arrested in Soho with über Monster Daniel Farson. In fear of being frisked back at the police station they swallowed all the hash they had on them and sat – high as kites – in a police cell for several hours before being released. By now the hallucinogenic quality of the hash had worn off and they had developed the most terrible munchies. So, Daniel Farson decided they should celebrate their new-found freedom by having a slap-up meal at Wheeler's. But the heady mixture of hash and seafood was not a happy one ... it led to instantaneous food poisoning and projectile vomiting over the restaurant's other patrons.

The child of another Soho habitué I spoke to complained that she would have to go and meet her mother in the French straight from school, still in her uniform, where she would be propositioned and leered at by a lot of dirty old Monsters. As well as Joshua Bowler and Daniel Thorold, Michael Law's youngest son (also named Michael) swam in the same rock pool and graduated to become a barman at the Colony Room.

To the young and uninitiated, the Monster Club of the 1980s was a steep learning curve in the University of Life. The first thing every potential Monster must master is 'the involuntary fall'. This means being able to fall when you don't want to. It usually takes a few minutes to learn this, and once you have mastered it you can fall anywhere in the street without the aid of an instructor. Then, having learned the rudiments of falling, one should try and master the subtle art of cadging drinks.

The easiest way to start off is to sit by the bar and face forward. In this position you can always hang onto the coat-tails of one of the more affluent drinkers if you feel you are getting out of your depth. Once you've built up enough confidence in the sitting position, try kneeling. In the kneeling position you can always grab on to someone if you lose control of your legs. You are now ready to practise some of the more intricate cadging tricks such as the *Champagne Siphon*, the *Pint Plough*, the *Vodka Pole Vault* and the *Gin and Tonic Star Jump* – all are easy to learn and should not take more than a couple of years to master with daily practice.

Before signing off this instructive section on the monstrous art of cadging, I'd like to add a list of don'ts that every wannabe Monster must pay attention to if they expect to excel at the sport:

1. Don't admit to people that you are an amateur and have never cadged before.
2. Don't drink near children. If it doesn't freak them out then, in all probability, they will laugh at you.
3. Don't use bad language when you fall. If you must be profane, be profane towards the barman who's just told you you've had enough and not towards the floor, where you're heading.
4. Don't take cheap potshots at tourists in between rounds. It's considered poor sportsmanship, even for beginners.

When not mingling with old Monsters, Henrietta's son was working with the Mutoid Waste Company: a wandering band of performance artists who transformed abandoned vehicles into fabulous creations which looked like something from the science fiction movie *Mad Max*. The Mutoid Waste Company had a place in the then industrial wasteland behind King's Cross station, which I visited whilst at art school. That's where I come into the picture: I met Joshua Bowler through drinking at the Colony. He has the dubious honour of being one of my first patrons, having bought a picture from me whilst I was still an art student. Although I never put two and two together at the time and realised that Josh's mum was in fact Henrietta Moraes, that legendary Queen of Bohemia.

A French Fable ...

Through Henrietta, Josh met Orlando Campbell, the son of another Soho drinking legend, and together they ran The Crucial Gallery which sold furniture and sculpture created from repurposed everyday objects. As Josh told *The New York Times*: 'I'm most interested in seeing an artist take an object and change its use, not its substance.' At the gallery, you might find the hood of an old black Mercedes converted into a cocktail cabinet or a desk made of melded glass. The whole aesthetic might now be mistaken for 'upcycling', but this 1980s trend was probably kicked off by the designer Ron Arad when he took two seats out of an old Rover car and repurposed them into a sofa. Back then, this sort of thing was the height of chic and The Crucial Gallery was considered so cool, it was '*crucial*'. As our mutual friend, the curator James Birch, told me:

> I met Henrietta through her son, Joshua. I used to go around for Sunday lunch and she'd be there. On one occasion she'd been in a pub around the corner with Lord Patrick Conyngham drinking amyl nitrate. Every time they breathed out again, they got high. So, there were these two red faced people at the dinner table. Henrietta

> was talking about someone dismissively then the person walked into the room: 'Oh, we've just been talking about you and not in very good terms.' At that time, Joshua was running a gallery … and Henrietta had stopped coming into Soho … she preferred to stay at home with her pet dachshund.

According to Marianne, one of the wonderful things about Hen was her love of dogs. She always had lovely dogs like her little dachshund Den, whom Marianne adored and found 'very nervy and a bit damaged – like his mistress'. It's said that dogs pick up their owners' traits and that some people even start looking like their pets. Although Hen didn't look like her dachshund, much of her memoir is devoted to dogs. But being Hen's pet was a precarious profession and when I was a young man there was a 'French Fable' recounted often at the bar of the French, which went something like this:

> Do you remember the time Henrietta forgot to close her fourth-floor window? Her dachshund went flying out of it pursuing a pigeon … then, a few weeks later she reversed a car over its replacement. Ha, ha, ha, ha, ha …

Needless to say, this anecdote caused much merriment amongst the other Monsters at the bar, but with death forever at her elbow, one wonders what Hen felt on 28 April 1992, when she heard that Francis Bacon had died. She had unexpectedly bumped into him on a bus some months earlier … he'd sat beside her making small talk about viewing the *Mona Lisa* in Paris when he suddenly changed tack, 'I've got a problem. Do you know anything about funeral arrangements?' Hen said she did not. 'When I die,' Francis told her, 'I don't want to have a funeral. How do I go about that?' She replied, 'I suppose you go to your solicitor.' – 'My solicitor is away on holiday. I don't want anything, anything, anything.'

Although Henrietta has been woven into the Francis Bacon legend, she was one of the few models used by him who did not attend his sumptuous 1971 exhibition at the Grand Palais, in Paris. Muriel Belcher, John Deakin and the rest of the Monster Club had climbed aboard Francis' freak show and fed upon the ensuing drama of the suicide of his lover and model George Dyer. Word spread like wildfire amongst the Monsters. 'Guess what?' they barked bitchily. 'She's committed Susan-cide.'

Francis' work is full of peculiar quirks … he painted a triptych of Mick Jagger to much fanfare but never once raised his brush for Marianne, and although Henrietta remained a constant presence in his studio, for the last few decades she no longer formed part of the drama of his daily life. However, Francis' death was a worldwide news item and a wake was held for him at the Colony Room. He'd always promised Henrietta a painting but never gave her one … he'd given his sister, Ianthe, a portrait of Henrietta instead.

After his death, Francis' work began to sell for millions at auction and Hen could be heard to complain about how much money was being made from her whilst she lived in abject poverty. However, in a filmed interview with Martha Parsey the following year, she dismissed her near mythical superstar status as Francis' muse and was quite sanguine about it all:

> Quite frankly, I think I was the only woman he knew who he could ask to take photographs of with no clothes on … I think it was really simple … things are always more simple than they appear. You try and invent great reasons for things when in fact things are often dead simple and I think that was it. I was the only girl he knew well enough.

Then, unsurprisingly, after a lifetime of partying, Henrietta began to suffer from a pain in her chest, which was diagnosed as cirrhosis of the liver. Deciding she wanted to live, Hen once again swore to give up drinking and began to attend those A.A. meetings that she loathed. Everyone looked so sickeningly happy and pleased to see one another but Henrietta couldn't see what there was to be so happy about. She felt terribly lonely now she'd stopped drinking whisky and vodka … she'd lost her two best friends: Johnnie Walker and Sally Smirnoff.

As if that wasn't bad enough, she felt tired all the time. Overweight and forever peeing, a life on the booze had led to diabetes and by not bothering to take her insulin injections she became so ill she was sent to hospital with a suspected heart attack and, like the demonically possessed child in *The Exorcist*, she projectile-vomited over two nuns in the back of the ambulance whilst her long-suffering son followed behind in his car.

Desperate to be a good son, Josh tried helping his mother to kick her addictions and redecorated her room to give her a fresh start. Once out of hospital, Henrietta went back to A.A. and on realising that there was a spiritual dimension to the meetings began to get better. But abstinence led to anxiety. She was terrified of attending parties as she'd never been to one sober. But she soon discovered that as people got drunk they seemed to get more boring.

Surveying Her Domain ...

Then came dachshund number three, the funny and energetic Max. Together they took long walks in Brompton Cemetery, one of Britain's oldest and grandest Victorian graveyards. Situated between the King's Road and Earl's Court, it's open daily to the public and dog walking is permitted on the indicated paths. Here, amidst some 35,000 monuments, ranging from simple headstones to substantial mausoleums, Hen indulged her fetish for melancholic strolls amongst rows of angels with missing limbs and the odd decapitated Virgin Mary.

In this pursuit she was not alone; joggers, cyclists and other dog walkers used the tree-lined paths, all of them unified in their wish to take a breath of fresh air down among the dead. Speaking of which, the place had more the air of a park than a cemetery. In this favourite spot Hen was interviewed and filmed by the artist Martha Parsey. You can see Hen clearly, as her beloved dachshund, Max, dashes around the tombs. The cemetery becomes a studio set as the last Queen of Bohemia strides around surveying her domain, passing every category of the human tribe: banker, lawyer, poet, mother, lover ... along with their calcifying statues, stumps, pillars and crosses – the famous and the infamous decay in tandem.

Opera singers share the soil with music hall artistes, entrepreneurs and journalists.

On her daily walk among the deceased, she headed down the central avenue, where many of the graves were ivy-covered, overgrown and dense with occult geometries, past the showiest mausoleums to the circular Jacobean theatre of the colonnades, made of Bath stone, and the beautiful neoclassical domed chapel. From here Hen would do an 'S'-shape past some of the more interesting mausoleums taking in the intricately carved Pre-Raphaelite tomb of the artist Valentine Prinsep and that of Barbe Marie Theresa Sangiorgi, wife of Soho restaurateur August Kettner.

A carved stone urn marks the grave of Marchesa Luisa Casati – an infamous Italian muse and patron of the arts, who, like Hen, had captivated the major artists of her day and became the subject of several significant works of art, as well as the object of much gossip. Discovering those who refused to be categorised in death as well as life, Hen comes across the crumbling grave of the composer Constant Lambert, former husband of Francis Bacon's other muse, Isabel Rawsthorne.

Amidst the mausoleums strong daylight throws bright shafts between the grey edifices like a projector lamp – figures vanish into alcoves and secret exits, as broad steps lead down to the underworld. It was also a necrophile park for hoodies hooked on narcotics and those seeking sexual solicitation. A popular cruising ground for gay men, Hen would stroll by guys hunkering down to give each other hand-jobs behind the tombstones. Sometimes the Park Police would sweep the graveyard to curb occurrences of 'antisocial behaviour' in this Arcadia where lost souls who are 'queerly departed' seek sex amongst the dearly departed, office workers with packed lunches masticate whilst others freely masturbate.

Then, having wound her way round, Hen would halt in front of a fascinating Egyptian-style mausoleum, which rises up majestically in the middle of the cemetery. Dwarfed in the presence of death and facing the largest and most elaborate construction in the entire place, she'd contemplate her own mortality. This mausoleum would be remarkable for its imposing stature alone, but there are those who maintain that it's also a fully functional time machine.

It was built for Hannah Courtoy, a mysterious woman who never married, but inherited a fortune from an elderly merchant for whom she had worked and whose name she later took. There are rumours that she was not only his lover, but also the mistress of kings, politicians and other powerful men. She and her daughters rest in a tomb designed by her two friends, Joseph Bonomi and Samuel Alfred Warner.

Warner was an inventor, the genius who invented the torpedo, and Joseph Bonomi a noted artist and Egyptologist, among the first to decipher the hieroglyphic texts found in the Valley of the Kings. It is said Bonomi discovered the secret of time travel from the hieroglyphs he found on one of his expeditions. Like many Victorians, Hannah was fascinated by Egyptian hieroglyphics and it is claimed that the two men convinced Hannah to finance their secret project – to design and build a time machine that looked like a mausoleum – and that they placed their invention in a cemetery, to ensure that no one would interfere with it over the passing decades, since cemeteries rarely change.

The mausoleum was finished in 1853 and, shortly after, Warner died in suspicious circumstances – some say because of what he discovered while working on the time machine, others claim that Bonomi killed Warner to stop him from revealing their project. Bonomi is buried in the cemetery too. On his headstone is an illustration of Anubis, the Egyptian god of death, looking in the direction of the mausoleum, which has strange wheel motifs on the bottom of its door and a large circular hole in the top with eight much smaller holes surrounding it – as if a dial or clock was supposed to fit there. For almost every structure in the cemetery there exists an architect's plan, but not for Hannah's mausoleum. Then, as if to add to the mystery, the key to it went missing, so no one has been able to see what's inside for more than 150 years …

If all this sounds far-fetched, dear reader, remember that Hen spent four years following ley lines, chasing UFOs and experiencing spectral visions. Recalling the Oscar Wilde line, 'He who lives more lives than one. More deaths than one must die' and having herself lived several lives in one lifetime, the idea of a mausoleum being a time machine appealed to her. She had loved and lost – and loved again – she had never got to say goodbye to so many of those she'd loved in her life: Elinor, Elizabeth, Francis, Muriel, Deakin and David Archer – all scattered to the wind. She wasn't there for any of them at the end. So many ghosts and yet …

I can see her clearly on the fleeting footage … as a crow cries and flaps its wings on the shoulder of an angel, she draws a deep breath and stirs from her thoughts. Snapping back to the present she suddenly realises that Max has gone ahead without her and calls out for him. As playful as ever, Max bounds out between two headstones, so excited and so full of life among the dead, he leads the way and together they wind their way back, leaving the cemetery by the same gate they entered.

Scotch Jimmy

After their walk in the cemetery, Hen attended her regular A.A. meeting with Max in tow. Needless to say, Hen's children were pleased that she had given up drinking. Old friends like Merilyn Thorold also reappeared in Hen's life, but there was a sense that an era was drawing to a close when their dear friend from the Colony Room, the artist Michael Andrews, became seriously ill and passed away in 1995.

After his funeral service, Hen and Merilyn distributed drinks from Merilyn's houseboat, *Wiljan*, which was coincidentally moored by St Mary's Church in Battersea, where the funeral was held. It had been a long time since she and Merilyn had returned from that summer holiday at Hydra. Merilyn had stuck by Hen through all her difficult times, but time was running out for both of them, and they were destined to die within months of one another.

However, Hen's life had now changed for the better. She became more stable without the influence of alcohol and stopped blaming others for her faults. Surely it must say something that to a counter-culture icon such as Marianne Faithfull, Hen was one of the freest people she'd ever known. The 'let's-drop-everything-and-do-this-ness' of Henrietta meant she was the greatest of company:

> She was witty, wonderfully warm and lovable and she had a good heart. A lot of times when I was really in deep shit, like when I was on heroin and really in a bad way, Hen would come over and look after me. She was incredibly kind-hearted and she loved me, I don't know why. She'd do very simple things that would reduce me to tears.

Marianne had given Hen the nickname 'Madre', a Spanish word meaning mother or matron. She certainly had a stern matronly presence about her and was great at taking control in a crisis. But, as Marianne could testify, giving up a lifetime of bad habits is hard and Henrietta would occasionally go for a trip down memory lane with her old mate Johnnie Walker:

> When she wanted to be, Hen could be absolutely charming to a fault but she did have a very grumpy side to her which manifested itself quite startlingly in a character she called Scotch Jimmy – a demon that appeared when she got really drunk and nasty – he only began to appear near the very end …

A Violent Diatribe

Meanwhile, Henrietta's long-lost husband, Dom Moraes, had published a second memoir, the aptly titled *Never at Home*. In it he describes their honeymoon in Athens with Bambi and the Eichmann trial, but deliberately cuts Henrietta out of the narrative, as if the wife he'd shared these experiences with had never existed. This must have raised a few eyebrows and her erasure from history may have prompted Hen to write her own version of events. As Marianne's friend, the author and curator Harriet Vyner, explained to me, if nothing else, everyone agreed that Hen writing her memoir might be a good way of her making some much-needed money:

> After spending so much time together drinking and taking drugs, it was only natural we should find ourselves going to A.A. After one

meeting, she gave me a proof copy of her autobiography, *Henrietta*, to look at. Even from reading the first few pages, I could tell it was magnificent. Then, when I mentioned in passing that I was going to see Lucian Freud for breakfast the next day she remarked, 'Oh, I wonder if you could ask him if I can use his portrait of me on the cover?' I agreed as I didn't think it would be a problem. The next morning, at breakfast, I mentioned the request to Lucian. At the very mention of Henrietta's name, he launched into a violent diatribe: 'Her morals are repulsive … she is completely untrustworthy', etc. etc. It went on for quite a long time as I sat in silence thinking, 'this is not going well, is it?' When Lucian finally reached the end of his tirade I said, 'So, that's a no, then is it?' – 'Oh, no! Of course, she can use the painting'. When I told Henrietta she was extremely happy … but I didn't fill her in on all the details of the conversation preceding the agreement.

Henrietta held her book launch in the French. Needless to say, her autobiography was a huge success and garnered excellent reviews. Her old friends in the press, such as Francis Wyndham (who'd acted as the witness at all three of her weddings), declared the book to be so brilliant it was 'impossible to put down'. Whilst her former Soho soulmate Jeffrey Bernard told the *Daily Telegraph*: 'Henrietta Moraes is one of the most courageous women I have ever come across.'

Yet no matter how warmly received and candid it might seem, Henrietta's memoir was also extremely guarded – a lot of people are left out and others mentioned minus their surnames. Obviously, the publisher had to be wary of potential legal action, what with all the drinking, drug-taking and other incriminating behaviour going on. Personally, I've always found that the first casualty of writing a historical account is the truth, no one seems to want to publish it because it's far too scary. But Henrietta's friend and literary agent, Alexandra Pringle, remembers the whole experience of working with her as being a journey of pure joy:

The I.C.A. (Institute of Contemporary Arts) held an event with Henrietta and Marianne Faithfull. They were incredibly funny

> together as they were both affectionate and rivalrous at the same time ... having just published competing autobiographies. Marianne came up to hug Henrietta and, completely by mistake, ripped the earring out of Henrietta's ear. Henrietta was convinced that Marianne had done it on purpose and muttered darkly to me about being Marianne's 'Minder' and how she'd come out of the toilet with needles falling out of her pocket. She was extremely catty about Marianne, but they were marvellous together!

With the resounding success of her book ringing in her ears, Hen set to work on a sequel, using her old nickname; it was tentatively titled: '*Piss off Darling*'. She also wrote several short stories. Towards the end of her first memoir, Henrietta proudly states that: 'My grandchildren and my dog have never seen me drunk, and I trust and pray they never will.' And it's true that Hen had now become the kind of loving maternal grandmother that she herself had never had, as John Dunbar informed me:

> Henrietta? Gawd ...! Mrs. Moraes! She could be quite heavy, she slightly scared me in a way. She somehow turned into Giles' Granny. Do you know Giles the cartoonist? He had a famous large lumbering granny figure, all in black, who appeared in his cartoon strips, well she got to be a bit like that – she certainly didn't suffer fools gladly. I got a phone call from her a couple of weeks before she died: 'Oh, I've got this wonderful new doctor who says I can drink!' and I was trying to say, 'No, no, Henrietta, it doesn't work like that.' She'd been very good and laid off it for a couple of years but eventually became miserable not drinking. Then she finally cracked and went out happy.

[illegible] Lady [illegible] the [illegible] and [illegible] [illegible] [illegible] Stuart Mackenzie [illegible]

[illegible] and [illegible] the [illegible] that [illegible] the King [illegible] had [illegible] [illegible] as [illegible] had [illegible] [illegible]

[illegible]

[illegible] and [illegible]

Chapter 16

Drawing to an End

So here we are, cooped up and hemmed in with a poverty-stricken Henrietta reduced to living in a one-room bedsit at 18 Edith Grove. Her daily routine now consisted of lying recumbent in bed, like the Queen of Sheba, rising late and wading through the World's End before strolling up the King's Road with her dog, Max, to buy a copy of her favourite newspaper, the *Daily Mail*, and sixty Camel cigarettes.

On her daily stroll she'd pass what was once Gerald McCann's Gloryhole boutique at 342a King's Road, where Gerald held court, back in the 1960s, in a pear-shaped room with puce wallpaper. Gerald was Muriel Belcher's favourite 'frock maker' and invented the 'kinky boot' as worn by Honor Blackman in the television series *The Avengers*, but with the days of designer boutiques receding behind her, the charity shops Hen passed by on the way were inspected for clothes, which she happily stole in the unshakeable belief that she herself was now a 'charity case'. Oxfam became her favourite place to shoplift from – on her daily pilgrimage to the chemist to collect those precious pills, which she popped with a ruthless professionalism. Yet, despite her diminished circumstances, she was still warm and witty and made life more thrilling for all those around.

She had no intention of growing old gracefully and at the age of sixty-five became the first punk pensioner promenading along the King's Road. Punk was, in a way, a product of the World's End and its emporium could be found at 430 King's Road where its main protagonists, Vivienne Westwood and Malcolm McLaren, used the former premises of Granny Takes a Trip to subvert British society.

Henrietta's continual survival against all the odds had made her into a living legend. In 1996 the National Portrait Gallery mounted an exhibition of John Deakin's photographs and being one of the few survivors of 1950s Soho, Henrietta wrote an article for the *Independent* on 6 April, titled 'The Curse of the Drinking Classes'. It was an inversion of Oscar Wilde's quip, 'drink is the curse of the working classes', in which she recalled her racy memories of Francis Bacon:

> When I was 18, I had spent all my mornings, afternoons and evenings with him ... Wherever he appeared, the air brightened, groups of people were animated, electricity buzzed, and bottles of champagne appeared. I had learned so much of the ways of the world from him, and though, at times, I had not properly understood half of his teaching, it had nevertheless, willy-nilly, been assimilated.

The *Guardian Weekend Magazine* also ran a feature on her titled 'The Queen of Soho', which was written by the journalist Patrick Cooney who took her back to revisit some of her old Soho haunts. Whilst reminiscing with Cooney in the French she gazed at a photo of Francis Bacon and remarked, 'Look at Francis! He's probably saying ... "How in God's name did you survive it all?"'

Marianne was able to help Hen out a bit towards the end by buying her a new set of teeth. After she'd started drinking again, Hen's inner demon 'Scotch Jimmy' had come out and someone had punched her, knocking her teeth out: 'Henrietta had been a really great beauty, and a face without your front teeth – it's just all caved in — and so I bought her some teeth and sent her to a good dentist.' But Marianne suspected Henrietta did not buy the plush ivory pegs she'd coughed up the money for. 'I think she got cheap teeth and then spent the rest of the money on booze,' she mused.

Hen was many things, but not a fool. She realised how ill she was and that her moneyed connections could not save her this time. Her son Joshua offered her sanctuary and once again persuaded her to give up alcohol for a while, but she plunged into a depression and was sectioned for attacking a police officer.

A Baptism of Fire

Then the last, but by no means least, important figure entered her life, the uproarious artist Maggi Hambling who became her lover. At the time, Maggi described the punk pensioner as her 'muse', they both had much in common and shared similar interests and tastes. To Hen, Maggi looked every inch the artist with her paint-spattered clothes and pale blue eyes heavily encircled with black eyeliner, which reinforced her penetrating stare. Like Hen, Maggi had been something of an *enfant terrible* of the British art world and always refused to be photographed without a cigarette in her paint-stained hands.

In 1997, the year before they met, Maggi had won a competition to create a public sculpture to commemorate Oscar Wilde. The director of the National Portrait Gallery invited Maggi to display her maquettes and sketches for the sculpture in the gallery. Along with the sculptures, Maggi had painted some portraits of Wilde, one of which depicted him on his deathbed staring at the wallpaper above his head. 'Before he died in the hotel in Paris where he lay ill, Wilde addressed the wallpaper: "One of us has to go, and I fear it will be me." What a great line to die on,' mused Maggi, 'and he's lasted longer than the wallpaper!'

Meanwhile, Henrietta had set her sights on enticing Maggi and luring her into her arms, as their mutual friend Alexandra Pringle confided in me:

> At that time, I was married to the art critic Tim Hilton, so my life was very much in the art world as well as the literary world ... and Henrietta was talking so vividly and excitedly about Maggi. I told Henrietta I had a kaftan I'd bought in Egypt but never worn and she said, 'Give it to me. I shall seduce Maggi with it!'

Maggi and Hen got together the following year, after the press controversy concerning the unveiling of Maggi's tribute to Wilde, which Henrietta would have certainly clocked in her copy of the *Daily Mail*. Installed behind St Martins-in-the-Fields, opposite London's Charing Cross station, the sculpture depicts Wilde rising from his coffin, laughing and smoking. It appealed to Henrietta's 'Wilde side', but the sculpture-cum-bench also received much derision. The art critic Tom Lubbock described it as 'wilfully tacky and silly' and the bronze cigarette in Wilde's hand has been hacked off and stolen many times, despite it being situated by a police station. Located on a dark side street, by a public toilet, over the years the sculpture has become a focal point for homeless people and drug addicts looking to score on the urine-streaked sidewalk.

So, what was the attraction for Henrietta? Well, for an artist, Maggi had a huge media profile. She had been the first artist in residence at London's National Gallery and as 'Maggi Hambling the television personality' she was beamed weekly into every sitting room in the land on Channel 4's game show *Gallery*, hosted by Colony Room habitué George Melly and devised by Daniel Farson. Maggi had always been drawn to those who'd inhabited the bohemian world of 1950s Soho. As a young art student, she had unwittingly followed in Henrietta's footsteps and gone through a baptism of fire at the Colony Room. Rather like someone stumbling upon a murder scene, Maggi's first visit to the Colony was indelibly stamped on her memory:

> I was taken there by the artist, Craigie Aitchison … we both got very drunk and ended up going back to a big house in Canonbury Square, which belonged to an old friend of Henrietta's, Marsh Dunbar. It was a very drunk party. I remember I went to bed with her in a room full of people. Early the next morning Craigie and I were desperately looking in the kitchen for some milk to put in our coffee. When we went back to the Colony the following week, Muriel seemed to quite like me, but Marsh Dunbar came in and looked right through me, as if she'd never seen me before, which put me right off and I left.

After that I didn't go back for years ... until I began to go with George Melly. There's that anecdote about a young man who waits outside the Colony every night for Francis Bacon to arrive. Finally, one night Bacon appears and the young man asks, 'I'm an artist will you come and look at my work?' – 'No, your paintings are dreadful' – 'But you haven't seen them' – 'No, but I've seen your tie!'

Henrietta never talked much about the past; she lived in the present moment ... but part of the appeal of the Colony was Francis Bacon. I once said to Henrietta: 'It's interesting that they say Francis Bacon didn't believe in God' and she said: 'Well, I'm not sure about that!' From what Henrietta said ... it was almost as if he was in search of God.

In the final months of Hen's life, Maggi Hambling looked after her. Together, they formed a sort of bohemian enclave that existed only unto themselves and they carved out their own bizarre support network as the two of them collaborated on a series of portraits. As with Joshua Bowler, Maggi was another person whom I'd originally come across whilst at art school, but it wasn't until some decades later, as I sat with Maggi in her London studio, that she told me about Henrietta:

Our first encounter was at a big Boxing Day lunch in Wiltshire ... five years earlier ... I met Henrietta again on 4 February 1998, two days after my father's funeral, at the end of a dinner following the Francis Bacon opening at the Hayward Gallery in London ... I was in quite a vulnerable state and as I got up to leave ... Henrietta was sitting on a table by the exit. She got up and said, 'Hello, when are you having me over for dinner?' I did invite her for dinner and she then wrote to me saying she needed £400 to settle some rather annoying bills and would I help her out? In exchange for which she would work. Well, the only thing I could think of was modelling ... that's how it started.

Looking back, Hen regretted that she'd never actually sat for Francis Bacon, an opportunity she was determined not to let slip by with Maggi. She wanted to spend what time she had left with an artist. Hen had an enquiring mind and was fascinated by the process of painting and drawing, as she explained to Martha Parsey:

> I never sat for him because he said people got too upset when they saw what he was painting ... I don't feel at all wounded, I never did. I was always rather cross that he painted from photographs because I wanted to sit for him really, because I liked talking to him very much. I had an awful lot of respect for him ... I would have accepted his interpretation of me whatever it was.

Now, once again, another figurative painter had found their muse in Henrietta. But what was her appeal to Maggi? After a long pause she raised her left hand on which she sported the chunky turquoise ring that had once belonged to Hen and took another deep drag on her fag before confiding in me:

> Henrietta's eyes looked into one's soul, at the same time exposing her own. She posed for me most Mondays for seven months ... until two days before she died. However arthritic or, on occasion, hung over, she courageously climbed onto the table; raw, intense, vulnerable and commanding. I became her subject rather than she mine. Her inspiration for me was a powerful mixture of attack, encouragement and wit: her defiant spirit of rebellion.

Drawing to an End ...

Hen was in awe of the ability of artists like Maggi and Francis to pare her down to her essence and in her filmed interview with Martha Parsey she displays great insight:

> What I do like about Francis' work is its prophetic quality. I thought, some time ago, all really great artists were prophets and he painted me with a hypodermic syringe in my arm ... I'd never really heard of drugs at that point of my life. I didn't take much notice of the hypodermic really. But later, I did muck about with

> drugs and get to know what a hypodermic was. But he put it there a good ten years before I'd even thought of it … I thought I'd never ever use one. I thought it was the sort of thing I didn't do, but then I thought I wouldn't ever drink before breakfast either!

Then, as if to confirm Henrietta's theory that all great artists are prophets, after months of working with Maggi something strangely prophetic happened. Maggi had drawn one of her props, a human skull, on the same sheet as Henrietta's head. 'My God,' cried Hen, 'you've made the skull look more alive than me.' For some, it was just another example of Hen's black humour, but Maggi began to notice her mood swings and wondered if she was secretly back on the sauce:

> She posed for me in a hat … Henrietta's daughter, Caroline, told me she always wore hats when she was drunk. Towards the end of September, the drink was driving her a bit mad. I remember going to collect her on a Monday and she was convinced that gas was escaping from her fire. I telephoned the gasman and there was no leak. Then, she went into the Mental Health Unit at the Chelsea and Westminster Hospital for two weeks.

Those who visited Hen in hospital say that she was away with the fairies and quite incoherent. When she came out she went to A.A. again, but as her friend and literary agent Alexandra Pringle told me, matters were not helped by two well-meaning model citizens:

> I was rung by Jerry Hall and Marie Helvin. They said, 'We want to buy the film rights to *Henrietta* and we are coming to your office … *right now!*' They arrived and we did the deal on the spot for £5000. I'd never done anything like it before, it was hilarious, I was calling Henrietta and saying, 'I've got Jerry Hall in my office' … and she was just dying of excitement. Then, when I got her the money, she started drinking again, almost immediately. I think the possibility of that film and the £5000 deranged her.

Having decided she should have a few drinks to celebrate, Hen began the last pub crawl to purgatory. After so many decades of drinking, the draw of the demon drink proved irresistible – its siren call causing her to crash upon the rocks and become shipwrecked on a sea of booze. As Maggi made sketch after sketch of her muse, Henrietta's very existence was drawing to an end:

> The drink was beginning to eat into her ... she was defying death. She knew it would kill her. There was something almost valiant about it ... obviously I tried to discourage her from drink. It was a battle between me and the drink and in the end, the drink won ... when she was drunk, she was monstrous ... it was heroic self-destruction. She defied death. She was very drunk in this drawing I did with my left hand. I was furious with her. She would sit for two minutes and then say: 'Oh, fuck it, I'm going downstairs to look for a drink' ... By December, Henrietta had become very fragile and was drinking only water, as it was the only liquid she could hold down, she began to rapidly lose weight and look surprisingly younger. She planned to write a sequel to her autobiography in which she would describe the pain of her life as opposed to the pleasure. Between us stood a bottle of water labelled: 'Delightfully Still' and I suggested the title for her new book might be: 'Still Henrietta', and she shot back, 'Why not "*Delightfully*"'?

By now, Henrietta was in pretty bad shape and she spent her last Christmas with Alexandra Pringle:

> Henrietta walked in, saw my then husband sitting there, and shouted, 'You're a shit, Tim Hilton! *You're a shit.*' She and my mother liked each other immediately and got on like a house on fire. Henrietta was really ill and kept vomiting, so my mother got her a bucket and sat next her as she vomited in to it. Henrietta was tremendously funny, incredibly witty ... I rather specialised in bohemian women.

Then, a few days later, came the New Year of 1999. The dawn of a new millennium, which the prophets of doom were predicting would give rise to a 'millennium bug' that would cause computers to crash and planes to fall from the sky whilst warning all and sundry that the end of the world was nigh.

On 5 January, Maggi telephoned Hen but got no answer so she decided to drive down to the World's End to see her the following morning. For such a place as the World's End, there might as well be no apostrophe in the word 'World's'. What may be seen by some as a name or an event was, for Hen, to be a death sentence.

World's End

And so here we are, dear reader, right back where we started … heading towards our final destination, the World's End … on a mission with Maggi and because today will be Henrietta's last day, it really is her world's end. It is 6 January 1999, as we join Maggi worriedly driving at breakneck speed towards Edith Grove, where she arrives to find Henrietta's door jammed and her hollering down from a window:

> From the bathroom window she enjoyed complaining how ludicrous it was that she couldn't get out. Max was lowered down in a travel bag on a length of electric cable and Henrietta then challenged me to enter the house through a very small high window, which I did … In her room, from her bed, she asked how long before he died Oscar Wilde had said those 'funny things' … referring to the famous wallpaper quote, when on his deathbed Wilde had said, 'This is a duel to the death. One of us must go, and I fear it must be me.' Staring up in her tiny room, Henrietta recited it perfectly. I furiously said she needed medical help. She responded by demanding I calm down, give her a hug and another cigarette. She died in an instant – whilst making her doctor laugh on the telephone.

A Lesson in How to Die …

When Henrietta died, she left her beloved dog Max to Maggi in her will – along with a large pile of unpaid bills. Her body was taken to the hospital where the staff gave Maggi permission to draw her:

> Our affair had been a dance of death with drink as the third party. Her parting gift to me was a lesson in how to die. Her hands, which were enormous, became small surprisingly quickly after she died. She was the most glamorous corpse I've ever seen.

On the morning of the funeral, Maggi went to the Chapel of Rest in Munster Road where she found Hen swaddled in gypsy clothes, replete with a red hat and cowboy boots. She was clutching a wand in one hand and in the other a small case containing pictures of her beloved dog Max. Maggi's drawings of Henrietta in her coffin show her looking rather cross, with one eye still open, as if she was still on the lookout for a livener … their mutual friend, George Melly, always joked with Maggi about her numerous deathbed drawings, because she was so keen on drawing cadavers he thought she ought to be nicknamed Maggi 'Coffin' Hambling. But not everyone was so enamoured by Maggi's coffin capers, as the artist Camilla Shivarg told me:

> The thing with Maggi Hambling always puzzles me because, I don't know if she's a bit of an ambulance chaser, but I don't ever remember seeing Henrietta with Maggi in my entire life. Then she published a book of drawings she'd made of Henrietta on her death bed. Horrible drawings. She even took over Henrietta's funeral, which I attended. Maggi was at the door greeting people, it really riled me the way she took over, there was something not right and she was perfectly rude to me as I came in. Although I'd known Henrietta since I was a baby Maggi raised her eyebrows at the sight of me as if to say: 'What the fuck are you doing here, Shivarg?' – as she used to call me when she was my tutor at art school. But then, like Henrietta, Maggi is another marvellous Monster …
>
> Funny thing was, despite dying penniless, Henrietta's funeral was fantastic. She had a horse drawn hearse with enormous black plumes which stopped the traffic … I wonder who paid for that?

Epilogue

Just like Oscar Wilde, Henrietta Moraes' legacy has far outlasted her wallpaper, although she's been given a rough ride posthumously in the press with headlines such as: 'The Naked Druggie Painted by Bacon Tips Out for a Record £7.9 M.' She's also been given short shrift by academics and art historians too. Check the index in the back of any book on Francis Bacon and you'll see she barely gets a mention.

Sharing the same model as Francis must have been an artistic fulfilment for Maggi. As part of the process she called 'positive grieving', Maggi continued to make artworks about Henrietta long after she died, because, as she says, 'If you've loved them, they don't die, they go on being alive inside you, don't they?'

In October 2001 an exhibition devoted to Maggi's artworks of Henrietta was held at Francis Bacon's former gallery, Marlborough Fine Art, where he'd originally exhibited his portraits of Hen back in 1963. Maggi's show consisted of thirteen sculptures and twenty-two paintings including a set of raw, fleshy oil studies of Hen's orifices on a dozen or so small canvases, grouped together as one work and titled *Prelude*. Other paintings depicted Hen drinking, laughing and looking certifiably stiff in her coffin.

Marianne Faithfull attended the private view and purchased a particularly poignant picture titled *Thames Walk, Battersea Park, 2000*. The inspiration for the piece came during a walk in Battersea Park, where Maggi and Henrietta used to take their dogs. Strolling along Maggi found an empty miniature bottle of rum and a bunch of wilting carnations nestling on a ledge, which moved her so much that she took them home and painted them. Whatever heart-wrenching story lay behind this scenario, it moved Marianne to tears:

> I love it because it carries a sense of loss and remembrance … Looking at it makes me think of her, dear brave, wild, chaotic, funny, heroically self-indulgent Hen. She was the epitome of that sort of bohemian life that's all gone now.

The exhibition also featured bronze sculptures of Hen's mouth glugging a can of Special Brew, perched, teetering, on the edge of her voluptuous lips. But one sculpture stood out from all the others: made of white plaster it depicted Henrietta's voracious mouth munching, which Maggi considers the most seminal of all her sculptures, *Henrietta Eating a Meringue*:

> When Henrietta was told she had diabetes, she tucked into cream cakes in a big way. It was part of her defiance … it was only a year later, when I started to paint the sea, that I realised I was trying to get that same movement into the paintings, the sea being like a great mouth. Eating the shingle, eating, eating, eating. You only realise these things afterwards … that Henrietta had inspired a whole new body of work, my series of sea paintings.

As for Dom Moraes, within a few years of deserting Hen his poetic muse had left him too. Instead, he travelled to almost every country in the world, writing journalism and travel books. In 1968, Dom settled back in India for good and went on to become one of the country's most well-known writers, a monumental figure in Indian English literature and India's Poet Laureate.

It's interesting that despite their estrangement Henrietta still kept Dom's surname. He must have meant a lot to her, especially after pursuing him for so many years. I wonder what Dom felt when he heard of her death. Did it cause him to reflect on the long and winding life he had lived? If so, he rarely spoke about it and divulged nothing.

After all, it was a yarn about a talented little boy, his brilliant father and a beautiful mother who was slowly losing her mind in a household of hysteria; a fairy tale about the coming of age of a precocious poet lauded by literary London; a fable about writing in war-torn Africa and hanging out with cannibals in the jungles of Indonesia; and a bodice-ripper about being seduced by bohemian Soho and Henrietta, before marrying Leela Naidu, once listed among the ten most beautiful women in the world. Whatever way you sliced the story, it too was drawing to an end, but would the truth ever be told?

A few years later, when the Gujarat riots erupted in 2002, Dom left for Ahmedabad as soon as the news of the death toll came through. Like Hen, Dom was still on the side of the underdog; even though he'd been diagnosed with cancer and was in considerable physical pain, he was one of the first journalists on the scene – something that his famous father would have applauded. But the stories Dom encountered, especially that of the eight-year-old girl who had been serially sodomised by policemen, shattered him. When he came back, his drinking escalated again. He spent his nights crying himself to sleep and his days downing Bloody Marys. He refused treatment for his cancer and nicknamed his tumour 'Gorgi'. Then, one afternoon, he retired for his daily nap and never woke up again.

One of the curious things about history is how it is continually being rewritten. For example, when Dom's obituary was published in *The Times* on 4 June 2004, it mentions him being married only twice – to Judith St Clare and Leela Naidu. But there is speculation that only Dom's first marriage to Henrietta was legitimate since they never divorced. However, *The Times* obituary completely cuts Hen out of Dom's life, despite him constantly referring to her as 'K' in his memoir *My Son's Father*.

The truth is, Henrietta had married three times in ten years: Michael Law, Norman Bowler and Dom Moraes. She'd also had a long affair with Lucian Freud and the Marquess of Milford Haven, a close friend of the Duke of Edinburgh and best man at his wedding to Queen Elizabeth II. Hen was one of the carefully chosen guests who attended the Marquess' sex parties at his Grosvenor Square flat, where the evenings began with card games such as 'Chase the Bitch' and 'Find the Lady', with the winners pairing off for sex in his luxury bedrooms.

Then, in 2009, ten years after Henrietta's death, Lord Glenconner (Colin Tennant), famous for turning the tropical island of Mustique into a celebrity playground, claimed he was the real father of Henrietta's son Joshua, born after a brief fling in 1955. When he and Joshua undertook DNA tests to prove they were father and son, Glenconner told the press that Lucian Freud 'was furious Joshua was mine, not his son', but I can't imagine Norman Bowler was too happy about it either, as James Birch told me:

> Joshua had naturally always thought that he was a product of Henrietta and Norman Bowler's relationship and took his father's surname. Joshua told me that the publisher of Henrietta's autobiography had said, 'Now your mother's died I think you should check your DNA.'

To unravel the final twist in Henrietta's tale, we have to go back to New Year's Eve 1954, to the Chelsea Arts Club Ball. For this unmissable event in the bohemian calendar, thousands arrived at the Albert Hall in a crush of crazy outfits. An eighty-legged insect weaves past a cute little drag queen astride a woolly giraffe, whilst Joan of Arc jives with a giant turkey trotting with a Sioux chieftain amidst various cowboys, teddy bears and red devils, all of whom scandalised the press with their 'outrageous' behaviour and gave a loud cheer as the balloons began to cascade from the ceiling at the stroke of midnight, welcoming in the New Year.

Amidst the throng, two young partygoers catch one another's eye, the future Lord Glenconner, then a handsome aristocratic heir called Colin Tennant (whose Uncle David ran Soho's infamously louche Gargoyle club) and Henrietta, the sexy Cinderella-like artists' model. Together they leave the party and take a taxi to Tennant's Knightsbridge home. It really wasn't Hen's idea, but it seemed like a good one at the time, and when she leaves … she leaves with a secret she will keep for the rest of her life.

Fast forward fifty years or so to 2010 and *The Times* newspaper reports that Henrietta's son has started investigating his parentage after his mother's demise. When a DNA test tells him that he's only a half-sibling to his sister Caroline, he begins to suspect Lord

Glenconner after a tip-off that he was seen leaving the 1954 New Year's Eve party with Hen:

> I sent him a letter. It was very tricky … I told him I'd been trying to sort through some of the confusion that my mother left behind when she died and that part of that was to do with the identity of my father … and I wondered whether it might be him.

But, as fate would have it, their paths had crossed thirty-five years earlier. As a child, Joshua was a schoolboy chum of Glenconner's son Charlie. After Josh had left school, he accepted a job from Glenconner and spent a year or so working in Mustique as a sports coach. Joshua told *The Sunday Times*: 'Colin became a hero of mine, which is rather extraordinary, given what has happened.' And Lord Glenconner agreed it had been 'quite magical', adding: 'What better Christmas present could there be for an old bloke than a son …?' But confessed that if he had known earlier it 'might have wrecked all our lives'. At the time he was hotly tipped to marry the Queen's sister, Princess Margaret, but now there was 'no embarrassment'.

The whole thing was so uncanny because, rather like a bizarre plot twist in one of Roald Dahl's *Tales of the Unexpected*, the party-loving lord had Lucian Freud's oil painting of Henrietta hanging on his study wall for over thirty years … staring down at him with an imploring look in her eyes, without him ever suspecting its poignancy: 'I always remember her as she was in that picture … a pensive girl with a blanket wrapped round her shoulders looking out the window at the ducks outside Lucian's studio.' As in most of Roald Dahl's stories our tale rests on a sharp punchline where there is little love for or between the people in it. In this respect, Henrietta's life and legacy (as in all of Dahl's *Tales of the Unexpected*) concludes with one of those snappy plot twists in which someone gets their grisly comeuppance and the characters are driven by their appetites to self-destruction.

In retrospect, Glenconner said Henrietta must have known that he was the father, 'but she never said a word to anyone and it is very much to her credit that she never tried to take advantage of me in any way'. Yet, despite what he may believe, there were no readily available pregnancy tests in those days and determining parenthood was not an exact science. Hen had slept with half a dozen men, any of whom could have been the father. But in light of Glenconner's response, Joshua admitted in *The Times* that he had to re-evaluate his wayward mother:

> Having someone turn round and say 'your mother behaved really well here' has really helped because it's easy to feel sour about how you were treated ... it underlines that, before the chaos took over, she had lots of nice friends and she was much loved. She at least had one relationship she didn't f*** up.

However, Joshua's own love life was just as complicated as his mother's, having fathered four children with three different women before training as a psychotherapist specialising in treating victims of trauma ... something which may have come in useful when dealing with his own shock at discovering he was the son of a lord. Josh told the press that he was 'proud to be a Tennant' because it gave him an anchor and an identity and suddenly made him feel that everything in his life made sense ... as he told *The Times*:

> If you are unhappy, you have a sort of fantasy that your father will be someone with a big white horse and a suit of armour and now that fantasy has come true. At least I expect he has a suit of armour in a cupboard somewhere.

But, according to friends, the news infuriated Lord Glenconner's long-suffering wife, who was forever cleaning up her husband's emotional mess. According to Lady Glenconner, her husband had a tendency to get over-excited and lose 'his rag in a spectacular fashion', occasionally hurling tables and chairs into the sea. A television documentary, *The Man Who Bought Mustique*, unflatteringly portrayed him as impatient, irritable and spoilt, and in her 2019 autobiography *Lady in Waiting*, Lady Glenconner recalls when Josh appeared on the scene:

> Colin had always had proteges, trying to advance the careers of young men ... he always got frightfully overexcited about everything, but it never lasted very long. I tried to be suitably enthusiastic and gave a house party at Glen for Josh and his family, introducing him to everybody to make him feel welcome. Colin opened his arms to him, taking him back to St Lucia with him to show his new son the island he so loved. Within about three days, he was on the telephone again. 'I can't stand it any longer, Anne!' he shouted, as if he thought I couldn't hear him all the way from St Lucia. I wasn't surprised and found it rather difficult myself that Josh had turned up after all that time.

Sadly for Josh, no sooner had he met his biological father than the louche lord dropped dead from a heart attack, disinheriting his children and leaving all his Caribbean property to a servant called Kent. As Josh discovered, being the son of Lord Glenconner was no less perilous than being that of Henrietta's. A bohemian streak had manifested itself in the party-loving peer which was to wreak havoc on his children. Of his three sons, his heir Charles died after years of heroin addiction, the second, Henry, died of Aids and the third was left severely disabled after a motorcycle accident, leading to dark rumours swirling around high society of a 'Curse of the Glenconners'. Now, with his fourth son, Joshua, born of a brief liaison with an artist's model, Lady Glenconner may have felt the curse was complete.

But had bad karma cursed Hen too? If she had deliberately set out to hide who'd sired her son, it had certainly put her on a disastrous course, leaving a lot of human wreckage in its wake. Everyone's life is full of 'What If?' moments but how different would Henrietta's life have been if she'd gone back to Glenconner, pregnant? Well, for a start she would never have nicked the boyfriend of her best friend and benefactor, John Minton, a course of action which precipitated his disastrous decline and suicide. Minton may well have lived on and visited Henrietta and Lord Glenconner on the tropical island of Mustique. Minton loved painting the Caribbean – he could have stayed with Hen and lived out much of the 1960s and 1970s with her on that small island in the West Indies which once epitomised the glamour of the jet set.

Together, they could have revelled in the mystique of Mustique and its rich reputation for a hedonistic way of life enjoyed by rock stars and royalty, all of which was salaciously reported on by the gutter press. Then, when not shaking her hips with their neighbour Mick Jagger, or sailing on Bob Dylan's yacht, Hen could have been a drinking partner for Princess Margaret – another promiscuous party girl who drank, smoked and screwed around with the 'fast set' – and unwittingly became a camp figure of fun. Together, they would have made a great double act – like two well-meaning but impulsive overgrown schoolgirls – Margaret and Hen could have lounged about sunbathing, as they enjoyed the local lads, who served them stark naked, except for a strategically placed coconut shell. With their tantrums, eccentricities and outrageous demands, they could have founded a new Monster Club on Mustique. Margaret's husband hated the island ... 'Mustake', he called it.

And what a 'Mustake' it would have been. Despite our flights of fancy, in all probability if Henrietta had returned to Glenconner pregnant, he would have persuaded her to have a backstreet abortion at one of those well-heeled Harley Street doctors that discreetly dealt with the aristocracy's 'little problems', at a time when the procedure was still illegal. Being several months pregnant, Hen would have had to have a late abortion with no anaesthetic. A truly brutal procedure. According to Caitlin Thomas' own account, the first (and last) Hen would have seen of Josh was as a fully formed baby reduced to 'scraps and chunks ... being callously chucked into a nearby pail', resembling something from a Francis Bacon painting.

As well as the loss of her son, having monstrous fun in Mustique would have also meant that Hen would never have sat for those photos by John Deakin which inspired Francis Bacon's iconic paintings of her and, in turn, Maggi Hambling would have never met and fallen in love with her. However, Maggi is quite fatalistic about it all. Her affair with Henrietta lasted less than a year, during which Henrietta was 'raging and violent' and even beat Maggi up, which she rather enjoyed. When I asked Maggi if Henrietta was the love of her life, she replied:

> She always said she was ... she was the most powerful muse. Henrietta was a force of nature, like the sea. I didn't stand a chance! I mean things happen, life happens and I think that phase of drawing Henrietta is one of the greatest series of drawings I've done. She had that thing of looking through you – no pretence – you couldn't have any secrets from her. I think that's why a lot of people found her so frightening.

But to Maggi, death has no dominion and Henrietta is still the perfect muse, inspiring and informing her artwork. Interestingly, in his preface to Maggi's book of drawings of Henrietta, the art critic John Berger says that drawing a face is 'one way of noting down a biography'. Despite her detractors, Berger compares Maggi to Rembrandt, realising that in most of Maggi's drawings 'Henrietta is not dead' and that 'the drawings are part of a love affair'. It is true that two decades after her death Henrietta is still a constant presence in Maggi's studio, which begs the question: Does she wish she'd met Henrietta earlier?

> Yes of course, of course. But again, I don't think there's any point in regretting anything. I'm pretty fatalistic, life gives you what it gives you. She was in command of all she surveyed, but she was also infuriating and impossible.
>
> She was a very moral woman. Although, some might consider her life immoral, but I think she was quite pure ... the *rawness* of her.

Afterword

If this is a confession, let's make it a brief one. This is a book I never had any intention of writing, and many discouraged me from doing so. When I finished my last book, *Queens of Bohemia and Other Miss-Fits*, I foolishly thought I could rest easy. However, my subconscious had other plans and rudely awoke me in the middle of the night by lobbing an ingenious grenade of epiphany at me, which blew my mind wide awake: 'I have enough information left over to write a biography on Henrietta Moraes.' A simple but revelatory idea that electrified me so much I couldn't go back to sleep.

After mulling it over for a few days, I wondered how to begin and whom to approach. Well, when Henrietta died, the art critic Tim Hilton wrote her obituary in *The Guardian* on 8 January 1999. So, before I began piecing together her 'portrait', I thought it wise to contact him. I wrote a letter to him in which I outlined my idea and stated that 'I would be very grateful if it were possible to speak to you concerning your memories and insights regarding Henrietta Moraes, and any of the other women who inhabited London's post-war creative scene'. To which I received this reply:

Dear Darren Coffield,

Fiona Green told me some months ago that she had given you my address. Now I have yours, and apologise immediately for the negative nature of my reply. I wish well to all young artists and writers and hope to give them good advice.

In the case of the book you are thinking of, however, it must be obvious to you (and any professional you consult) that there are insuperable difficulties before you.

First of all, the people that interest you are dead and cannot be interviewed. So also with the various friends who once had reminiscences.

Secondly, what is there to commemorate about such women. They produced nothing or next to nothing that would give them a place in the history of 20th-century culture.

- Except perhaps Elinor Bellingham-Smith. But her best work was done in rural West Anglia, where she belonged. See the nice little RA exhibition of about twenty or more years ago.

Everyone knows that the real heroines of Soho were the wives and daughters who slaved for little reward in Italian and French cafes and restaurants.

Your projected book will find much opposition from feminists. In fact, though, they may not be able to read what you say, for the chances of publication are slim.

This century cares less and less about the London bohemia of the last century. I remember some years back that John Moynihan's very full account of his parents and their friends could not find a publisher …

I think you should try something else, if you truly wish to write about old artistic life.

A good plan would be to go to the archives in the Tate library. They have been collecting information (and interviews) about people in the art world. Not much is generally known about this archive and little of it has been made public. Why not go there, look through the catalogue lists, and see if there is anything that appeals to you as a subject?

Yours,

Tim Hilton

Following in the wake of Tim Hilton's letter consigning Henrietta Moraes to the dustbin of history, others in the art world also made it clear not to bother them. They warned me off her … well, who wouldn't? To them, she was merely a dirty joke. After all, they've been stuck in the laundromat of the London art world, laundering dirty money for so long that they've lost their sense of smell. But I haven't. No one is going to bin Hen whilst I'm around, she's not the two-dimensional cardboard cutout character that art historians portray her as … besides I couldn't have the injustice of it all on my conscience any longer.

Acknowledgements

Firstly, I would like to pay tribute to the people who helped me with the book but sadly passed away before publication: Christopher Barker, Marianne Faithfull, David Marrion, Diana Melly, Ken Thomson and Daniel Thorold, all of whom were extremely generous with their time and energy; they will be greatly missed.

Secondly, I must say a huge thank you to Maggi Hambling for her support, Sarah Lucas for her foreword, David Venn for his endless editorial insights and to all those who contributed: Geoffrey Aquilina Ross, Ros Baronio Archer, James Birch, Charlotte Black, Orlando Campbell, Leigh Casey, Cressida Connolly, Matthew Connolly, John Dunbar, Rose Fenton, Helen Frank, Prue Freeman, Fiona Green, Peter Ho, Dafydd Jones, Michael Law, Trisha Locke, Hugh Monk, Tim Motion, Tom Onions, Alexandra Pringle, Jane Rankin-Reid, Jo Reed Turner, Jonathan Ross, Camilla Shivarg, Emelia Thorold and Harriet Vyner.

I am also indebted to the many authors, their estates and literary executors for allowing me to quote from their various texts, books and memoirs: *Anything Once* (copyright © Joan Wyndham, 1993) reproduced by kind permission of Camilla Shivarg; *The Arms of the Infinite: Elizabeth Smart and George Barker* (copyright © Christopher Barker, 2006) reproduced by kind permission of Christopher Barker; *Faithfull: An Autobiography* (copyright © Marianne Faithfull, 1994) and *Marianne Faithfull: Memories, Dreams and Reflections* (copyright © Marianne Faithfull, 2007) reproduced by kind permission of Nicholas Dunbar; Peter

Levi's correspondence and photographs (copyright © Peter Levi, 1961) reproduced by kind permission of Matthew Connolly; *Model and Artist: Henrietta Moraes and Francis Bacon* (copyright © Martha Parsey, 1993) reproduced by kind permission of Martha Parsey; *Prince Charming* (copyright © Christopher Logue, 1999) reproduced by kind permission of Rosemary Hill; *Norman's London* (copyright © Frank Norman, 1969) reproduced by kind permission of Geraldine Norman; *Restless Lives: The Bohemian World of Rodrigo and Elinor Moynihan* (copyright © John Moynihan, 2002), *Not All a Ball* (copyright © John Moynihan, 1970) and the gossip column *In London Tonight* (copyright © John Moynihan, 1960) reproduced by kind permission of Leo Moynihan.

I am grateful to James Moores and Edward Suckling of the John Deakin Archive for both their patronage and permission to reproduce John Deakin's photographs; Conor Macklin of the Grosvenor Gallery for sharing his knowledge of F.N. Souza and his circle, as well as Dom Moraes' friend Jeet Thayil, and Sarayu Ahuja of Dom Moraes Estate for their help and encouragement.

Lastly, I am truly thankful for the unstinting support of my family and friends, without which I would never have written *Hen*.

Notes

Chapter 1 Law of the Jungle

For Gaston Berlemont on Henrietta see *Queens of Bohemia and Other Miss-Fits* by Darren Coffield (The History Press, 2024) p. 218. Henrietta complains about her meal ticket, Tony Hubbard, in *Never a Normal Man* by Daniel Farson (Harper Collins, 1997) p. 115 and talks about her early life in *Queen* magazine (23 September 1965 Vol. 423, No. 5552). Paul Potts quoted from his memoir *Dante Called You Beatrice* (Eyre & Spottiswoode, 1960) p. 218; Henrietta remembers Sid the Swimmer in 'The Curse of the Drinking Classes' (*Independent*, 5 April 1996). Michael Law quotation from Nigel Richardson's *Dog Days in Soho: One Man's Adventure in Fifties Bohemia* (Gollancz, 2000) p. 101. For Francis Bacon's 'ghastly English laws' see *Tales from the Colony Room: Soho's Lost Bohemia* by Darren Coffield (Unbound, 2020) p. XV. Background information gleaned from 'Queen of Soho' by Patrick Cooney (*Guardian Weekend Magazine*, 22 August 1998); *Henrietta* by Henrietta Moraes (Penguin, 1995); *Never a Normal Man* by Daniel Farson (Harper Collins, 1997); *Tears Before Bedtime* by Barbara Skelton (Hamish Hamilton, 1987) and my interviews with Di Hall and Diana Melly. I am also grateful to Harriet Vyner for interviewing Marianne Faithfull on my behalf.

Chapter 2 The Colony

Muriel Belcher quotations taken from *Tales from the Colony Room: Soho's Lost Bohemia* by Darren Coffield (Unbound, 2020) pp. 1–35. Henrietta mentions Francis Bacon's 'force field' in 'Queen of Soho' by Patrick Cooney (*Guardian Weekend Magazine*, 22 August 1998). Information and quotes from Francis Bacon, George Melly and David Marrion concerning Muriel Belcher taken from *Tales from the Colony Room* pp. 1–35. For further information on Muriel Belcher see *The French: A Personal History* by Sandy Fawkes (Lewis/Botham, 1993); *Club International Magazine* Vol. 3, No. 12 (December 1974) and *Queen* magazine (November 1969 Vol. 433, No. 5684). Frank Norman quote from *Norman's London* by Frank Norman (Secker & Warburg, 1969) p. 187. For the hold-up at the Gargoyle see *Queens of Bohemia and Other Miss-Fits* by Darren Coffield (The History Press, 2024) p. 223. Henrietta mentions Muriel in the documentary *The*

Life and Unsteady Times of John Deakin, directed by John Christie (Without Walls, 1991: www.youtube.com/watch?v=TqzMDMEpa-Y.

Chapter 3 Chelsea Girls

Information on the Chelsea Set taken from *High Diver* by Michael Wishart (Blond & Briggs, 1977); Henrietta's partying gleaned from *Which Yet Survive: Impressions of Friends, Family and Encounters* by John Mills (Quartet, 2017). For Henrietta on Lucian Freud see Martha Parsey's film *Model and Artist; Henrietta Moraes and Francis Bacon* (www.mphqprojectspace.com/category/exhibiitons, 1993). Elinor Bellingham-Smith quotes on John Minton and Henrietta are taken from John Moynihan's memoir *Restless Lives: The Bohemian World of Rodrigo and Elinor Moynihan* (Sansom & Company, 2002) pp. 19, 127, 154 & 167. For Henrietta on the Chelsea Set, see 'Queen of Soho' by Patrick Cooney (*Guardian Weekend Magazine*, 22 August 1998) and for Norman Bowler's take on it all read *My God, Is That the Time?* (Auroville, 2005) pp. 54–55. Further information obtained from my interviews with Diana Melly and Jo Reed Turner.

Chapter 4 Dom

Dom Moraes quoted from his memoir *My Son's Father* (Penguin, 1990) p. 131; Paul Potts quoted from Daniel Farson's article 'Soho Serendipity' (*Wheeler's Review*, Spring, 1975); Henrietta recalls David Archer and John Deakin in *Tales from the Colony Room* by Darren Coffield (Unbound, 2020) p. 94; Henrietta calls David Archer an entrepreneur in the BBC documentary *A Gentleman of Soho* (BBC Radio 3, 14 July 1974); Henrietta in the Colony quote from *Tales from the Colony Room* p. 94; Bernard Kops recalls Dom Moraes (*The Guardian*, 4 June 2004); Christopher Logue discusses David Archer's shop in *Prince Charming* (Faber & Faber, 1999) pp. 184–186; Dom's love for Henrietta quoted from *My Son's Father* (Penguin, 1990) p. 174, in which he gives Henrietta the non de plume 'K'. Other background information from Daniel Farson's *Never a Normal Man* (Harper Collins, 1997) and *Sacred Monsters* (Bloomsbury, 1988). Stephen Fothergill charts David Archer's decline in *The Last Lamplighter: A Soho Education* (London Magazine Editions, 2000).

Chapter 5 University Challenge

Henrietta mentions her food poisoning and the Turkish lady in *Queen* magazine (23 September 1965 Vol. 423, No. 5552). Dom opening up Henrietta's mind from *My Son's Father* (Penguin, 1990) p. 184; Michael Southgate quoted from my interview; Bernard Kops quoted from Dom's obituary (*The Guardian*, 4 June 2004) and Ved Metha from his memoir *Up at Oxford* (John Murray, 1993) p. 221. Further information obtained from James Birch, Camilla Shivarg and Dom's friend Jeet Thayil, author of *The Book of Chocolate Saints* (Faber & Faber, 2019) in which the novel's protagonist, Newton Francis Xavier, is a confection of Dom Moraes and F.N. Souza.

Chapter 6 Fin de Partie

Ved Metha quotations from *Up at Oxford* (John Murray, 1993) pp. 202 and 221; Patrick Garland quotes from Philip Hoare's obituary of Henrietta (*Independent*, 16 January 1999); Dom Moraes mentions his problems at Oxford in *Gone Away: An Indian Journey* (World Books, 1961) p. 10. Further background information from my interviews with Jeet Thayil, Conor Macklin, Diana Melly and James Birch.

Chapter 7 The Smart Set vs. the Chelsea Set

George Barker quote from *By Heart: The Life of Elizabeth Smart* by Rosemary Sullivan (Flamingo, 1992) p. 340 and for Elizabeth Smart at *Queen* magazine see pp. 290–296; Elizabeth Smart mentions Henrietta in her diaries *On the Side of Angels* ed. by Alice Van Wart (Flamingo, 1995) p. 42; Henrietta's wedding quoted from the gossip column *In London Tonight* by John Moynihan (*Evening Standard*, 5 December 1960); Christopher Barker quotes about Henrietta, Brian Higgins and Elizabeth Smart from *The Arms of the Infinite* by Christopher Barker (Pomona, 2006) pp. 261–262. For more Higgins see *Never at Home* by Dom Moraes (Penguin, 1994) p. 98; Joan Wyndham quotes taken from *Anything Once* (Flamingo, 1993) pp. 61–63; for Veronica Hull and Robin Cook read *The Hidden Files* by Derek Raymond (Little Brown, 1992) pp. 277–279. Further information from my interviews with Paddy Swift's friend Tim Motion, Christopher Barker, Camilla Shivarg and Diana Melly.

Chapter 8 The Honeymoon from Hell

Information taken from my interviews with Mim Scala, Christopher Barker and Camilla Shivarg. For Dom's take on Bambi see *Never at Home* (Penguin, 1994) p. 20; Henrietta mentions their honeymoon in her autobiography *Henrietta* (Penguin, 1995). Postcard to Peter Levi courtesy of Matthew Connolly; Dom's quotes on the Eichmann trial see *Never at Home* (Penguin, 1994) pp. 28 and 33; Henrietta on their voyage to Britain, *Henrietta* (Penguin, 1995) p. 62; Dom lies about his mother in Ved Metha's *Up at Oxford* (John Murray, 1993) p. 212 and fears her in *Never at Home* (Penguin, 1994) p. 7. Mim Scala paints the scene vividly in his memoir *Diary of a Teddy Boy* (Headline Publishing, 2000).

Chapter 9 Non-Dom

Bernard Kops on Dom Moraes (*The Guardian*, 4 June 2004). Information concerning Hussein Shariffe, F.N. Souza and Gallery One courtesy of Conor Macklin of London's Grosvenor Gallery and their exhibition catalogue *Gallery One and the Indian Avant Garde* (Grosvenor Gallery Fine Arts, 2023). Viscountess

Bridgeman and Emelia Thorold quoted from my interviews. Henrietta talks about being photographed by John Deakin in the documentary *The Life and Unsteady Times of John Deakin*, directed by John Christie (Without Walls, 1991: www.youtube.com/watch?v=TqzMDMEpa-Y) and also in *Francis Bacon Revelations* by Mark Stevens and Annalyn Swan (William Collins, 2021) p. 491. Henrietta recalls Lucian Freud and Francis Bacon in Patrick Cooney's 'Queen of Soho' interview (*Guardian Weekend Magazine*, 22 August 1998); John Moynihan reminisces about Henrietta, John Deakin and Francis Bacon in *Not All a Ball* (MacGibbon & Kee, 1970) p. 183; Thea Porter quoted from 'Muriel's Academy' (*Harpers & Queen* magazine, November 1982) p. 222. Further information from Ros Baronio Archer, David Marrion, Marianne Faithfull, Annie Freud and Patrick Hughes.

Chapter 10 The Cat Bungler of Bohemia

Information regarding Henrietta's drug use collated from her numerous interviews, but here she is quoted from Patrick Cooney's 'Queen of Soho' (*Guardian Weekend Magazine*, 22 August 1998). Henrietta also writes about it eloquently in 'A Life of Drugs' (*Sunday Times Magazine*, 6 September 1964), from which I have also quoted. Henrietta mentions her lack of role models in *Queens of Bohemia and Other Miss-Fits* by Darren Coffield (The History Press, 2024) p. 222. Further information from John Dunbar, Marianne Faithfull, Jo Reed Turner, Fiona Green and Diana Melly who proved invaluable, as did her memoir *Take a Girl Like Me: Life with George* (Vintage, 2006).

Chapter 11 Hen the Heroine

Information collated from my interviews with Geoffrey Aquilina Ross, John Dunbar, Rose Fenton, Barry Miles, Camilla Shivarg, Jo Reed Turner, Marianne Faithfull and *Groovy Bob* by Harriet Vyner (Faber & Faber, 1999). Henrietta writes about being introduced to LSD in her memoir *Henrietta* (Penguin, 1995), and George Melly discusses LSD in *Style into Revolt* (Allen Lane/Penguin, 1970) p. 109. Many thanks to Richard Adams and James Birch for sourcing Henrietta's exposé of 'The Process' cult in *OZ* magazine (No. 4, May 1967) (www.openculture.com/2016/03/download-the-complete-archive-of-oz.html). Unsurprisingly, numerous articles and conspiracy theories about the Process Church abound on the internet (burningambulance.com/2018/06/12/the-process).

Chapter 12 Paint Your Wagon

For dining out at the Baghdad House with Mick Jagger read the selected diaries of Cecil Beaton, *Self Portrait with Friends* ed. Richard Buckle (Pimlico, 1991) p. 382. Further information taken from my interviews with Geoffrey Aquilina Ross and Trisha Locke. For Marianne Faithfull on Brian Jones and the Rolling Stones see *Faithfull: An Autobiography* by Marianne Faithfull and David

Dalton (Little, Brown and Company, 1994) p. 172. For tales of the wagon trail and quotes from David Tomlin and Iggy the Eskimo visit atagong.com/iggy/archives/2018/10/paint-your-wagon-iggy-movie-unearthed.html. Further information from John Dunbar and Marianne Faithfull's interview with Harriet Vyner. Keith Richards quoted from his autobiography *Life*, co-written with James Fox (Orion, 2010) p. 205. Henrietta mentions the wagon trail in her memoir *Henrietta* (Penguin, 1995), and her son, Joshua, mentions his mother in 'Joshua Bowler: The Daddy of All Mustique Secrets' (*The Times*, 17 March 2010).

Chapter 13 Making Hay

Nigel Waymouth quote from www.tumgik.com/tag/nigel%20waymouth. Further information from Marianne Faithfull and Harriet Vyner. For Henrietta's job interview and aptitude for work, I've quoted from *Marianne Faithfull: Memories, Dreams and Reflections* (Fourth Estate, 2007) p. 158. April Ashley discusses Richard Booth in her second memoir (co-written with Douglas Thompson), *The First Lady* (John Blake, 2006) p. 136. In April's first memoir (co-written with Duncan Fallowell) she recalls Viva King, *April Ashley's Odyssey* (Jonathan Cape, 1982) pp. 201–203. Further information from April Ashley's obituary (*The Times*, 29 December 2021) and Richard Booth's obituary (*The Times*, 23 August 2019). Marianne recalls Henrietta working for Richard Booth in *Marianne Faithfull* p.159.

Chapter 14 Faithfull Friends

Background information taken from Henrietta's autobiography *Henrietta* (Penguin, 1995) and Marianne's memoir *Marianne Faithfull: Memories, Dreams and Reflections* (Fourth Estate, 2007) p. 158. Lucian Freud on Henrietta and her lack of knickers, *The Lives of Lucian Freud: Youth* by William Feaver (Bloomsbury, 2019) p. 569. Further information from Charlotte Black, Peter Brunton, John Dunbar, Marianne Faithfull, Trisha Locke, Mim Scala, Ken Thomson and Harriet Vyner.

Chapter 15 Hen Today, Gone Tomorrow

Information from Mel and June Andrews, James Birch, Orlando Campbell, John Dunbar, Michael Law, Alexandra Pringle, Daniel Thorold and Nigel Richardson's *Dog Days in Soho: One Man's Adventure in Fifties Bohemia* (Weidenfeld & Nicolson, 2000). Joshua Bowler and The Crucial Gallery quoted from *The New York Times* article 'On Foot in a London Village' (www.nytimes.com/1988/03/20/travel/on-foot-in-a-london-village-portobello-art-festival.html). For Henrietta on the bus with Bacon see *Francis Bacon Revelations* by Mark Stevens and Annalyn Swan (William Collins, 2021) p. 692. For Henrietta on modelling see Martha Parsey's film *Model and Artist: Henrietta Moraes and Francis Bacon* (www.mphqprojectspace.com/category/exhibiitons, 1993). Henrietta on her grandchildren never seeing her drunk quoted from *Henrietta* (Penguin, 1995) p. 213.

Chapter 16 Drawing to an End

Information from James Birch, Marianne Faithfull, Maggi Hambling, Alexandra Pringle, Camilla Shivarg and Harriet Vyner. Henrietta on Bacon quoted from 'The Curse of the Drinking Classes' (*The Independent*, 5 April 1996) and Patrick Cooney's article 'Queen of Soho' (*Guardian Weekend Magazine*, 22 August 1998). Henrietta on sitting for Bacon and the prophetic nature of his work taken from Martha Parsey's film *Model and Artist: Henrietta Moraes and Francis Bacon* (www.mphqprojectspace.com/category/exhibiitons, 1993). For Maggi Hambling's work with Henrietta see *Maggi and Henrietta* (Bloomsbury, 2001); 'A Life in Pictures, Interview with Maggi Hambling' by Lynne Barber (*The Observer*, 3 December 2007) and 'Maggi Hambling's Deathly Visions' (*The New Yorker*, 10 May 2022).

Epilogue

As well as information from my interviews with Maggi Hambling and James Birch, I have referred to Tim Hilton's obituary of Henrietta Moraes (*The Guardian*, 8 January 1999); Dom Moraes' obituary (*The Times*, 4 June 2004); Lord Glenconner's obituary (*The Times*, 30 August 2010) and the following press stories have been gleaned for information and quoted from: 'Lord Glenconner, 83, Discovers Long Lost Lovechild' by Daniel Foggo (*The Sunday Times*, 10 January 2010); 'Joshua Bowler: The Daddy of All Mustique Secrets' by Tim Mutton (*The Times*, 17 March 2010); 'Lord Glenconner Leaves His Caribbean Estate to Faithful Servant' (*The Times*, 18 June 2011); 'Court Settles Inheritance Row over Glenconner Will' by David Brown (*The Times*, 4 March 2014); 'Irish Outsider Artist and Former Oil Man Bill Griffin' by John P. O'Sullivan (*The Sunday Times*, 19 June 2016); 'Partying Lord Glenconner "Stole Land" for His Very Own Love Island' (*The Times*, 23 June 2018) and 'Interview: Sue MacLaine, Artist and Star of Still Life: An Audience with Henrietta Moraes' by Jackie McGlown (*The Scotsman*, 8 August 2012). For Caitlin Thomas' account of late-term abortion, see Caitlin Thomas, *My Life with Dylan Thomas: Double Drink Story* (Virago, 2013) p. 148. Lady Glenconner quoted from her autobiography *Lady in Waiting* (Hodder & Stoughton, 2019) p. 301; John Berger quoted from *Maggi and Henrietta* (Bloomsbury, 2001).

Bibliography

Ashley, April and Fallowell, Duncan, *April Ashley's Odyssey* (Jonathan Cape, 1982)

Ashley, April and Thompson, Douglas, *The First Lady* (John Blake, 2006)

Barker, Christopher, *The Arms of the Infinite* (Pomona, 2006)

Beaton, Cecil, ed. Richard Buckle, *The Selected Diaries of Cecil Beaton* (Pimlico, 1991)

Blackwood, Caroline, *In the Pink* (Bloomsbury, 1987)

Bowler, Norman, *My God, Is That the Time?* (Auroville, 2005)

Coffield, Darren, *Tales from The Colony Room: Soho's Lost Bohemia* (Unbound, 2020)

Coffield, Darren, *Queens of Bohemia and Other Miss-Fits* (History Press, 2024)

David, Hugh, *The Fitzrovians: A Portrait of a Bohemian Society 1900–1955* (Sceptre, 1989)

Enroth, Ronald, *Youth, Brainwashing and the Extremist Cults* (Zondervran/ Paternoster Press, 1980)

Faithfull, Marianne, *Marianne Faithfull: Memories, Dreams and Reflections* (Fourth Estate, 2007)

Faithfull, Marianne and Dalton, David, *Faithfull: An Autobiography* (Little, Brown and Company, 1994)

Farson, Daniel, *Never a Normal Man: An Autobiography* (Harper Collins, 1997)

Farson, Daniel, *Sacred Monsters* (Bloomsbury, 1988)

Farson, Daniel, *Soho in the Fifties* (Michael Joseph, 1987)

Fawkes, Sandy, *In Praise of Younger Men* (Hamlyn, 1979)

Fawkes, Sandy, *The French: A Personal History* (Lewis/Botham French House, 1993)

Feaver, William, *The Lives of Lucian Freud: Youth* (Bloomsbury, 2019)

Fothergill, Stephen, *The Last Lamplighter: A Soho Education* (London Magazine Editions, 2000)

Gere, Charlie, *World's End* (Goldsmiths Press, 2022)

Glenconner, Lady, *Lady in Waiting* (Hodder & Stoughton, 2019)

Grosvenor Gallery, *Gallery One and the Indian Avant Garde* (Grosvenor Gallery Fine Arts, 2023)

Hambling, Maggi, *Maggi and Henrietta* (Bloomsbury, 2001)

Hooker, Denise, *Nina Hamnett: Queen of Bohemia* (Constable, 1986)

Lessing, Doris, *Walking in the Shade: Autobiography 1949–62* (Harper Collins, 1997)

Logue, Christopher, *Prince Charming* (Faber & Faber, 1999)

Luke, Michael, *David Tennant and the Gargoyle Years* (Weidenfeld & Nicolson, 1991)

Melly, Diana, *Take a Girl Like Me: Life with George* (Vintage, 2006)

Melly, George, *Style into Revolt* (Allen Lane/Penguin, 1970)

Metha, Ved, *Up at Oxford* (John Murray, 1993)

Mills, John, *Which Yet Survive: Impressions of Friends, Family and Encounters* (Quartet, 2017)

Moraes, Dom, *Gone Away: An Indian Journey* (The Reprint Society/World Books, 1961)

Moraes, Dom, *My Son's Father: An Autobiography* (Penguin, 1990)

Moraes, Dom, *Never at Home* (Penguin, 1994)

Moraes, Henrietta, *Henrietta* (Penguin, 1995)

Moynihan, John, *Not All a Ball* (MacGibbon & Kee, 1970)

Moynihan, John, *Restless Lives: The Bohemian World of Rodrigo and Elinor Moynihan* (Sansom & Co., 2002)

Norman, Frank, *Norman's London* (Secker & Warburg, 1969)

Peppiatt, Michael, *Francis Bacon in Your Blood* (Bloomsbury Circus, 2015)

Plante, David, *Difficult Women* (Futura, 1984)

Potts, Paul, *Dante Called You Beatrice* (Eyre & Spottiswoode, 1960)

Raymond, Derek, *The Hidden Files* (Little Brown, 1992)

Richards, Keith and Fox, James, *Life* (Orion, 2010)

Richardson, Nigel, *Dog Days in Soho: One Man's Adventure in Fifties Bohemia* (Weidenfeld & Nicolson, 2000)

Sandhu, Sukhdev, *London Calling: How Black and Asian Writers Imagined a City* (Harper Perennial, 2004)

Scala, Mim, *Diary of a Teddy Boy* (Headline Publishing, 2000)

Schoenberger, Nancy, *Dangerous Muse: A Life of Caroline Blackwood* (Wiedenfeld & Nicolson, 2001)

Sinclair, Andrew, *Francis Bacon: His Life and Violent Times* (Sinclair-Stevenson, 1993)

Skelton, Barbara, *Tears Before Bedtime* (Hamish Hamilton, 1987)

Smart, Elizabeth, ed. Alice Van Wart, *On the Side of Angels* (Flamingo, 1995)

Stevens, Mark and Swan, Annalyn, *Francis Bacon: Revelations* (William Collins, 2021)

Sullivan, Rosemary, *By Heart: The Life of Elizabeth Smart* (Flamingo, 1992)

Thayil, Jeet, *The Book of Chocolate Saints* (Faber & Faber, 2019)

Vyner, Harriet, *Groovy Bob* (Faber & Faber, 1999)

Wishart, Michael, *High Diver* (Blond & Briggs, 1977)

Wyndham, Joan, *Anything Once* (Flamingo, 1983)

Index